WHO FREED THE SLAVES?

WHO FREED THE SLAVES?

The Fight over the Thirteenth Amendment

Leonard L. Richards

The University of Chicago Press CHICAGO AND LONDON

Leonard L. Richards is an award-winning historian and the author of seven books, including *Gentlemen of Property and Standing; Anti-Abolition Mobs in Jacksonian America; The Life and Times of John Quincy Adams; The Slave Power: The Free North and Southern Domination, 1780–1860; Shays's Rebellion: The American Revolution's Final Battle*; and *The California Gold Rush and the Coming of the Civil War*. A professor of history at the University of Massachusetts for many years, he has also taught at San Francisco State College and the University of Hawaii.

The University of Chicago Press, Chicago 60637
The University of Chicago Press, Ltd., London
© 2015 by Leonard L. Richards
All rights reserved. Published 2015.
Printed in the United States of America

24 23 22 21 20 19 18 17 16 15   1 2 3 4 5

ISBN-13: 978-0-226-17820-2 (cloth)
ISBN-13: 978-0-226-20894-7 (e-book)
DOI: 10.7208/chicago/9780226208947.001.0001

Library of Congress Cataloging-in-Publication Data
Richards, Leonard L., author.
Who freed the slaves? : the fight over the Thirteenth Amendment /
Leonard L. Richards.
pages
Includes bibliographical references and index.
ISBN 978-0-226-17820-2 (cloth : alk. paper) — ISBN 978-0-226-20894-7
(e-book) 1. United States. Constitution. 13th Amendment—History.
2. Slaves—Emancipation—United States—History—19th century.
3. Ashley, James Mitchell, 1824–1896. 4. United States. President (1861–
1865 : Lincoln). Emancipation Proclamation. 5. Slavery—Law and
legislation—United States—History—19th century. I. Title.
KF4545.S5R53 2015
342.7308'7—dc23
2014023200

For my grandchildren:
Paige, Tyler, Margot, Hazel, Samuel, Eliza, and Hadleigh

The Thirteenth Amendment to the Constitution of the United States

Ratified December 6, 1865

SECTION 1.

Neither Slavery nor involuntary servitude, except as a punishment for crime whereof the party shall have been duly convicted, shall exist within the United States, or any place subject to their jurisdiction.

SECTION 2.

Congress shall have the power to enforce this article by appropriate legislation.

Contents

Acknowledgments

This project, even though it took just two years to write, actually began some forty years ago, back in the days when I was a graduate student seeking a dissertation topic. At the time, I benefited from the sage advice of Wilson Smith, my main adviser, along with that of Daniel Calhoun and Paul Goodman. All three told me that the topic I had chosen, Northern opposition to the antislavery movement, had to be narrowed. It was just too broad to be done effectively. So I began looking for narrower topics and settled on two, Northerners who mobbed abolitionists and Northerners who opposed the Thirteenth Amendment. I spent about a summer working on both and then decided to concentrate on the mobs.

In the years that followed, although my research interests went in a different direction, the discarded topic never completely vanished from my thoughts because, every year, I taught one or more courses that dealt with the death of US slavery. And, to my dismay, whenever the abolition of slavery came up for classroom discussion, no one in the class ever singled out the proponents of the Thirteenth Amendment for special credit. Clearly, those tenacious warriors along with their equally pugnacious adversaries had been long forgotten.

Otherwise, the explanations I got from students for slavery's demise changed over the years. In the beginning, back in the late 1960s, Lincoln had a lot of bad press. Scores of articles had been published portraying him as a bigot, and some of that information had trickled down to my students. So at first virtually no one said: "Lincoln freed the slaves." Nearly all, however, attributed the end of slavery to the Emancipation Proclamation. At this point, most then went on to explain that "Lincoln reluctantly did it just to keep England out of the war." That became the standard answer, repeated one semester after another. Then, gradually, the notion that Lincoln was at best a "reluctant" emancipator disappeared. But the other notion—that the Emancipation Proclamation ended slavery—remained the norm. Few knew anything about the Thirteenth Amendment, and virtually no one knew that getting it through Congress was an uphill battle.

A few years back, I mentioned this fact to some high school history teachers who were taking a course I was teaching in the Teaching American History program. One member of the class decided to poll his fellow history teachers, both in our class and elsewhere, and find out how much they knew about the end of slavery. The results, he said, were "terrible." So I decided to write this book, never realizing that Steven Spielberg was about to incorporate several of the long forgotten warriors into the movie *Lincoln*, which undoubtedly made millions of moviegoers realize for the first time that the Thirteenth Amendment—and not the Emancipation Proclamation—ended US slavery, but which still adhered to the long-standing tradition of giving Lincoln most of the credit.

In putting this book together, I have had plenty of help. First of all, I owe a big thanks to my students, both at the University of Massachusetts and in the Teaching American History program. I tried much of the basic story out on them, and time and again they pushed me for more information. So much of the explanatory material is there largely because of them. I also owe a big thanks to my colleagues at the University of Massachusetts, especially to Bruce Laurie, Ron Story, Robert Jones, and Barry Levy, who for decades have listened to my ramblings and provided me with sound advice. I also owe a very large debt to many archivists and librarians, especially those at the University of Massachusetts and the American Antiquarian Society, who for the past forty years have found the microfilm, microfiche, and obscure books I needed and in recent years have directed me to key websites. Special thanks are also due to the anonymous reviewers who made valuable suggestions for improving the manuscript and to Timothy Mennel, Nora Devlin, and Yvonne Zipter of the University of Chicago Press, who shepherded the manuscript through publication.

Prologue

WEDNESDAY, JUNE 15, 1864

James Ashley never forgot the moment. After hours of debate, Schuyler Colfax, the Speaker of the House of Representatives, had finally gaveled the 159 House members to take their seats and get ready to vote.

Most of the members were waving a fan of some sort, but none of the fans did much good. Heat and humidity had turned the nation's capitol into a sauna. Equally bad was the stench that emanated from Washington's back alleys, nearby swamps, and the twenty-one hospitals in and about the city, which now housed over twenty thousand wounded and dying soldiers. Worse yet was the news from the front lines. According to some reports, the Union army had lost seven thousand men in less than thirty minutes at Cold Harbor. The commanding general, Ulysses S. Grant, had been deemed a "fumbling butcher."

Nearly everyone around Ashley was impatient, cranky, and miserable. But Ashley was especially downcast. It was his job to get Senate Joint Resolution Number 16, a constitutional amendment to outlaw slavery in the United States, through the House of Representatives, and he didn't have the votes.

The need for the amendment was obvious. Of the nation's four million slaves at the outset of the war, no more than five hundred thousand were now free, and, to his disgust, many white Americans intended to have them reenslaved once the war was over. The Supreme Court, moreover, was still in the hands of Chief Justice Roger B. Taney and other staunch proponents of property rights in slaves and state's rights. If they ever got the chance, they seemed certain not only to strike down much of Lincoln's Emancipation Proclamation but also to hold that under the Constitution only the states where slavery existed had the legal power to outlaw it.[1]

Six months earlier, in December 1863, when Ashley and his fellow Republicans had proposed the amendment, he had been more upbeat. He knew that getting the House to abolish slavery, which in his mind was the root cause of the war, was not going to be easy. It required a two-thirds vote. But he had thought that Republicans in both the Senate and the House might somehow muster the necessary two-thirds majority. No longer did they have to worry about the united opposition of fifteen slave states. Eleven of the fifteen were out of the Union, including South Carolina and Mississippi, the two with the highest percentage of slaves, and Virginia, the one with the largest House delegation. In addition, the war was in its thirty-third month. Hundreds of thousands of Northern men had been killed on the battlefield. The one-day bloodbath at Antietam was now etched into the memory of every one of his Toledo constituents as well as every member of Congress. So, too, was the three-day battle at Gettysburg.

If Republicans held firm, all they needed to push the amendment through the House was a handful of votes from their opponents, either from the border slave state representatives who had remained in the Union or from free state Democrats. It was his job to get those votes. He was the bill's floor manager.

Back in December, Ashley had been the first House member to propose such an amendment. Although few of his colleagues realized it, he had been toying with the idea for nearly a decade. He had made a similar proposal in September 1856, when it didn't have a chance of passing.

He was a political novice at the time, just twenty-nine years old, and known mainly for being big and burly, six feet tall and starting to spread around the middle, with a wild mane of curly hair and a loud, resonating voice. He had just gotten established in Toledo politics. He had moved there three years earlier from the town of Portsmouth, in southern Ohio, largely because he had just gotten married and was in deep trouble for helping slaves flee across the Ohio River. He was not yet a Congressman. Nor was he running for office. He was just campaigning for the Republican Party's first presidential candidate, John C. Frémont, and Richard Mott, a House member who was up for

James M. Ashley, congressman from Ohio. Brady-Handy Photograph Collection, Library of Congress (LC-BH824-5303).

reelection. In doing so, he gave a stump speech at a grove near Montpelier, Ohio.[2]

The speech lasted two hours. In most respects, it was a typical Republican stump speech. It was mainly a collection of stories, many from his youth, living and working along the Ohio River. Running through it were several themes that tied the stories together and foreshadowed the rest of his career. In touting the two candidates, he blamed the nation's troubles on a conspiracy of slaveholders and Northern men with Southern principles, or as he called them "slave barons" and "doughfaces." These men, he claimed, had deliberately misconstrued the Bible, misinterpreted the Constitution, and gained complete control of the federal government. "For nearly half a century," he told his listeners, some two hundred thousand slave barons had "ruled the nation, morally and politically, including a majority of the Northern States, with a rod of iron." And before "the advancing march of these slave barons," the "great body of Northern public men" had "bowed down . . . with their hands on their mouths and mouths in the dust, with an abasement as servile as that of a vanquished, spiritless people, before their conquerors."[3]

Across the North, many Republican spokesmen were saying much the same thing. What made Ashley's speech unusual was that he made no attempt to hide his radicalism. He made it clear to the crowd at Montpelier that he would do almost anything to destroy slavery and the men who profited from it. He had learned to hate slavery and the slave barons during his boyhood, traveling with his father, a Campbellite preacher, through Kentucky and western Virginia, and later working as a cabin boy on the Ohio River. Never would he forget how traumatized he had been as a nine-year-old seeing for the first time slaves in chains being driven down a road to the Deep South, whipping posts on which black men had been beaten, and boys his own age being sold away from their mothers. Nor would he ever forget the white man who wouldn't let his cattle drink from a stream in which his father was baptizing slaves. How, he had wondered, could his father still justify slavery? Certainly, it didn't square with the teachings of Christ or what his mother was teaching him back home.

Ashley also made it clear to the crowd at Montpelier that he had violated the Fugitive Slave Law more times than he could count. He had actually begun helping slaves flee bondage in 1839, when he was just fifteen years old, and he had continued doing so after the Fugitive Slave Act of 1850 made the penalties much stiffer. To avoid prosecution, he and his wife had fled southern Ohio in 1851. Would he now mend his ways? "Never!" he told his audience. The law was a gross violation of the teachings of Christ, and for that reason he had never obeyed it and with "God's help . . . never shall."[4]

What, then, should his listeners do? The first step was to join him in supporting John C. Frémont for president and Richard Mott for another term in Congress. Another was to join him in never obeying the "infamous fugitive-slave law"—the most "unholy" of the laws that these slave barons and their Northern sycophants had passed. And perhaps still another, he suggested, was to join him in pushing for a constitutional amendment outlawing "the crime of American slavery" if that should become "necessary."[5]

The last suggestion, in 1856, was clearly fanciful. Nearly half the states were slave states. Thus getting two-thirds of the House, much less two-thirds of the Senate, to support an amendment outlawing slavery was next to impossible. Ashley knew that. Perhaps some in his audience, especially those who cheered the loudest, thought otherwise. But not Ashley. Although still a political neophyte, he knew the rules of the game. He was also good with numbers, always had been, and always would be. Nonetheless, he told his audience to put it on their "to do" list.

Five years later, in December 1861, Ashley added to the list. By then he was no longer a political neophyte. He had been twice elected to Congress. Eleven states had seceded from the Union, and the Civil War was in its eighth month. As chairman of the House Committee on Territories, he proposed that the eleven states no longer be treated as states. Instead they should be treated as "territories" under the control of Congress, and Congress should impose on them certain conditions before they were allowed to regain statehood. More specifically, Congress should abolish slavery in these territories, confiscate all rebel lands, distribute the confiscated lands in plots of 160 acres or fewer to loyal citizens of any color, disfranchise the rebel leaders, and establish new governments with universal adult male suffrage. Did that mean, asked one skeptic, that black men were to receive land? And the right to vote? Yes, it did. And if such measures were enacted, said Ashley, he felt certain that the slave barons would be forever stripped of their power.[6]

Ashley's goal was clear. The 1850 census, from which Ashley and most Republicans drew their numbers, had indicated that just a few Southern families had the lion's share of the South's wealth. Especially potent were the truly big slaveholders—families with over one hundred slaves. There were 105 such family heads in Virginia, 181 in Georgia, 279 in Mississippi, 312 in Alabama, 363 in South Carolina, and 460 in Louisiana. With respect to landholdings, there were 371 family heads in Louisiana with more than one thousand acres, 481 in Mississippi, 482 in South Carolina, 641 in Virginia, 696 in Alabama, and 902 in Georgia.[7]

In Ashley's view, virtually all these wealth holders were rebels, and the Congress should go after all their assets. Strip them of their slaves. Strip them of their land. Strip them of their right to hold office. Half-hearted measures, he contended, would lead only to half-hearted results. Taking away a slave baron's slaves undoubtedly would hobble him, but it wouldn't destroy him. With his vast landholdings, he would soon be back in power. And with the right to hold office, he would not only have economic power but also political power. And with the end of the three-fifths clause, the clause in the Constitution that counted slaves as only three-fifths of a free person when it came to tabulating seats in Congress and electoral votes, the South would have more power than ever before.

When Ashley made this proposal in December 1861, everyone on his committee told him it was much too radical ever to get through Congress.[8] He knew that. But he also knew that there were men in Congress who agreed with him, including four of the seven men on his committee, several dozen in the House, maybe a half-dozen in the Senate, and even some notables such as Representative Thaddeus Stevens of Pennsylvania and Senator Ben Wade of Ohio.

The trouble was the opposition. It was formidable. Not only did it include the "Peace" Democrats, men who seemingly wanted peace at any price, men whom Ashley regarded as traitors, but also "War" Democrats, men such as General George McClellan, General Don Carlos Buell, and General Henry Halleck, men who were leading the nation's troops. Also certain to oppose him were the border state Unionists, especially the Kentuckians, and most important of all, Abraham Lincoln. Against such opposition, all Ashley and the other radicals could do was push, prod, and hope to get maybe a piece or two of the total package enacted.

Two years later, in December 1863, Ashley thought it was indeed "necessary" to strike a deathblow against slavery. He also thought it was possible to get a few pieces of his 1861 package into law. So, just after the House opened for its winter session, he introduced two measures. One was a reconstruction bill that followed, at least at first glance, what Lincoln had called for in his annual message. Like Lincoln, Ashley proposed that a seceded state be let back into the Union when only 10 percent of its 1860 voters took an oath of loyalty.

Had he suddenly become a moderate? A conservative? Not quite. To Lincoln's famous 10 percent plan, Ashley added two provisions. One would take away the right to vote and to hold office from all those who had fought against the Union or held an office in a rebel state. That was a significant chunk of the population. The other would give the right to vote to all adult black males. That was even a bigger chunk of the population, especially in South Carolina and Mississippi.[9]

The other measure that Ashley proposed that December was the constitutional amendment that outlawed slavery. A few days later, Representative James F. Wilson of Iowa made a similar proposal. The wording differed, but the intent was the same. The Constitution had to be amended, contended Wilson, not only to eradicate slavery but also to stop slaveholders and their supporters from launching a program of reenslavement once the war was over. Then, several weeks later, Senator John Henderson of Missouri and Senator Charles Sumner of Massachusetts introduced similar amendments. Sumner's was the more radical. The Massachusetts senator not only wanted to end slavery. He also wanted to end racial inequality.

The Senate Judiciary Committee then took charge. They ignored Sumner's cry for racial justice and worked out the bill's final language. The wording was clear and simple: "Neither slavery nor involuntary servitude, except as a punishment for crime, whereof the party shall have been duly convicted, shall exist within the United States, or any place subject to their jurisdiction."[10]

On April 8, 1864, the committee's wording came before the Senate for a final vote. Although a few empty seats could be found in the men's gallery, the women's gallery was packed, mainly by church women who had organized a massive petition drive calling on Congress to abolish slavery. Congress for the most part had ignored their hard work. But to the women's delight, thirty-eight senators now voted for the amendment, six against, giving the proposed amendment eight votes more than what was needed to meet the two-thirds requirement.

All thirty Republicans in attendance voted aye. The no votes came from two free state Democrats, Thomas A. Hendricks of Indiana and James McDougall of California, and four slave state senators: Garrett Davis and Lazarus W. Powell of Kentucky and George R. Riddle and Willard Saulsbury of Delaware. Especially irate was Saulsbury. A strong proponent of reenslavement, he made sure that the women knew that he regarded them with contempt. In a booming voice, he told them on leaving the Senate floor that all was lost and that there was no longer any chance of ever restoring the eleven Confederate states to the Union.[11]

Now, nine weeks later, the measure was before the House. And its floor manager, James Ashley, expected the worst. He kept a close count. And, as the members voted, he realized that he was well short of the required two-thirds. Of the eighty Republicans who were in attendance, seventy-nine eventually cast aye votes and one abstained. Of the seventeen slave state representatives in attendance, eleven voted aye and six nay. But of the sixty-two free state Democrats, only four voted for the amendment while fifty-eight voted nay. As a result, the final vote was going to be ninety-four to sixty-four. That was eleven shy of the necessary two-thirds majority.

The outcome was even worse than Ashley had anticipated. "Educated in the political school of Jefferson," he later recalled, "I was absolutely amazed at the solid Democratic vote against the amendment on the 15th of June. To me it looked as if the golden hour had come, when the Democratic party could, without apology, and without regret, emancipate itself from the fatal dogmas of Calhoun, and reaffirm the doctrines of Jefferson. It had always seemed to me that the great men in the Democratic party had shown a broader spirit in favor of human liberty than their political opponents, and until the domination of Mr. Calhoun and his States-rights disciples, this was undoubtedly true."[12]

Despite the solid Democratic vote against the resolution, there was still one way that Ashley could save the amendment from certain congressional death. And that was to take advantage of a House rule that allowed a member to bring a defeated measure up for reconsideration if he intended to change his vote. To make use of this rule, however, Ashley had to change his vote before the clerk announced the final tally. He had voted aye along with his fellow Republicans. He now had to get into the "no" column. That he did. The final vote thus became ninety-three to sixty-five.[13]

Two weeks later, Representative William Steele Holman, Democrat of Indiana, asked Ashley when he planned to call for reconsideration. Ashley told him not now but maybe after the next election. The trick, he said, was to find enough men in Holman's party who were "naturally inclined to favor the amendment, and strong enough to meet and repel the fierce partisan attack which were certain to be made upon them."

Holman, Ashley knew, would not be one of them. Although the Indiana Democrat had once been a staunch supporter of the war effort, he opposed the destruction of slavery. Not only had he just voted against the amendment—he had vehemently denounced it. Holman, as Ashley viewed him, was thus one of the "devil's disciples." He was beyond redemption. And with this in mind, Ashley set about to find at least eleven additional House members who would stand their ground against men like Holman.[14]

Chapter One

THE OLD ORDER AND ITS DEFENDERS

From James Ashley's perspective, his failure on June 15 to get the Senate resolution outlawing slavery through the House stemmed from just one odious fact. Too many House members were like William Steele Holman of Indiana. They had been "molded and stamped with the brand of the slave barons," and even three years of the bloodiest war in the nation's history hadn't broken the hold the slave barons had on them.[1]

This servility, contended Ashley, trumped everything else. Backstage, in his pursuit of more votes, he had repeatedly urged Holman and others to follow instead the teachings of Christ and do what they knew was "right." At the same time, he had insisted that the proposed amendment would benefit everyone but the "privileged" elite. Not only would it end chattel slavery in the South and stop Chinese coolies from being enslaved in the Far West. It would also be a godsend for all free workers. It would guarantee their right to work free of undue coercion, and it would elevate those at the bottom who now had to compete with slave labor. No longer would poor whites in the South have to work for "slave wages." No longer would they be under the thumbs of slave masters who denied them the benefits of free schools, a free press, and free speech. Like free laborers elsewhere, they would have a chance to get ahead and enjoy a better life.[2]

Yet, try as he might, Ashley's powers of persuasion had fallen largely on deaf ears. Holman and others hadn't budged. Instead, they had attacked the proposed amendment from all sides, repeatedly lambasting it as unconstitutional and as a violation of states rights but also insisting that it would prolong the war, make peace impossible, ruin the

Northern economy, cause the North to be overrun with black vaga-
bonds, and undermine the property rights of all white Americans.
The speeches had ranged in quality, from racist rants to carefully con-
structed constitutional arguments that legal scholars would later ana-
lyze meticulously.[3] But did any of this matter? In Ashley's view, it was
all window dressing, just a bunch of afterthoughts to justify the habit
of always deferring to the slave barons.

This servility, lamented Ashley, was monstrous. Not only had it determined the outcome of the June vote, but it had governed national
politics for decades as well. Some of his Republican colleagues even
dated it back to the time of Washington and Jefferson. They insisted
that many Northern members of Congress, and especially Northern
Democrats, had been subservient to slaveholding interests from the
very beginning.[4] Ashley, however, refused to accept this view. He
maintained that Congress had once been different.

The Founding Fathers, said Ashley, had not designed a Constitution that was proslavery. Their masterpiece had simply been hijacked
by the likes of John C. Calhoun with the help of men like Holman. Not
all Southern slaveholders, moreover, were slave barons. In his mind,
two of his boyhood heroes, Thomas Jefferson and Andrew Jackson,
were noteworthy exceptions. Although both had owned hundreds of
slaves over the course of their lifetimes, they had always put the country and its future far above their interests as slaveholders. They had
never catered solely to the interests of the Deep South.

Ashley also insisted that Jackson and other leaders of Democratic
Party, which was the party of his youth as well as Holman's youth,
had once "shown a broader spirit in favor of human liberty than their
political opponents." The big change, said Ashley, had come in 1841
when he was just sixteen years old working on a steamboat on the
Ohio River. With the death that year of President William Henry Harrison and the "acting presidency" of John Tyler, the party of Jackson
had fallen into the hands of John C. Calhoun and his states' rights disciples, and so began "the organized conspiracy of the slave barons,
which culminated in the Rebellion."[5]

As Ashley told the story, the first time he himself had to cope with
this "conspiracy," face to face, came three years later.[6] In May 1844,
he attended the Democratic national convention in Baltimore. Even
though he was only nineteen years old, he went as a dedicated sup-

porter of Martin Van Buren, the Little Magician of New York, who was making his third bid for the presidency.

The former president had a majority of the delegates pledged to him, but he had also indicated that he opposed the immediate annexation of slaveholding Texas. To derail his candidacy, a pro-Texas contingent led by Robert J. Walker of Mississippi got the convention to uphold a rule that had been virtually ignored four years earlier. It required the Democratic nominee to have a two-thirds majority. Van Buren couldn't get the two-thirds, and after nine ballots the nomination went to James K. Polk, a Tennessee slaveholder. Ashley, like many of Van Buren's supporters, left Baltimore convinced that the "slave oligarchy" had cheated his man out of the nomination.

For the next decade, Ashley wavered, sometimes supporting the Democratic nominee, sometimes a third-party candidate. Then in January 1854, Senator Stephen A. Douglas, Democrat of Illinois, delivered the final, crushing blow. The Illinois senator was anxious to organize into territories the northern half of the Louisiana Purchase, land that had been closed to slavery since the Missouri Compromise of 1820, partly to facilitate the building of a transcontinental railroad that would run from his hometown of Chicago to the gold country in northern California. Blocking his way was Senator David R. Atchinson, who represented a slaveholding constituency across the Missouri River from the land in question. Not only had Atchinson promised his constituents that they would be able to take their slaves into the new territory, he had virtually staked his political career on that promise as well. Joining Atchinson were several powerful Southern senators who insisted that no bill would pass unless it contained a clause repealing the Missouri Compromise. Douglas gave in to their demands, and President Franklin Pierce, a New Hampshire Democrat, used all the power of his office to get forty-four Northern House Democrats to vote for the repeal.

For Ashley, that was the last straw. The Kansas-Nebraska Act of 1854 alienated him from the Democratic Party forever. As the bill made its way through Congress, all hell broke out in the North, and Ashley joined the many thousands who lambasted Douglas and other "Janus-faced northern Democrats" for yielding to the slave barons. At a convention in Maumee, Ohio, he helped organize a new anti-Nebraska party. Then he flirted briefly with another new party, the Know-Nothings, which to his disgust turned out to be more anti-Catholic than antislavery. Within two years, he was campaigning for the new Republican Party. And in 1858, he was the Republican candidate for Congress in the large Toledo district. He won by a narrow margin. In 1860, Ashley backed Salmon P. Chase, a fellow Ohioan and another former Democrat, for the Republican presidential nomination. When the nomination went to Abraham Lincoln, Ashley campaigned hard for the party's nominee. He also ran for a second congressional term and was reelected.

From the beginning, Ashley was deemed a "wild-eyed radical." His willingness to help runaway slaves form their own church, as well as his support of school desegregation and voting rights for women and blacks, distinguished him from virtually every other politician in his district.[7] He had his prejudices, to be sure. He was definitely an anti-Catholic. He assumed that whites were superior to blacks. The very thought of interracial marriage disgusted him. He also indicated on more than one occasion that given the level of white racial prejudice, blacks might be better off leaving the country and taking refuge in Central America or, even, going "back to Africa" as the American Colonization Society proposed. But, unlike virtually every Northern Democrat and many of his fellow Republicans, Ashley never pandered to Northern racism. On the contrary, he spoke out forcefully for granting blacks the same rights as white citizens—including the right to vote, the right to hold office, the right to sit on juries, and the right to join the militia—even when it clearly hurt him politically.

Following Lincoln's election in 1860, Ashley added to his radical credentials. The Republican victory triggered a national crisis, as seven Deep South states pulled out of the Union, beginning with South Carolina on December 20 and ending with Texas six weeks later. The outgoing administration of James Buchanan, a Pennsylvania Democrat who owed his presidency mainly to the slave states, fretted and then fretted some more. Few in Washington had any idea what the incoming president would do. Elected by a minority of the voters, Lincoln said little publicly about what his policy might be, while in private he opposed any plan, arrangement, or compromise that left the slightest room for slavery's expansion. Meanwhile, politicians in Washington and elsewhere scurried about trying to find a formula that would bring the Deep South back into the Union.

Ashley didn't join them. Instead, he opposed compromising in any way with the Deep South "conspirators." The federal government must stand firm, said Ashley. And, if war broke out, it must move quickly and decisively. Declare martial law. Blockade Southern ports. Hang rebel leaders. And confiscate all rebel property, including slave property. Was that legal? It definitely was, said Ashley. As John Quincy Adams had pointed out to Congress nearly twenty years earlier, the war power clause of the Constitution gave the president, as commander-in-chief of the armed forces, all the legal authority he needed to emancipate every single slave in any state that dared to rebel. And the faster Lincoln did that, said Ashley, the better.[8]

That winter and spring, however, Ashley was a lone voice shouting in the wilderness. The *Toledo Blade*, the party's chief newspaper in his district, even took him to task. The editor of the *Blade*, Clark Waggoner, thought Ashley's views were incendiary and told his readers as much. If there was a war, contended Waggoner, it should not be fought to destroy slavery and the slave oligarchy as Ashley insisted but to restore the Union as it had been before the war. He also called on Ashley to moderate his views. Instead, Ashley fired back with a series of letters to the editor. Thus Toledo's two leading Republicans got into a war of words, one saying that anything short of the destruction of slavery would be a victory for the slave barons, the other calling for the restoration of the old order.[9]

The Republican editor, Clark Waggoner, clearly had the upper hand in 1860–61. He both had more influence locally and his views resonated among most of Ashley's fellow congressmen. Compromise was in the air.

On December 4, even before South Carolina officially seceded, the House of Representatives voted 145 to thirty-eight to create the Committee of Thirty-Three, a special committee of "one from each state," to deal with the crisis. Everyone knew what the committee was to do. It was to work out some sort of "compromise" with the Deep South leaders. Ashley was one of the thirty-eight to vote no. In debate, he lambasted the committee and its proposals, especially those coming from William Kellogg, an Illinois Republican, whom he hoped to see "kicked by a steam Jackass from Washington to Illinois." Kellogg should be against cutting a deal with the Deep South "conspirators,"

John J. Crittenden, senator from Kentucky.
Matthew Brady photograph, 1855, Library of Congress.

of giving in to any of their demands. The Congress had being doing that for years, said Ashley, and look what it gotten them. Just more demands.[10]

Many in Congress also sought guidance from the leaders of the eight slave states that bordered the South but still remained in the Union. What would they do? Ashley, however, thought seeking their advice was absurd. The border-state leaders were just dealmakers for the Deep South "conspirators." Nonetheless, all eyes that December turned to Senator John J. Crittenden of Kentucky, a good-natured, proslavery Unionist who always had a chaw of chewing tobacco in his mouth.[11] He had been chewing since he was a boy, and his teeth had turned brown. At age seventy-four, he was at the tail end of long and distinguished career.

Crittenden had first entered Kentucky politics in 1811, when he was twenty-one years old. When he took his first seat in the US Senate in 1817, he was only twenty-seven years old—three years shy of the constitutional requirement. He had served for two years before the Kentucky governor realized that the appointment was illegal and had him removed from office. Subsequently, Crittenden had been Speaker of the Kentucky House of Representatives, governor of Kentucky, attorney general of the United States on two different occasions, and US senator on three different occasions.

On the issues that led to the secession crisis, Crittenden's family was hopelessly split. His son Thomas would end up fighting for the Union, his son George for the Confederacy. Years before, the family had also split over the behavior of his nephew William, a twenty-eight-year-old West Point graduate who in 1851 had led over one hundred Southern volunteers on a futile filibustering expedition to seize Spanish Cuba, with its three hundred thousand slaves, and add it to the United States. Captured by Cuban authorities, William and fifty of his American comrades had been executed by a firing squad.[12]

Torn almost as much as Crittenden's family was the white population Crittenden represented. Historians would later say that the Civil War in Kentucky was really a "brother's war," with one brother going one way, the other the opposite way. That is clearly an exaggeration. In the end, for every white brother who fought for the Confederacy, two fought for the Union, and a whopping seven out of ten sat out the war. No state east of the Mississippi had a greater percentage of non-participants.[13]

While support for the Union was strong among some of Crittenden's followers, lackadaisical among others, support for slavery was widespread. Crittenden himself owned nine slaves on the eve of the Civil War. He had made his career mainly as a lawyer-politician and now had just household servants. But among his constituents and within his family were numerous planters, men and women who owned twenty or more field hands, and he was answerable to them and well aware of it.

Roughly 19 percent of all Kentuckians were slaves, and their masters had long had inordinate political power. In 1792, when the slave population was barely 16 percent, proslavery men had gotten a clause written into the state constitution that explicitly protected slavery. It prohibited the legislature from passing laws for the emancipation of slaves without getting the prior consent of their owners and without granting full compensation "in money for the slaves so emancipated." This article, the first in a state constitution, was later copied by other Southern states. Years later, in the state's constitution of 1850, proslavery forces in Kentucky had made emancipation virtually impossible. They had established a series of hurdles, so that would-be emancipationists would first have to get the backing of two consecutive legislative sessions, then the people, then a constitutional convention, before any legal change could take effect.[14]

By this time, the demand for more slaves in Kentucky had lessened. Up until the early 1820s, Kentucky planters had imported thousands of slaves each year from Virginia. Since then, they had exported more slaves than they imported, and for at least thirty years the Crittendens and many other Kentucky planters had fattened their pocketbooks by selling off surplus slaves to the southwest—to the new labor-starved cotton plantations in Arkansas and Mississippi and to the dangerous and pestilent sugar plantations in Louisiana. It was a lucrative business, and by the 1850s Kentucky ranked third in the slave export trade. Only Virginia and South Carolina exported more slaves per year than Kentucky.

Thus every year, several thousand Kentucky-born slaves were on the road, the men in chains, heading south and west. Some were accompanied by their masters, but probably two out of three were in the hands of slave traders who had roamed the state looking especially for able-bodied young men who would fetch a good price in Natchez, New Orleans, and other Deep South markets. This trade, in turn, had probably ripped apart one out five slave families in Kentucky. Yet, at the same time, it had increased the value of every slave in Kentucky and had enriched nearly every Kentucky planter.[15]

This lucrative business, however, was vulnerable. For nearly thirty years, Northern abolitionists had denounced it for ruining black families. Then in 1852, Harriet Beecher Stowe had made it the centerpiece of her best selling novel *Uncle Tom's Cabin*, and thousands of her readers had called on Congress to outlaw it. Could that be done? Yes, said pundits, under the interstate commerce clause of the Constitution. That also was what Harriet Beecher Stowe indirectly called for. And that, declared the editor of the *Kentucky Statesman*, was something that Crittenden and other Kentucky politicians must stop from ever happening.[16]

Besides representing a state where slaveholders had inordinate power, and one that had been enriched by the interstate slave trade, Crittenden also represented a state that held Lincoln and his party in contempt. In the 1860 presidential campaign, Crittenden himself had done much to promote this scorn. He had denounced Lincoln and his followers as fanatics who thought it was "their duty to destroy the white man" so that "the black man might be free." He had also said that "should Lincoln be elected," the South "could not submit to the consequences" and therefore would "secede from the Union." He had insisted that the only way to avert this catastrophe was by supporting the Constitutional Union Party and its choice for president, the Tennessee slaveholder John Bell, whose platform contained only one plank: the preservation of the Union.[17]

Many white Kentuckians either saw the world as Crittenden did or adhered to his advice. Bell won 45 percent of the Kentucky popular vote and all twelve of the state's electoral votes. He beat John C. Breckinridge, a native son and the favorite of the Deep South, by eight percentage points. He trounced Lincoln, the other native son, by a sixty-to-one margin. In the four-man race, Lincoln finished dead last, with less than 1 percent of the popular vote and a total of only 1,364 votes. Even his old friend Joshua Speed, now a prosperous Kentucky slave owner, opposed him. Lincoln got only ten votes in the counties in which his family had once lived, and only five votes from Fayette County, the home of his in-laws, the Todds. The Todds, like the Crittenden family, were hopelessly divided. Of Mary Todd Lincoln's thirteen siblings, eight ended up supporting the Confederacy and five the Union. The most controversial was her sister Emilie, whose husband died fighting for the Confederacy, and who came to live in the White House but refused to take an oath of allegiance to the Union.

Following Lincoln's election, Crittenden hoped to find some way to appease South Carolina and stop the disunionists in their tracks. That was expected of him. For he held the same senate seat as Henry Clay, the silver-tongued Great Pacificator who had been credited by many in Congress with bringing about sectional peace on at least three different occasions, first in 1820, then again in 1833, and still again in 1850. Now, many in Congress sought another peacemaker. They thus turned to Crittenden, the man who had worked in Clay's shadow for most of his career. Was he up to the task? Might he be another Clay? Might he find a way to put the country back together?

To that end, Crittenden in December 1860 proposed that Congress pass six constitutional amendments and four resolutions that protected slavery. He called for extending the old Missouri Compromise line to California, banning slavery above the line, but allowing it to expand below the line in all territories "now held, or hereafter acquired," which many assumed meant slaveholding Cuba. He also pressed for a series of amendments that would prohibit Congress from abolishing slavery on all federal property located within the slave states, from abolishing slavery in the District of Columbia as long as it was legal in Maryland and Virginia, and from interfering with the interstate slave trade, the lucrative business that was clearly crucial to his slave-owning constituents. He wanted still another amendment, which was also a special concern to his border-state constituents, that mandated that Congress compensate the owners of runaway slaves. Finally, he called for a sixth amendment that made perpetual the other five amendments, along with the three-fifths clause and the fugitive slave clause of the Constitution. On top of all this, he wanted the Northern states to repeal their personal liberty laws and to bar all blacks from voting, and Congress to stiffen the penalties for violating the Fugitive Slave Law of 1850, the one that Ashley had told his constituents that he would never obey.

Arguing that this "compromise" package was the last, best hope to avert disunion, Crittenden took it to the Senate floor. Many border-state politicians liked it, many Northern Democrats supported it, but the Republican majority regarded it as complete "surrender" to the slave states, and offstage Lincoln urged its defeat. On January 16, with the fourteen senators from states that had seceded or were about to secede not voting, the Senate rejected it by a 23–25 vote, with Republicans providing all twenty-five of the nay votes.[18]

Crittenden then returned to Kentucky and worked hard to get his fellow Kentuckians to rebuff secessionist overtures from South Carolina and the other Deep South states. In May, he chaired a convention in Frankfort, Kentucky, where he successfully thwarted secessionist agitators. In a special election in June, he was sent back to Congress, this time as a member of House of Representatives.

The Kentucky senator was not the only national figure that December who called for a constitutional amendment to protect slavery. So, too, did some Republicans, along with many Northern Democrats.

One plan may have had Lincoln's blessing. On the evening of December 20, in Springfield, Illinois, the president-elect had a long talk with Thurlow Weed, the most influential wheeler-dealer in the Republican Party and the right-hand man of New York senator William Henry Seward, Lincoln's choice for secretary of state. Weed, in turn, passed along the gist of this meeting as well as some written proposals to his friend Seward. The New York senator then drafted a consti-

William H. Seward, senator from New York. Prints and
Photographs Division, Library of Congress (LC-USZ62-21907).

tutional amendment that would have prohibited future amendments
from interfering with slavery in states where it already existed.

Was Seward simply doing Lincoln's bidding? That is a matter of dispute. What isn't in dispute is that Seward had high hopes for this proposal. He thought that it would convince Southerners that the Republican Party had no intention of destroying slavery in the states where
it existed. It would thus turn the secessionist tide, causing unionism
to flourish in the upper South and disunion to wither and die in the
lower South. Unfortunately, the diminutive New York senator underestimated the strength of the secessionist movement.

Once Seward introduced this proposal, every Republican in Congress took notice. Not only had Lincoln chosen Seward to be his secretary of state, but the fifty-nine-year-old senator was also a powerful
figure in his own right. He had been the governor of New York before
becoming the party's leading voice in the Senate for more than a decade. He had also been the first choice of many Republicans for the
presidential nomination in both 1856 and 1860. On the advice of his
friend Weed, he had withdrawn his name from consideration in 1856,
a decision that many thought cost him the 1860 nomination. And in
1860 he had lost to Lincoln on the third ballot. He had scores of ad-

mirers, men who loved his storytelling, his wit, his vitality, and his enormous capacity for hard work. He also had his detractors, men who thought he was incredibly vain, duplicitous, and underhanded.[19]

Seward presented his proposed amendment to the Senate just before Christmas 1860. Four days later, his ally in the House of Representatives, Charles Francis Adams of Massachusetts, offered a different and much wordier version, whereby the only way slavery in any state could be abolished was if every slave state so agreed. It went to the House Committee of Thirty-Three, which had been formed to handle such matters. The committee approved Adams's wording, twenty-one to three. Then the committee's chairman, Thomas Corwin of Ohio, sounded out other party members and learned to his chagrin that the language was too strong and probably wouldn't get the two-thirds vote needed for passage. So on February 26, Corwin proposed a substitute: "No amendment shall ever be made to the Constitution which will authorize or give to Congress power to abolish or interfere, within any State, with the domestic institutions thereof, including that of persons held to labor or service by the laws of said State." The substitute was exactly what Seward had proposed in the Senate, with the addition of just one word—the word "ever." The committee endorsed the substitute.

Then the next day, to James Ashley's horror, this revised amendment came before the House for a vote. Seven slave states were now out of the Union, and none of their representatives were there to vote. Now known as the Corwin Amendment, the measure came well short of the necessary two-thirds majority, receiving 123 aye votes to seventy-one nays. The nays consisted of seventy Republicans and one Democrat, John Hickman of Pennsylvania. The next day, one of the nay voters, David Kilgore of Indiana, moved to reconsider. The motion to reconsider passed, 128 to sixty-five. A new vote on the Corwin Amendment then passed, 133 to sixty-five.

The revised amendment was then rushed to the Senate, which had three days left before the session expired. Taking charge was Lincoln's long-time rival, the Little Giant from Illinois, Stephen A. Douglas. The five-foot-four-inch Democrat was anxious to get the amendment passed. But before he could push it through, Charles Sumner of Massachusetts intervened. He tried to block the vote, insisting that the previous day's journal was in error and needed to be corrected. He got a one-day delay. The next day, debate was furious. Then, on Sunday, Douglas succeeded. The final vote was twenty-four to twelve, the exact number needed for passage. All twelve no votes came from Republicans.[20]

James Ashley thought that day should live in infamy. It proved once again that the slave barons were in control. But outgoing president James Buchanan was delighted with the result—so delighted that he signed the amendment even though the Constitution didn't call on him to do so. As for incoming president Lincoln, the *New York Tribune* reported that he had advised Republicans from his home state of Illinois to vote for it.

The amendment then went to the states for approval. It was ratified by Ohio on May 13, 1861, and by Maryland on January 10, 1862. But, thanks to the outbreak of the Civil War, it never came close to getting the required support of three-fourths of the states. It thus failed to become the thirteenth amendment to the Constitution.[21]

Two days after the Corwin Amendment was sent to the states for ratification, Abraham Lincoln was sworn in as president. In his inaugural address, he gave the amendment his stamp of approval. He also pleaded for the preservation of the Union. At the same time, he refused to recognize secession and said that any violent acts against the United States were "insurrectionary or revolutionary" and that the Union would "defend and maintain itself." He insisted that while the federal government would not initiate hostilities, it would "hold, occupy, and possess" the federal forts and other federal properties in the seven seceded states as well as collect the import duties in those states.

Lincoln thought that his inaugural address would reinforce unionist sentiment throughout the South, keep the upper South from seceding, and eventually overcome secessionist sentiment in the lower South. Unfortunately, like William Seward, he grossly overestimated unionist sentiment in the South, especially in the seven seceded states. It was much weaker than he imagined. Two days after his inaugural address, the Confederate Congress responded. It authorized the raising of a hundred thousand troops. Newspapers across the Deep South endorsed the action and praised the manliness of their new government. Many thousands volunteered.

The crisis came to a head when Lincoln had to make a decision about lightly garrisoned Fort Sumter. Located in the entrance of Charleston's harbor, it had become the symbol of the whole federal property controversy. It had supplies for just six weeks. Lincoln decided to send a naval expedition bearing provisions. Confederate authorities, in turn, demanded that the fort be evacuated. Then, when that demand was refused, Confederate artillery on April 12, 1861, opened fire and forced the fort's surrender.

In response, Lincoln called on the states for seventy-five thousand troops. That led to the second secession crisis. Rather than provide men to be used against fellow Southerners, Virginia seceded from the Union on April 17 and joined the Confederacy, and within six weeks Arkansas, Tennessee, and North Carolina followed. To tighten Virginia's adherence to the Southern cause, the Confederacy then moved its capital north from Montgomery to Richmond.

That left only four slave states—Delaware, Maryland, Kentucky, and Missouri—still in the Union. Three of these states—Maryland, Kentucky, and Missouri—had strong secessionist movements and would provide roughly eighty thousand troops for the Confederacy. Meanwhile, thousands of men from the Appalachian hill country of eastern Tennessee and western North Carolina would fight for the Union, and the western counties of Virginia would break away from Virginia and under the auspices of the Lincoln administration form the new state of West Virginia.

Following the firing on Fort Sumter, Ashley spent the next few weeks rallying recruits at war rallies in Indiana, Illinois, and Ohio. He liked what he saw. He became convinced that the "mad action" of the slave barons had made antislavery sentiment grow faster in just thirty days than it had in thirty years. He hoped that the Lincoln administration would take advantage of this "golden moment" and take steps to destroy slavery. One step would be for the president and his men to appoint true Republicans to oversee the four slave states that still remained in the Union. But that, he noted, hadn't happened. Instead, Lincoln seemed to be listening to conditional Union men like Kentucky's John Crittenden.

All these men talked about, complained Ashley, was reconciliation. They also refused to recognize that slavery was the sole cause of the rebellion, and until it was destroyed there would be no peace. They even insisted that soldiers be used as slave catchers. That was not only immoral and disgraceful, said Ashley, it was also absurd. Returning fugitive slaves to their masters was the last thing the army should be doing. Instead, it should be disrupting slavery at every opportunity. Conditional unionists like Crittenden, concluded Ashley, were "worse than undisguised traitors."[22]

Such thinking was not unique to Ashley. It was commonplace among Ashley's fellow Ohio radicals. Since the 1840s, many of them had insisted that the political leaders of Kentucky and other Southern states spoke only for the slave-owning aristocracy. Ignored entirely, they said, were nonslaveholding whites. Not only were these ordinary men and women left out in the cold, but for generations, their aspirations had also been trampled on. To them, slavery was a curse, and the slaveholding elite knew it. Thus, once the Republicans ended the control of men like Crittenden, these ordinary folk would rise up and be heard. That, said Ashley, was a sure thing.[23]

Many Ohio radicals also expected to see slaves rise up and challenge the system. With this in mind, one of their aging mentors, sixty-six-year-old Joshua Giddings, called for an emancipation proclamation in the first month of the war. Nothing, wrote Giddings, would do more damage to the Southern war effort than such a proclamation. It would strike "such terror to the whole south" that it would "compel every fighting man to remain at home and look to their negroes instead of going into the army to kill our friends."[24] Unfortunately, noted Ashley, men like Giddings didn't have the president's ear.

Yet, while Crittenden and other conditional unionists did have the president's ear, the war created situations that they couldn't control. The first one that captured Ashley's attention began with three slaves—Shepard Mallory, Frank Baker, and James Townsend.

Their owner, Confederate Colonel Charles K. Mallory, had hired them out to build fortifications for the 115th Virginia Militia at Sewell's Point in Hampton Roads, Virginia. After about a week of work, the three men learned that their master planned to hire them out to another Confederate unit, located somewhere in North Carolina, far away from home. Rather than go there, they seized a canoe and paddled across the James River toward Fortress Monroe, a Union installation near the mouth of Chesapeake Bay.

On the evening of May 24, 1861, they approached the picket guard and told him their story. The next day, the guard brought them before the fort's commander, Major General Benjamin F. Butler. After quizzing the three men, Butler decided that he was justified in confiscating

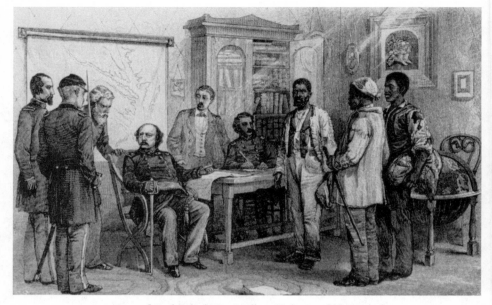

General Butler declaring Mallory, Baker, and Townsend
contraband of war. 1861 engraving, Library of Congress.

them as "property designed, adapted, and about to be used against the
United States." He declared them contraband of war and put them to
work at the fort building a bakery. The following day, one of Colonel
Mallory's subordinates, Major John B. Cary, appeared at the fort under
a flag of truce and demanded that the three men be returned under the
Fugitive Slave Act of 1850. Butler informed him that the act applied
only to citizens of the United States, and as a Virginia secessionist the
colonel was no longer a citizen.

News of the actions of Shepard Mallory, Frank Baker, and James
Townsend traveled rapidly through the slave grapevine. Three days
after their successful canoe ride, eight more slaves appeared at the
fort's gates. The next day, fifty-nine more presented themselves. By
August 1861 some nine hundred fugitives sought and gained refuge at
Fortress Monroe. By March of the following year, the total was about
fifteen hundred, with about 850 being women and children. By the
end of 1862, the total was nearly five thousand. By May 1863, the number exceeded ten thousand.

Some came by sea, many by land. Dressed in men's clothing, one
woman walked alone through some two hundred miles of Confeder-

ate territory to get to the fort. Called to testify before the American Freedmen's Inquiry Commission, Captain Charles Wilder, the superintendent of contrabands, explained that she was not the only one who traveled so far. "They came from all about," said Wilder, "from Richmond and 200 miles off in North Carolina."[25]

Although slaves from as far away as Richmond and North Carolina essentially freed themselves, walking miles through swamps and hostile territory, much of credit went to General Butler, who quickly became an antislavery hero. For such accolades, the forty-two-year-old general had a strange background. A New Hampshire native, he had made a name for himself as a Massachusetts trial lawyer and as an active member of the state's Democratic Party. Like most Democrats in Massachusetts at the time, he had little success in state politics, serving just one term as a state representative, one term as a state senator, and losing two gubernatorial races. But more noteworthy was his record. He was identified with the proslavery wing of the Democratic Party. In the 1860 presidential election, he had even supported the proslavery candidate, John C. Breckinridge, and had run for governor on the Breckinridge ticket. Despite his Southern sympathies, however, Butler was quick to volunteer for the Union cause once the war began. A brigadier general of the Massachusetts militia, he led forces that secured Baltimore for the Union and, as a major general, captured Fort Hatteras and Fort Clark in North Carolina. He was then assigned to Fortress Monroe in southeast Virginia.[26]

Ashley met Butler soon after the general made his momentous decision. He thought the general's refusal to return Mallory, Baker, and Townsend to their master was a great step forward. He also liked the general, and the two soon became close political allies. After some delay, Lincoln's secretary of war, Simon Cameron, also approved Butler's decree. That, too, pleased Ashley. The White House, he concluded, might prove to be more forceful than he had at first realized.[27] That hope, however, was shattered when he returned to Washington.

In Washington, the Republicans had firm control of Congress. With eleven of the fifteen slave states now out of the Union, the South had lost control of national politics, especially in the Senate. For years, proslavery Southerners in the Senate had enjoyed the whip hand, as there had always been a handful of free state senators who would vote with them on North-South issues, men like William Gwin of Califor-

nia and Daniel S. Dickinson of New York. Now, while the proslavery
contingent could still count on Northern senators like Indiana's Jesse
Bright, their own numbers had dwindled. The exodus of their Southern brethren had left Republicans in control—not just of the House
but also of the Senate, by a sixteen-vote margin.

Nonetheless, when the emergency summer session of Congress
opened, proslavery men still seemed to have a larger voice in both
houses than their numbers warranted. John J. Crittenden again took
center stage. He no longer represented Kentucky in the Senate. He was
now a member of the House of Representatives. Yet he was still widely
regarded as the chief spokesman for the four slave states that still remained in the Union. As such he drafted a resolution in July 1861 that
required the Union government to take no action against the institution of slavery.

The resolution blamed "the present deplorable civil war" on "the
disunionists of the Southern States." But, at the same time, it also declared that the Union was not waging war "in any spirit of oppres-
sion, nor for any purpose of conquest or subjugation, nor purpose
of overthrowing or interfering with the rights or established institutions of those States, but to defend and maintain the supremacy of the
Constitution and to preserve the Union, with all the dignity, equality,
and rights of the several States unimpaired." The resolution, in short,
promised that slavery would still be intact whenever the war ended
and the seceding states returned to the Union.

Shortly thereafter, Senator Andrew Johnson of Tennessee offered
a similar resolution in the Senate. At this point Crittenden's replacement in the Senate, John C. Breckinridge, broke ranks with his fellow
Kentuckian. He chastised Crittenden and Johnson for blaming the war
on the Confederacy. He blamed the war instead on the Republican
Party, only to have one of his long-time followers, Henry Rice of Min-
nesota, openly renounce his leadership.[28]

Where did the White House stand? It backed the two resolutions.
Of all the problems that faced Lincoln in July 1861, nothing worried
him more than what Crittenden's Kentucky might do. How deep was
their loyalty to the Union? Would tampering with slavery drive them
out of the Union? If the Kentuckians left, what would happen in slaveholding Missouri? And in slaveholding Maryland? He feared the worst.
Hence, in his message to Congress on July 4, he had made it clear that

he had "no purpose, directly or indirectly, to interfere with slavery in those States where it exists."

The approval of the White House undoubtedly added weight to the two resolutions. In the early months of the war, even antislavery radicals who hoped that the war would destroy slavery were hesitant to criticize the administration's policies. Preserving Northern unity was essential. It was at the top of the agenda. So when the resolutions came up for a vote on July 22 and 25, respectively, both the House and the Senate voted overwhelmingly in their favor. Only seven Republicans voted no, and two dozen abstained.

James Ashley abstained. He later said that it was "the most cowardly act" of his life. Nothing shamed him more. If he'd had any guts, he would have followed the lead of two of his fellow House Republicans, John F. Potter of Wisconsin and Albert G. Riddle of Ohio, and voted against this "humbug" resolution.[29]

Within a few weeks, Ashley had a chance to partially redeem himself. He was not alone in his hatred of the Crittenden and Johnson Resolutions. Nor was he alone in his hatred of Fugitive Slave Act.

Among the House members who shared his views was Owen Lovejoy. A fifty-year-old Illinois Republican who many thought looked too well fed and sweet tempered to be a true radical, he was the younger brother of Elijah Lovejoy, a famous abolitionist newspaper editor who had been killed by a proslavery mob in Alton, Illinois, in 1837. On his brother's grave, he had sworn never to forsake the antislavery cause. And, like Ashley, he had openly defied the Fugitive Slave Act on numerous occasions.

On July 2, Lovejoy addressed the House. He proposed that the House go on record that it was "no part of the duty of the soldiers of the United States to capture and return fugitive slaves." His resolution passed, but to Ashley's dismay it had no teeth. It was nonbinding. It simply recommended that Union generals stop using their men as "slave catchers."[30] Would Democratic generals like George McClellan and Don Carlos Buell abide by this recommendation? The answer was no.

Also sharing Ashley's views was Zachary Chandler in the Senate. An uneducated, self-made, hard-drinking man in his late fifties, he had been sent to the Senate in 1857 by the Republican Party's more radical elements in central and western Michigan. Like Ashley, he was a rough but effective debater who seldom pulled his punches. He essentially agreed with Ashley that Southern slave masters had long dominated the federal government, especially the Senate, and insisted that no compromise should ever be made with the "Slave Power."

On July 5, to Ashley's delight, Chandler introduced a punitive confiscation bill. It called on the federal government to seize the property of all the top Confederate leaders—the governors, legislators, judges—as well as "all military officers above the rank of lieutenant." These individuals were also to be "forever disqualified" from holding any office. To Ashley's dismay, Chandler lacked the votes to get his bill passed, but he wasn't alone in his thinking. There were other confiscation proposals, generally less stringent than his, being bandied about.[31] Did any of these bills have a chance? Ashley hoped so.

Then, on July 21, Ashley and the other proponents of confiscation got an unexpected boost. The Union army at Bull Run suffered a humiliating defeat. While half of the Union forces probably fought bravely and stood their ground, the other half ran back to Washington.

On talking to the returning soldiers, one congressman after another learned that slaves "by the thousand" had been instrumental in the Confederate victory. They had been used to dig trenches and build fortifications. They drove teams. They did the cooking. They tended the wounded. They did dozens of camp chores. After several interviews, Congressman James G. Blaine, a Maine Republican, concluded that he had grossly underestimated the impact of the South's slave population. It had freed up hundreds of thousands of Southern white men to kill his constituents and other Northern farm boys. He was thus duty-bound to make the Southern slave owners pay dearly.[32]

By this time, reports of the actions of Mallory, Baker, and Townsend had also made their way to Congress. Although the Kentucky delegation was up in arms about the hundreds of slaves who were freeing themselves and taking refuge at Fortress Monroe, others applauded the bravery of these men, women, and children who had walked miles through hostile Confederate territory to get to the Union stronghold. What was the Congress as a whole to do about it? Was the Congress to back General Butler? Or the other Democratic generals, men like Don Carlos Buell, Henry Halleck, and George McClellan, who were returning slaves to their masters?

Except for a few congressmen like John Potter of Wisconsin and Albert Riddle of Ohio, most members of Ashley's party had formally endorsed the position of Crittenden and his fellow Kentuckians. They had voted for the Crittenden and Johnson Resolutions. They had agreed that Congress had no right to legislate against slavery in a state. But what about individuals who allowed their slaves to be used against the United States? Couldn't such traitors be punished? Didn't the laws of war authorize the seizure of any property, including slave property, used to aid the war effort directly?

With such questions in mind, Republicans on the Judiciary Committee crafted the First Confiscation Act. It authorized the federal government to seize any property, including slave property, used by the Confederacy to aid the war effort directly. The measure came up for a vote in early August, the last days of the short summer session. Its sponsors insisted that the bill didn't break new ground. It wasn't a law against a state. It was a law that applied only to individuals who had taken up arms against the United States. It was essentially a restatement of a basic law of war that had been recognized by virtually every country in the world.

That argument, however, failed to win over border-state congressmen and Northern Democrats. They denounced the bill. They said it went too far. They claimed that it violated the Constitution. All but three voted against it. Ashley, Chandler, and their fellow Republicans, however, were in the majority. With eleven slave states now out of the Union, they had more than enough votes. All but six Republicans voted for the bill. The measure thus passed the House, sixty to forty-eight, and the Senate, twenty-four to eleven.[33] On August 6, the last day of the session, it reached the president's desk.

Lincoln was reluctant to sign it. Union troops had just been routed at Bull Run and forced to flee back to Washington. Didn't that make the bill seem like an act of desperation? He also feared that the measure might be struck down by the Supreme Court, which was still in the hands of Chief Justice Roger B. Taney and other proslavery men. Finally, the lack of bipartisan support bothered him. He worried that the act might push the border states, especially Kentucky and Missouri, into secession in order to protect slavery within their boundaries. At the same time, however, Lincoln also faced overwhelming pressure from his fellow Republicans, including his party's most powerful senators, to sign the measure.

In the end, Lincoln approved the bill but gave his attorney general, Edward Bates, no instructions on its enforcement. And Bates, a staunch conservative, had no desire to make sweeping changes in the slave states. Moreover, he didn't have the manpower to enforce any congressional act even if he wanted to. The only government agency that had the necessary manpower was the army, so enforcement, if there was to be any, rested with Lincoln as commander-in-chief. What would he do? Would he force Democratic generals like George McClellan, Henry Halleck, and Don Carlos Buell to abide by the clear intention of Congress? Or would he allow them to ignore Congress, go their own way, and return fugitives to bondage? He essentially did the latter.

Thus, to the disgust of Ohio volunteer John Beatty, his commander General Buell continued to make him hunt down runaways and return them to their masters. It was the policy of an "amiable idiot," wrote Beatty. Only a fool like Buell would "fritter away the army and the revenue of the government in the insane effort to protect men who have forfeited all right to protection."[34]

Three weeks after Lincoln signed the Confiscation Act, its underlying principles received their first test.

The commander of the Western Department of the Union Army was Major General John C. Frémont, who was a folk hero. Thousands of children had grown up hearing stories about how the Pathfinder, as he was known, and his men had scaled "the savage battlements of the Rocky Mountains," carrying the American flag to places it had never been before. Thousands of settlers had made the long trip from Nebraska to California with Frémont's *Travels* serving as their only guidebook. Thousands had hailed him as the "great explorer," the man who had provided more usable information about the West than all before him. He also had been the Republican Party's first presidential candidate. In 1856 he had won eleven of the sixteen free states, 114 electoral votes, and roughly one-third of the popular vote. Had he carried Pennsylvania and Indiana, or Pennsylvania and Illinois, he would have won the presidency.

On July 25, the Pathfinder entered Saint Louis and found the city in the midst of a guerrilla war. He also received reports indicating that "nearly every county" in Missouri was in "insurrectionary condition," that the enemy was being financed by many of the state's bankers and

"Col. Fremont Planting American Standard on Rocky Mountains."
1856 Republican election poster, Library of Congress.

wealthy slave owners, and that Confederate troops were advancing along the Southern frontier. He was short of men, money, and ammunition. His army consisted mainly of ninety-day volunteers who were threatening to leave once their terms expired. Some of his men were robbing the locals blind, which in turn had exacerbated guerrilla activity.

Then the news got worse. On August 10, one of his key commanders, Brigadier General Nathaniel Lyon, launched an attack on Confederates at Wilson's Creek. The battle was bloody, with each side suffering about thirteen hundred casualties. But the Confederates succeeded in killing Lyon, in routing a column led by Colonel Franz Sigel, and in forcing a Union retreat. Their success buoyed Southern sympathizers throughout the area, stimulated even more giving by the state's pro-Southern bankers and planters, and the Confederacy soon recruited forty thousand men and began a campaign to recover southern Missouri, while Confederate guerrillas terrorized settlements around Saint Louis.

In response, Frémont went after all Missourians who opposed him, not just the rebels in arms but also the bankers and wealthy planters who had financed them. He had banks seized and their officers replaced by "good" Union men who put the squeeze on the pro-Confederate planters, calling in their loans and launching lawsuits against them, driving many into bankruptcy and spurring their sons to join the guerrillas. Worried about Confederate plots within Saint Louis, he declared martial law throughout the city on August 14. Then on August 30, he declared martial law once more, this time throughout the entire state, proclaiming that "anyone found with arms within Union lines" would be "shot upon being found guilty by a court-martial" and that the property, real and personal, of all persons who took up arms against the Union or assisted those who did so would be "confiscated to the public use, and their slaves, if any they have, . . . declared free." Frémont's proclamation electrified much of the North. Republican newspapers, by and large, sang his praises. Secretary of War Simon Cameron telegraphed his hearty approval. Someone had finally taken vigorous action.[35]

One unhappy reader, however, was Cameron's boss, Abraham Lincoln, the commander-in-chief. He hadn't been alerted in advance by the general. He, like most of his countrymen, learned about Frémont's proclamation from the press. And his main worry was keeping Kentucky in the Union. Accordingly, he acted quickly to repair the damage. He wrote Frémont and ordered him not to shoot any guerrillas without getting prior approval, for the Confederates would undoubtedly shoot "our best men" in retaliation. He also told the general that freeing rebel slaves would "alarm our Southern Union friends, and turn them against us — perhaps ruin our rather fair prospect for Kentucky." He then asked Frémont to modify his order so that it complied with the Confiscation Act, which permitted the seizure of slaves, but only slaves used directly in the Confederate war effort, and said nothing specifically about declaring slaves "free."[36]

Instead of treating Lincoln's letter as a direct order, Frémont sent his wife, Jessie, to Washington to confer with the president. The daughter of one of the nation's most illustrious senators, Thomas Hart Benton, she had literally been raised in Washington politics. She also was famous in her own right. At a midnight meeting, she tried to convince Lincoln that her husband's judgment was better than his. Lincoln didn't budge. On his desk were scores of letters and telegrams from border-state unionists protesting Frémont's action. More were on the way.

Especially blunt were those from Lincoln's oldest and best friend, the Kentuckian Joshua Speed. Wrote Speed: "Do not allow us by the foolish action of a military popinjay to be driven from our present active loyalty." Speed further warned that "our Constitution and laws prohibit the emancipation of slaves among us—even in small numbers. If a military commander can turn them loose by the threat of a mere proclamation—it will be a most difficult matter to get our people to submit to it." Warned Speed again, two days later: "So fixed is public sentiment in this state against freeing Negroes . . . that you had as well attack the freedom of worship in the North or the right of a parent to teach his child to read as to wage war in the state on such principles."[37]

Jessie Benton Frémont thus failed in her quest. On September 11, the day after her visit, Lincoln publicly revoked her husband's edict. Six weeks later, he removed Frémont from his command. The decision generated a huge backlash. Back in Missouri, Frémont had plenty of critics, men and women who regarded him as an impetuous fool. But he also had the backing of a large number of officers to whom he had given irregular commissions, the Germans of Saint Louis whose causes he had embraced, and antislavery radicals who thought that fighting against slaveholders, without fighting against slavery, was like fighting with one arm tied behind one's back.

Unionists in Missouri thus split into two camps, with the more conservative element rallying behind the president, the more radical behind the general. Leading the conservatives was Frank Blair, whose brother Montgomery was Lincoln's postmaster general. Leading the radicals was his cousin, B. Gratz Brown. Both men were Kentucky-born. Both came from wealthy, slave-owning, political families. And both were former Democrats. Yet, despite their similar backgrounds, they were at loggerheads over what Lincoln had done and the direction that the war was taking.[38]

Lincoln's decision also stirred up Republicans nationally. No action that he took in his four years as president inspired more letters to the White House. They came by the hundreds. The Harvard poet James Russell Lowell captured the spirit of many. "How many times," asked Lowell, "are we to save Kentucky and lose our self respect?" And while some Democratic newspapers enthusiastically backed the president, some Republican papers treated Lincoln's rebuke of Frémont as a giant step in the wrong direction. Declared John Medill of the *Chicago Tribune*: "The President's letter to General Frémont has caused a funereal gloom over our patriotic city. We are stricken with a heavier calamity than the battle of Bull Run. It comes upon us like a killing June frost, which destroys the coming harvest. It is a step backwards, and backward steps seldom lead to good results."

Echoing Medill was Erastus Wright, one of Lincoln's friends from Springfield, Illinois. Wrote Wright: "I have just returned from Chicago where 25,000 were assembled at the State Fair—Freemonts [*sic*] Proclamation was the key note. 99 of every 100 said amen! The Laws of War Justified it, and the necessities of the case required it. . . . Genl Freemont has the hearts of the People." Echoing Wright was still another old friend, Illinois senator Orville H. Browning: "It is in no spirit of fault finding that I say I greatly regret the order modifying Genl Frémont's proclamation. That proclamation had the unqualified approval of every true friend of the Government within my knowledge. I do not know of an exception. Rebels and traitors, and all who sympathize with rebellion and treason, and who wish to see the government overthrown, would, of course, denounce it. Its influence was most salutary, and it was accomplishing much good. Its revocation disheartens our friends, and represses their ardor."[39]

Worse still were the letters that Lincoln and his secretaries never saw. Especially harsh was Senator Benjamin Wade of Ohio. One of Ashley's closest associates, Wade was known to his friends and admirers as Bluff Ben. Tough and tenacious, much like a bulldog, he had already concluded that incompetent generals and timid politicians had botched the Northern war effort and cost the lives of hundreds of his constituents. On learning about Lincoln's decision to countermand Frémont's order, he exploded. He fired off an angry letter to Senator Zachary Chandler of Michigan, a fellow radical. Never one to mince words, Wade blamed the decision on Lincoln's "imbecility and perverseness." Insisting that Lincoln's decision had done more harm to the Union war effort than General Irwin McDowell had done "by retreating at Bull Run," he told Chandler that it was so wrong-headed that it "could only come of one born of 'poor white trash' and educated in a slave State."[40]

Pressure from leading Republicans, radicals like Wade, and especially conservatives like Orville Browning, eventually forced Lincoln to give Frémont another appointment. In March 1862, he named Frémont head of the army's new Mountain Department, serving in West Virginia. There, Frémont proved to be no match for one of the heroes of the Confederacy, Lieutenant General Thomas J. "Stonewall" Jackson, who in a series of brilliant tactical maneuvers eluded Frémont's men for eight days and then whipped them at Cross Keys on June 8.

Browning's letter also led to a strong reply from the president, one that would later be quoted by historians time and again. "I think to lose Kentucky," wrote Lincoln, "is nearly the same as to lose the whole game. Kentucky gone, and we cannot hold Missouri, nor as I think, Maryland. These all against us, and our job is too large for us. We would as well consent to separation at once, including the surrender of this capitol."[41]

Among the Republicans who were disheartened by Lincoln's action was James Ashley. The president's "border-state policy" made him sick. That the president gave in to men like John Crittenden, contended Ashley, effectively put them in charge of the government. Were they loyal to the Union? No, said Ashley, their first loyalty was to slavery and the small slaveholding aristocracy that ran their home states.

Far more important than having the support of men like Crittenden, argued Ashley, was winning the support of the Confederacy's 3.5 million slaves. After all, slave labor was essential to the Confederate war effort. It freed up hundreds of thousands of Southern white men to attack and kill Northern volunteers. But slave labor wasn't willing labor. It could be turned. And it should be turned at once. For every slave who came over to the Union side, the North in effect would gain two workers—the one the South lost, and the one the North acquired. To simply ignore those numbers, said Ashley, made no sense whatsoever.

To Ashley's further horror, Lincoln's border-state policy and the Crittenden-Johnson Resolution had been embraced by a new party that had sprung up in much of North, including in his home state of Ohio and in his home district of Toledo. Once the war began, several prominent Republicans and some War Democrats clamored for the formation of a new party, a Union party, that would insist on victory but not the subjugation of the South and the destruction of slavery. The editor of the *Toledo Blade*, Ashley's old nemesis Clark Waggoner, pushed this idea to the hilt. Throughout Ohio, the pressure to form a Union party was strong, and the two major parties sent men to a Union convention at Columbus on September 5.[42]

Ashley attended the convention and was enraged by everything he saw. He wrote his friend Salmon Chase, now Lincoln's Treasury secretary, that never before had he met "so many doughfaces and cowards" in a political convention. The Democrats were bad, but the Republicans were even worse. The party seemingly had sent its "doughiest" men to Columbus. To attract Union Democrats, these men had even agreed to the gubernatorial nomination of David Tod, the chairman of the 1860 Democratic convention. How could any "true" Republican do that? How could any Republican support Tod? Just a short time before, the man had opposed "coercing" the Southern states to remain in the Union. And years earlier, he had campaigned vigorously for much harsher treatment of Ohio's black population. Even worse, said Ashley, was the new party's platform. By declaring that the war was being waged solely "to defend and maintain the supremacy of the Constitution, and to preserve the Union," it had essentially adopted the Crittenden-Johnson Resolution. Ashley warned Chase that if he should ever embrace this platform it would be the end of their political friendship.[43]

To Ashley's further dismay, the Union Party did well in the fall election. Tod was easily elected, and the party won both houses of the state legislature. After the election was over, Ashley went on a speaking tour across the state, lambasting the new party's platform, and reiterating his conviction that the aim of the war was to destroy the slave barons and the labor system that had made them so rich, so powerful, and so disloyal. At a huge rally at Toledo on November 26, he summed up his position: "The overthrow of slavery will not only end the war, but beyond all doubt, save the Union and preserve constitutional liberty, by making us what we ought to be, a homogeneous people."[44]

Equally troubling to Ashley were the actions of Frémont's replacement in Saint Louis, Major General Henry W. Halleck. Like Frémont, the forty-six-year-old Halleck had made a name for himself in the Far West. He had been an important figure in the writing of the California Constitution and had made a fortune in the state as a successful lawyer and land developer. Unlike Frémont, he was a West Point graduate, a Democrat, and sympathetic to the South. Also unlike Frémont, he was a cautious man who never made impulsive decisions and never openly defied his superiors. He had been dubbed Old Brains because of his military scholarship. His forte was administrative detail rather than battlefield tactics. Lincoln once described him as "little more than a first rate clerk."[45]

On taking over for Frémont in Saint Louis, Halleck became the senior Union army commander in the Western theater. He immediately put his administrative talent to work and straightened out the chaos that Frémont had left. He also gave his subordinates, who included Ulysses S. Grant and William Tecumseh Sherman, very specific orders on how to deal with fugitive slaves. On November 19, he issued General Order No. 3, which stated that under no circumstances were they to welcome fugitives into their camps. Instead, they were to expel all fugitives within their camps and drive back all those who approached their lines. Two months later, Halleck reaffirmed this order when Grant set out to capture Fort Henry and Fort Donaldson. He told Grant that it "does not belong to the military to decide upon the relation of master and man."[46]

As far as Grant was concerned, an order was an order. When Frémont issued a proclamation freeing the slaves of Missouri rebels, Grant followed it to the letter. When Lincoln overruled Frémont, Grant assumed that he was not suppose to touch slavery and accordingly returned at least one fugitive to his master. Then when Grant received Halleck's General Order, he made sure it was obeyed. He told one skeptical subordinate that it had to be followed regardless of what the subordinate thought. As for Sherman, he liked Halleck's policy. He had no desire to protect and feed runaways, especially women and children, who might come into his camp. He thought it would be too expensive and that it would hamstring an army that was on the move.[47]

That December, Ashley finally had his chance at redemption. When Congress convened for its normal winter session, the makeup was more to his liking. There were now 106 Republicans, forty-two Democrats, and twenty-eight border-state unionists in attendance. Gone were several of slavery's most outspoken defenders. No longer did he have to listen to Henry C. Burnett, Democrat of Kentucky, constantly harass House Republicans with points of order and objections. Burnett was now a colonel in the Confederate army. Another Kentuckian, Senator John C. Breckinridge, had left to become a Confederate brigadier general, while Missouri senators Trusten Polk and Waldo P. Johnson had departed to become Confederate colonels. Soon another headache would depart, Indiana senator Jesse Bright. Technically a free state legislator but also a long-time owner of Kentucky land and slaves, he would be expelled from the Senate in February for his blatant pro-Confederate sympathies.

As the new session opened, a new controversy arose. At issue was Secretary of War Simon Cameron's annual report. The sixty-two-year-old Pennsylvanian had leaked it to the press without bothering to clear it with the White House. Never a team player but one of the most successful political bosses in the nation's history, Cameron had bargained his way into Lincoln's cabinet because he had so much power in Pennsylvania politics. The Czar of Pennsylvania, as he was called, not only was known for being powerful, he also had a reputation for being corrupt—so corrupt that he had been given another nickname, The Great Winnebago Chief, allegedly for swindling Indians out of everything they had. A wheeler-dealer of the first order, he had made a fortune in newspapers, railroads, and manufacturing. Rich and influential, he had trouble deferring to the president. Indeed, according to Lincoln's private secretary, he was even "openly discourteous to the President."[48]

Cameron's report was a bombshell. One paragraph declared: "Those who make war against the Government justly forfeit all rights of property, privilege and security derived from the Constitution and laws against which they are in armed rebellion; and as the labor and service of their slaves constitute the chief property of the rebels, such property should share the common fate of war to which they have devoted the property of loyal citizens. It is as clearly the right of the Government to arm slaves when it may become necessary as it is to use gunpowder or guns taken from the enemy." These were not merely strong words, but strong words from a top government official. Newspapers across the country thus reprinted them word for word.

On reading Cameron's words, Ashley was pleased. So was the radical wing of the Republican Party. But the Lincoln administration was furious. Not only had the secretary of war clearly embraced the position that the army should never be returning runaway slaves to bondage, he had, in fact, gone much further. He had even advised the army to arm rebel slaves if need be. How would this sit with the Kentuckians? And with other Union slave owners? Everyone knew the answer.

It would alienate them. Arming rebel slaves, declared the *Louisville Journal,* was an abomination. It would "introduce into a war that is now humane and holy a savage ferocity and brutality that every Christian man and woman should shudder to contemplate."[49]

So, to no one's surprise, President Lincoln ordered the secretary of war to recall the official copies of his report and to delete the offending passage about arming slaves. Lincoln thus made it clear that he and his war secretary were not on the same page. A month later, in January 1862, Lincoln sacked Cameron for a host of reasons—mismanagement, corruption, and abuse of patronage, as well as the unauthorized call to arm black men—and sent him off as minister to Russia.

The Cameron incident, just like the Frémont incident, distanced radical Republicans like Ashley from the president and his men. Yet, while the radicals couldn't control the actions of the White House or get Lincoln to abandon his border-state policy, they had growing power in the House of Representatives.

Leading them was Thaddeus Stevens of Pennsylvania, the chairman of the House Ways and Means Committee. He was an adroit parliamentarian, the "evil genius of the Republican party," according to many border-state politicians and Northern Democrats. They hated him and loved to make fun of his clubfoot and especially his ill-fitting, dark brown, and wavy-haired wig. But that did them little good when he rose to speak, for he was the master of harsh wit, sarcasm, and satire. Hands loosely locked before him, never changing his expression, seldom making a gesture, he could always be counted on to slowly, calmly, and ruthlessly rip their arguments to shreds.

As a lawyer in Lancaster and Gettysburg, Stevens had a long history of helping black men and women. He had defended many fugitive slaves without fee. And, in a sensational case, he had helped win the acquittal of some thirty men who had been charged with treason for killing Edward Gorsuch, a Maryland slaveholder in pursuit of four runaway slaves. Stevens had also been accused many times of living in sin with a mulatto woman, his housekeeper, Lydia Smith. Now, at age sixty-nine, he called for the type of all-out war that Lincoln hoped to avoid. Rather than simply trying to bring the South back into the Union and coddling the border slave states, he called for "a revolution," a war that would destroy the Old South, free every slave, slay every traitor, burn every rebel mansion.[50]

Thaddeus Stevens, congressman from Pennsylvania. Prints and Photographs Division, Library of Congress (LC-USZ62–15441).

On December 4, the wily Pennsylvanian was handed a golden opportunity to rally his troops. The Indiana Democrat William Steele Holman made a tactical mistake. Holman wanted to assure everyone once again that proslavery men had nothing to fear. So he moved that the House go on record again in support of the Crittenden-Johnson Resolution. He indicated that he was willing to support the administration's war policies if the Republicans were still willing to adhere to the proslavery promises made in the July resolution. Would they do so? The answer was no. By an overwhelming Republican vote, orchestrated by Stevens, the House tabled Holman's motion, seventy-one to sixty-five, and thus refused to reaffirm the Crittenden Resolution. Ashley consequently had a chance to redeem himself.[51]

A week later, Ashley and his fellow radicals went after Halleck's Order No. 3. They accused Old Brains of being proslavery. To his defense came Missouri Representative Frank Blair, a strong supporter of Lincoln's decision to revoke Frémont's emancipation decree. On the House floor, Blair read an undated letter that he had received from Halleck. It was cautiously worded, typical of Halleck. In it, the general said that he was "ready to carry out any lawful instructions in regard to fugitive slaves, which my superiors may give me," and that he would "enforce any law that the Congress may pass."[52]

That hardly placated Ashley and the radicals. For them, it was just double-talk. Hadn't Congress already passed such a law? Hadn't it already specified what to do with slaves who were being used by the Confederate army to build fortifications, dig ditches, cut down timber, and do all the menial work around camp? Didn't the general realize that such work freed up many thousands of white rebels to man guns on the front line and thus kill and maim his own men? Surely, Old Brains must have some idea what the enemy was doing.

For radical Republicans like Ashley, the Halleck incident underscored a larger question. Namely, what was Congress to do about Democratic generals who refused to attack the private property of traitors? Lincoln, it was clear, was going to be of no help. He mandated that generals like Frémont adhere to a narrow interpretation of the Confiscation Act but allowed generals like Halleck to flout it. Thus, if Congress wanted the generals to move against rebel property, Congress would have to enact a tougher law.

On December 3, immediately after the opening prayer, Illinois senator Lyman Trumbull announced that he intended to introduce such a bill. What he had in mind, he indicated, was a bill that provided for the seizure of all rebel property, whether used directly to support the war or owned by a rebel a thousand miles away from the battlefield. Trumbull also minced no words about the slaves of rebellious masters. Under his bill, every one of their slaves would be "declared and made free."[53]

Trumbull's words immediately captured the attention of official Washington. The fifty-eight-year-old Illinois senator was a formidable figure. He had a long and distinguished record and until recently had been more influential than Lincoln in Illinois politics. Born and raised in Connecticut, he had spent four years in Georgia teaching school and studying for the bar. While there, he had concluded that slavery was a barbaric institution, one that degraded both blacks and whites. On moving to Illinois, he had become one of the state's top lawyers, arguing eighty-seven cases before the state's supreme court. He had subsequently been elected to the court and to the legislature. In the legislature, he had sponsored a bill to register free blacks so that they wouldn't be identified as fugitive slaves and returned to their alleged masters. He had also defended blacks who were accused of being runaway slaves.

Like Ashley, Trumbull had once been a Jacksonian Democrat. And like Ashley, he had broken with the party of his youth when Stephen A. Douglas introduced the Kansas-Nebraska Act. In 1855, the Illinois state legislature had chosen him over Lincoln to represent the state in the US Senate. And in 1861, he had shown more "guts" than Ashley. He had voted against the Crittenden-Johnson Resolution. Yet, he was never regarded as a "wild-eyed" radical like Ashley. He was seen as a "judicious" man, "cold and calculating," a highly skilled courtroom lawyer, and partly for that reason he had been given the powerful position of chairman of the Senate Judiciary Committee.

Would Trumbull's proposed bill bring a dramatic change to the war? Would it force Democratic generals to go after rebel property? Would it also force Lincoln to abandon his abominable border-state policy? Ashley, among others, had high hopes that Trumbull's bill would be a giant step in the right direction.

Chapter Two

LINCOLN AND EMANCIPATION

From the outset of the war, James Ashley denigrated Lincoln's border-state strategy. He rejected the notion, long popular among historians, that it was the "wisest" of a lot of bad options. In his judgment, securing the enthusiastic aid of the Confederacy's 3.5 million slaves was far more important than having the half-hearted support of eight hundred thousand white Kentuckians. He also couldn't fathom why anyone would give men like John Crittenden, men he regarded as traitors at heart, a veto over national policy.

To Ashley's further disgust, the president in the early months of the war seemed to have no desire to destroy slavery quickly, much less strip the slave barons of their wealth and power or even treat them as man stealers who had no legitimate property rights in slaves. The president not only overruled Frémont but, in addition, he repeatedly tried to coax Crittenden and others into accepting a program of state emancipation done gradually with federal compensation. Technically, that compensation would go to the state, but undoubtedly it would end up in the hands of the state's slaveholders. Also included would be federal money to encourage ex-slaves to leave the country.

If the border states were to adopt this program, said Lincoln, there would be no rough spots. The process would take ten, twenty, or thirty years. The changes would come gently, like the "dews of heaven." And the planters would end up with all of their wealth. Instead of having it in slaves, they would have it in dollars, and mainly in dollars that came out of the pockets of their Northern countrymen. That, in Ashley's eyes, not only would set a bad precedent but would also leave several million black Americans with no hope of freedom and the slave barons with too much wealth and power.

None of the key elements in Lincoln's plan were new. They all had been around for years.

In 1780, Pennsylvania had enacted gradual emancipation. The law freed the future offspring of all Pennsylvania women currently in bondage. These unborn children, however, were not truly "free" on birth. They had to serve their mothers' masters without compensation until they reached age twenty-eight. Four years later, Rhode Island and Connecticut passed similar laws with less stringent service requirements. Connecticut imposed service to age twenty-five, while Rhode Island required males to serve until age twenty-one and females until age eighteen. Fifteen years later, in 1799, New York also freed the unborn, with the requirement that males serve until age twenty-eight and females until age twenty-five. And in 1804, New Jersey also enacted gradual emancipation, obligating the males to serve until age twenty-five and the females until age twenty-one. These laws did not come easily. In New York and New Jersey especially, slave owners fought them tooth and nail.

On the national stage, Southerners led by Congressman William Laughton Smith of South Carolina had belittled the entire movement. Essentially blaming it on Pennsylvania Quakers, Smith and his cohorts had claimed that its sponsors were not true Americans and that, on the contrary, though these Quaker pacifists had been present during the American Revolution, they had refused to take up arms against British redcoats. Instead of joining the fight for freedom, they had sat on their hands and been willing to let true Americans live in abject slavery under King George III. Smith and others also insisted that Northerners just wanted to be rid of an economically burdensome slave population, perhaps sell them off to Southern buyers, and that the whole program would fail because slave mothers were simply incapable of teaching their children good habits. Worse yet, the end result would be "amalgamation," the mixing of black blood and white, the mongrelization of America.

This mocking approach remained the norm for nearly forty years. Then in 1819, when Missouri applied for statehood, all hell broke loose. Representative James Tallmadge of New York moved that gradual emancipation be imposed on Missouri. Initially, the motion caught

James Tallmadge, congressman from New York. From the
Biographical Directory of the United States Congress.

Southern leaders by surprise. Not only was Tallmadge a freshman congressman, he was also a lame duck. He hated Washington and had decided not to run again. Nonetheless, when the territory of Missouri petitioned for statehood, he proposed two amendments, one prohibiting "the further introduction of slavery" into Missouri, the other providing that slaves born in Missouri after it became a state "shall be free, but may be held to service until the age of twenty-five years."

Those words led to a congressional donnybrook that lasted the better part of two years. Southerners no longer just belittled Northerners. They were livid. Threats of disunion and civil war became commonplace. Jefferson said it alarmed him like "a fire bell in the night." Pointing at Tallmadge, Thomas Cobb of Georgia screamed: "You have kindled a fire which all the waters of the ocean cannot put out, which seas of blood can only extinguish."[1]

In the end, it took all of Henry Clay's manipulative genius to bring the battle to a close. To get Missouri in as a slave state with no strings attached, the adroit Kentuckian had to use all his powers as Speaker of the House. After several false starts, he worked out a deal that enabled Massachusetts to split in two, with one half becoming the new state of Maine (thereby giving New England two additional senators), and that banned slavery in all parts of the Louisiana Purchase above the 36°30' latitude line with the single exception of Missouri. He then got fourteen Northern House members to vote to admit Missouri as a slave state, and thirty-seven of his Southern followers to vote for the prohibition of slavery in the northern half of the Louisiana Purchase. The rest of the Southern delegation, however, never accepted the second part of Clay's "compromise." They denounced it as the bitterest pill that the South ever had to swallow.

Just as gradual emancipation was an old idea, so too was compensating slave owners for the loss of their slaves. Compensation was a key ingredient in all the gradual emancipation laws. Not only did the unborn children have to work for their mother's master until they reached a certain age, ranging from age eighteen to age twenty-eight, the owners also had the right to sell or will these youngsters before they came of age.

In addition, some states offered other sweeteners. In New York, where the fight over gradual abolition went on for years, the final bill included a clause that many thought was a gift to slave owners. It permitted a master to renounce his or her rights to a child within one year of the child's birth. The abandoned child, then, would become a ward of the local overseer of the poor, who in turn would bind the boy or girl out, often to the owner of the child's mother, the same person who had just renounced ownership. The costs were to be borne by the state, which was to pay $3.50 per month to whomever was responsible for raising the child. If the owner played it right, then, he or she could get not only the child's labor until age twenty-eight but also $3.50 per month for raising the youngster. The costs of this clause, however, created a backlash. Other New Yorkers complained that they were being unfairly taxed to enrich slaveholders. They demanded the clause's repeal and eventually got it.[2]

On the national scene, there had also been proposals for compensating slaveholders who gave up slavery. Most of these schemes involved the nation's western lands. When Virginia and other states ceded their western land claims to the federal government, antislavery advocates saw an opportunity. They proposed that money derived from the sale of these lands be used to rid the country of slavery.[3] In 1790, Elbridge Gerry of Massachusetts put this idea before Congress. Ten years later, in 1800, George Thacher, also of Massachusetts, offered a similar plan. These proposals, however, never got off the ground. Both men were roundly denounced by representatives from South Carolina, first William Laughton Smith and Thomas Tudor Tucker, and then by John Rutledge Jr. In the years that followed, others would make similar proposals, with the same negative results.

In 1819, ex-President James Madison secretly worked out a similar scheme. In a letter to Robert J. Evans, which he insisted be kept private, the third Virginia president offered a detailed plan. He had obviously given the matter much thought. He figured that $600 million would be needed, and to reach the necessary amount the government would have to sell off three hundred million acres of western lands at $2 an acre or two hundred million acres at $3. The government then could bank the money in a land fund, draw interest, and slowly rid the nation of slavery. A few years later, Madison's predecessor, Thomas Jefferson, also toyed with the idea. Still frightened by the Missouri crisis, he mulled over the possibility of using the public lands to eradicate slavery gradually. The lands, he pointed out, had been initially ceded "for the general good of the whole." Why not use them, then, for this noble purpose?[4]

Neither Jefferson nor Madison went public with these proposals. One who did was Representative Henry Meigs of New York City. In 1820, he was one of the fourteen Northern congressmen who had voted with the South on the admission of Missouri as a slave state. For doing so, he would later be lambasted by men like Ashley as a "doughface," a Northern man with Southern principles. Yet Meigs, like Jefferson, also worried about the growing tensions between North and South, and he thought one way to solve them was to give the planters western lands for gradually abandoning slavery. On at least three occasions, he tried to rally Southern support. His most detailed plan, which he offered in 1821, called for the federal government to set aside five hundred million acres, and when a slave owner decided to give up slavery, he could exchange his slaves for land certificates equal to the value of his slaves, the value to be decided by a three-man committee, including one member that the slaveholder essentially picked. This proposal received such a sarcastic response from John Floyd of Virginia that Meigs asked that it be tabled. Floyd agreed, and the tabling motion passed sixty-six to fifty-five.[5]

And so it went. In 1837, there was a bill before the Senate against emancipating slaves in the nation's capital. Henry Clay tried to amend it. He wanted to include the words "unless compensation were made to the proprietors of slaves." South Carolina's John C. Calhoun then rose and vilified Clay. He accused the Kentuckian of acting from expediency rather than principle. Those were fighting words in much of the South. Nothing could be worse, added Calhoun, than granting Congress the power to appropriate "public funds to purchase and emancipate slaves." It was the "most dangerous and unconstitutional" concession that could be made. Clay immediately backed down.[6]

Twelve years later, Calhoun was still on the attack. He rounded up forty-eight Southern congressmen to sign a protest that he had written against those who wanted to keep slavery out of the land taken from Mexico. In signing the protest, the men also had to agree to denounce the British for using government funds to end slavery in the British West Indies. The result was a disaster, argued Calhoun. It left the islands in the hands of blacks. It prostrated the whites. The same would happen here, in the United States, if the compensationists ever got their way.[7]

The third part of Lincoln's preferred program was also an old chestnut. The idea of shipping ex-slaves out of the country had been bandied about for at least seventy years. In the eyes of Jefferson and others, simply turning slaves loose was impossible even if slave owners were somehow compensated for their losses. Whites and blacks, Jefferson contended, could never live together peacefully as free men; racial distinctions would either have to be wiped out through intermarriage and interbreeding, or one race would eventually exterminate the other. Such thinking, which was widespread in Jefferson's America, had led to one program after another to ship emancipated blacks out of the country. Defenders of slavery, like William Laughton Smith of South Carolina, simply sneered at such "fanciful schemes." Shipping millions of blacks out of the country would cost half the national income, and it hardly made sense for a nation that was short of both capital and labor to be spending millions getting rid of labor.

Nonetheless, there were plenty of wishful thinkers, and in December 1816 at the Davis Hotel in Washington, gentlemen reformers launched the biggest and most notable of these movements, the American Colonization Society. Supported by such illustrious men as President

James Monroe, Chief Justice John Marshall, and Speaker of the House Henry Clay, the new society claimed that the answer lay in shipping free blacks "back to Africa." According to staunch supporters, African colonization would rid the country of the poor and despised free blacks, encourage planters to emancipate their slaves, and provide a nucleus of black missionaries to carry the Gospel to the Dark Continent. Zealots claimed divine inspiration.

More aggressive than its predecessors, the American Colonization Society sent out agents to whip up support among men of prominence. Soon churches, charitable groups, and even state governments began contributing money, and Congress appropriated $100,000 to aid the society. With this largesse, the society in 1821–22 helped found the colony of Liberia on the west coast of Africa as a refuge for freedmen. And in honor of President Monroe, a strong supporter, the capital was named Monrovia. Yet even with the contributions and support of men of power, the society managed to send only fourteen hundred blacks across the Atlantic by 1831 and only six thousand by the outbreak of the Civil War.

Meanwhile, African colonization generated intense hostility from both sides of the political spectrum. On the one hand, it infuriated Northern free blacks, especially when it was used to stir up white mobs that drove them out or their homes and burnt their churches. Nearly all of them saw the movement as forcible expulsion. This view, in turn, was soon embraced by most abolitionists, especially by the country's best known abolitionist, the Boston newsman William Lloyd Garrison. Saving his sharpest barbs for the Colonization Society, Garrison said that its only purpose was to bolster southern slavery by annually sending "hundreds of worn-out slaves . . . off to die, like old horses."[8]

Equally hostile were planter-politicians from the Deep South. Even though the movement clearly had the support of Henry Clay and other border-state politicians, they saw it mainly as a front for Northern "fanatics" who wanted to destroy slavery. In 1824, Governor John Wilson of South Carolina called on his state legislature to condemn this "invasion" of Southern rights "at the threshold." The state senate did so gladly. And by 1827, the Carolinians were joined by the Georgians, who formally castigated African colonization as "especially ruinous to the prosperity, importance, and political strength of the southern States."[9]

Willard Saulsbury, senator from Delaware. Brady-Handy Photograph
Collection, Library of Congress (LC-BH83-3539).

In short, the three prongs of Lincoln's preferred program—gradual
emancipation, compensation, and colonization—had a checkered history. Lincoln, however, was more than committed to it. He was persistent.

In October 1861, the president asked Joseph Kennedy, superintendent of the federal census, for figures on the slave population of Delaware.[10] He picked Delaware because he knew that it had the fewest
slaves by far of the Union slave states. Delaware, however, was anything but Lincoln country. Both senators were proslavery Democrats.
One was Willard Saulsbury, who hated Lincoln to such an extent that
he later denounced him on the Senate floor as "an imbecile" and "the

weakest man ever placed in a high office." Ordered to take his seat, Saulsbury pulled out a revolver and threatened to kill the sergeant at arms.[11] Less flamboyant but equally hostile was Delaware's other senator, James A. Bayard Jr. He believed that the seceding states should be allowed to go their own way and opposed all acts to suppress the rebellion. Citing the property rights of owners, he also opposed tampering with slavery in any way.

Although the two Delaware senators fought one another for control of the state's Democratic Party, neither was in danger of being replaced by the state legislature. They also had the backing of most of the state's voters, especially its rural voters, who in 1860 overwhelmingly rejected Lincoln's candidacy in favor of his exact opposite, John C. Breckinridge, the choice of the Deep South. Statewide, Breckinridge won 45.4 percent of the vote to John Bell's 24.1 percent and Lincoln's 23.7 percent.

Nonetheless, when Superintendent Kennedy reported back to Lincoln, the president thought he just might have a winning hand. There were only 1,798 slaves in Delaware's three counties, just 1.6 percent of the total population, and three-fourths of them lived in Sussex County, which bordered Maryland. Statewide, there were also 19,829 free blacks, which indicated that slavery was dying of its own accord. And of the state's 90,589 whites, only 587 owned slaves. Surely, here was the place to start.

So in November, Lincoln drafted a bill offering $400 per slave if Delaware agreed to gradual emancipation. The money, totaling $719,200, would be paid in 6 percent US bonds, doled out in thirty-one annual installments. From the date the act became effective, all newborns of slave women would be freeborn, but the female children would be required to serve until age eighteen and the male children until age twenty-one. The draft proposal also called for the immediate emancipation of all slaves thirty-five or older, with other living slaves receiving freedom when they reached thirty-five, and slavery being completely abolished by January 1, 1893, or maybe some earlier date, perhaps 1872. If 1872, then compensation could be compressed into ten payments.

Before submitting this proposal to Congress, however, Lincoln decided that he had to clear it with the Delaware legislature. For this purpose, he invited George Fisher, the state's lone congressman and his only congressional supporter in Delaware, to a meeting in Washington. He offered Fisher $300 per slave, $100 less than he planned, but Fisher, himself a slaveholder, wouldn't have it and successfully bargained Lincoln up to $500 per slave. Afterward, the president sent Fisher drafts of two bills that Fisher could submit to the Delaware legislature. Fisher drummed up some support for the one that would end slavery in 1872. He also arranged a meeting between Lincoln and one of his few slave-owning supporters in the state, Benjamin Burton of Indian River Hundred, who owned sixteen slaves, a large number by Delaware standards. Burton told Lincoln that the state's "farmers" (i.e., slave owners) would go along with the plan if the price was fair.

Fisher then went to the state capitol in Dover and, with the help of Republican Nathaniel B. Smithers, drew up a bill and presented it to the General Assembly. It would free all slaves over thirty-five at once, and all others by 1872. The compensation rate was to be set by a local board of assessors, and payments were to average about $500 per slave. Payment was to come from a pool of $900,000 to be provided by Congress, which, he assured legislators, was safely in Republican hands.

It was a good deal, contended Charles I. Du Pont, a retired banker, wool manufacturer, and railroad tycoon. He thought it would "prove a God send to many a slave owner."[12] But both of the state's US senators vehemently opposed it. So did most state Democrats, who dubbed their opponents "Black Republicans" and equated Lincoln's compensation scheme with racial equality, racial intermarriage, and the destruction of white society. In February 1862, Fisher somehow managed to get the measure through the state Senate by a five-to-four vote, thanks to two Democrats, Wilson Cannon and Jacob Moore, who voted with the Unionists. Then he learned in a straw poll that the bill would fail in the House, maybe by just one vote, maybe by more. He withdrew the measure.

Despite this failure, Lincoln still had high hopes. On December 3, 1861, in his annual message to Congress, the president suggested that Congress set aside money for states voluntarily freeing their slaves and allocate funds to colonize those ex-slaves, contrabands, and possibly free blacks as well to Liberia, Haiti, or some other foreign land. Then on March 6, in a special message, he called on Congress to offer federal compensation to "any state which may adopt the gradual abolishment of slavery."

This was not simply a humanitarian gesture, said Lincoln. It was a means for shortening the war, for if the border states abolished slavery it would reduce the lure that the Confederacy had for them, and that in turn would cause the Confederacy to lose hope in winning the allegiance of the border states and, thus, cause the rebellion to collapse. To those who said the program was too expensive, he told them that the costs of just eighty-seven days of war would provide money enough to buy out all the slave owners in all the border states. And to border-state slaveholders who might refuse this offer, Lincoln warned them that it was "impossible to foresee all the incidents which may attend and all the ruin which may follow" the war's continuation.[13]

Lincoln also invited the border-state representatives to a private meeting at the White House. He appealed to them personally to support compensated emancipation. He also assured them that his plan envisioned colonization of freed slaves outside the United States. By this time, he had his eye on a new site for colonizing ex-slaves— Chiriquí (now Barú) on the Isthmus of Panama, which he had been told was rich in coal. Lincoln also again warned his visitors that the war created situations that were difficult to control. He got some support from two Missourians, Senator John B. Henderson and Representative John W. Noell. The others wanted no part of it.[14] In the end, Congress adopted Lincoln's proposed resolution on April 10, after a vote of ninety-seven to thirty-six in the House and thirty-two to ten in the Senate. All the Republicans supported the proposal, but voting no were both Delaware senators, as well as John Crittenden and nearly 90 percent of the border-state House members.

For most border-state men, supporting Lincoln's compensation plan was simply out of the question. It took too much political courage. The folks back home wouldn't stand for it. It was tantamount to committing political suicide.

Few border-state representatives had any doubts on this score, but if they did, all they had to do was listen to the hard-luck story now being told by one of their fellow House members, George Fisher of Delaware, a state where, as mentioned earlier, only 587 citizens owned slaves. Because Fisher had tried and failed to get such a proposal through the Delaware legislature, he was now in deep political trouble. Democrats had stigmatized him as a "blackhearted abolitionist who desired not only to steal all the negro slaves in Delaware from their masters but to elevate them above the white race . . . and to compel by law the intermarriage of whites and blacks." As a result, moaned Fisher, he was now in danger of losing his House seat, even though in all likelihood he was going to be running against a man who was on his deathbed, the former governor William Temple.[15]

Meanwhile, while every Republican seemingly backed Lincoln's compensation plan, much of that support was paper-thin. James Ashley, for one, had a more radical agenda. The last thing he wanted to do was compensate man stealers for the loss of their slaves. Chosen by his party in December 1861 to chair the House Committee on Territories, Ashley met with Ben Wade, a fellow Ohio radical and the chairman of the Senate Territorial Committee, in the office of their mutual friend, Lincoln's Treasury secretary Salmon P. Chase. There, the three men agreed that while no state could legally leave the Union, once one did, the state "lapsed into the condition of a Territory with which we could do what we pleased."[16]

Shortly after this meeting, Ashley left Washington to attend his mother's funeral. In his absence, he had William Vandever, an Iowa Republican, introduce a resolution to the House Territorial Committee "to inquire into the legality and expediency of establishing territorial governments within the limits of the disloyal states and districts, and to report by bill or otherwise." The resolution was adopted.

Then on returning to Washington, Ashley himself worked out the details. They were far more radical than anything Lincoln imagined. Ashley wanted temporary governments established for the rebel "territories." Each territory would have a governor, a legislative council of seven to thirteen members, and a judiciary. The old state laws, including the old laws protecting slavery, would be null and void, and the legislative council would be forbidden to pass any laws that might reestablish slavery. The public land was to be seized and used to compensate members of the armed services and loyal citizens, black as well as white. The plots were "not to exceed 160 acres." The territories were to have public schools open to all children, black as well as white. All those who had taken an oath to the United States but had joined the Confederacy were forbidden to hold public office. All adult males who had been loyal to the United States, black as well as white, could vote and sit on juries.[17]

On February 24, Ashley managed to get this bill through his committee on a four-to-three vote. But the minority members, led by

James Craven of Indiana and Aaron Harding of Kentucky, attacked it in two reports. They complained bitterly that the bill's main purpose was to emancipate all the slaves in the conquered territory and to grant the former slaves all the rights and privileges of white citizens. The bill was then lambasted by George Pendleton, Democrat of Ohio. He said that the legislation should be titled "a bill to dissolve the Union and abolish the Constitution of the United States." He moved that it be tabled. The House agreed, sixty-five to fifty-six. Not only did border-state unionists and free state Democrats vote against Ashley's measure, so too did twenty-two Republicans. Nonetheless, Ashley had the support of fifty-six Republican colleagues, and that was enough to get him to try again.[18]

At the same time that Ashley's radical program was being slapped down in Congress, the proposal of compensated emancipation scored a victory. In December 1861, Senator Henry Wilson of Massachusetts introduced a resolution to end slavery in the District of Columbia. He was joined by Representative John Hutchins of Ohio in the House.

The two motions came as no surprise. Since the formation of the federal city in 1801, there had been vehement opposition to slavery within its borders. It was a national disgrace, said antislavery men and women. Not only did Southern congressmen bring their slaves to Washington, but slave traders used the city as a major gathering point for slaves that they bought from hard-pressed Chesapeake farmers and shipped off to the Deep South. Every day, visitors to Washington encountered black men in chains being driven through the streets, bound for ships that would take them to New Orleans and other slave markets. Again and again, foreign commentators called attention to the slave pens that were within a stone's throw of the nation's capitol. In the 1830s, this spectacle had led to limited support for the American Antislavery Society, which every year bombarded Congress with massive petitions to end both slavery and the slave trade in Washington, DC, "the so-called temple of liberty." In 1850, the society's supporters seemingly had won half a loaf, when Congress agreed to abolish the slave trade in Washington but not the institution of slavery.

Also clear was Lincoln's position on this matter. As early as 1848, he had opposed the American Antislavery Society's call for the immediate abolition of slavery in the District of Columbia "without compensation to slaveholders." Instead, he had insisted that emancipation should be gradual and the slave owners should be paid for their lost property. Ten years later, in his famous debates with Stephen A. Douglas, he had reiterated this position. He had argued that, while Congress undoubtedly had the right to abolish slavery in the District, it should not do so unless it agreed to emancipate the slaves gradually and pay their owners compensation.

In December 1861, both Senator Wilson and Representative Hutchins rejected Lincoln's plea for gradual emancipation. They called instead for immediate abolition. Their proposals were then referred to the appropriate Senate and House committees. In the House committee, James Ashley fashioned a bill that would have freed the district's thirty-one hundred slaves immediately "after the passage of the act." Ashley was then contacted by his friend Salmon P. Chase, Lincoln's Treasury secretary, and then by Lincoln himself. They suggested that the bill should compensate loyal slave owners by paying them a "ransom" of no more than $300 per slave. Lincoln also wanted the emancipation to be gradual.

Ashley objected. He thought the president's compensation policy as well as his border-state policy was wrong-headed. He opposed appropriating "a million of dollars from the National Treasury to pay the slave-owners of the District of Columbia for their slaves" because he was against "officially recognizing property in man" and "was confident that before the close of the war slavery would be abolished without compensation." He also believed "that at least two-thirds of the so-called 'loyal slave-owners' in the District of Columbia who applied for and accepted compensation for their slaves would at that time have welcomed Jefferson Davis and his government in Washington with every demonstration of joy." Nonetheless, Ashley knew enough not to fight Lincoln, Chase, and the party hierarchy. So he went along with their ransom proposal. But he didn't agree with Lincoln's demand for gradual emancipation. On this point, he had the support of the party and thus prevailed.[19]

Meanwhile, in the Senate, Lot Morrill of Maine steered through a proposal that matched the one being generated in the House. The final measure in both houses called for immediate abolition, compensation to loyal owners of up to $300 per slave, and the creation of a board of commissioners to award compensation to loyal slaveholders up to a total of one million dollars. It also repealed the Maryland slave statutes that had been in force in the district since 1801.[20]

During debate, Senator Garrett Davis of Kentucky tried to kill the bill. He defended slavery at great length and spoke of the "horrors" of black men immediately becoming free. Others joined him, and soon racists had a field day. Lurid predictions of race war, the mixing of the races, and the mongrelization of America became commonplace. Davis then offered as an amendment a poison pill, a new section mandating that the emancipated slaves be deported. On March 24, he got half the Senate to support his amendment, nineteen to nineteen, forcing Vice President Hannibal Hamlin to cast the decisive no vote.

The sponsors of the bill then decided that they didn't have enough votes to get the bill through the Senate. So they agreed to include money for voluntary colonization, with payments up to $100 for each slave choosing emigration. On April 6, the revised bill passed the Senate, twenty-nine to fourteen. And on April 11, after a grueling six-hour session, it passed the House, ninety-two to thirty-eight. As usual, John Crittenden and most of the other border-state representatives voted against the bill. So, too, did most Northern Democrats.

Lincoln received the revised bill three days later but dallied for another two days before signing it. He liked the provision that provided steamship tickets to Liberia or Haiti for any freed slave who cared to go. But he didn't like the provision that called for immediate abolition and expressed regret that "families would at once be deprived of cooks, stable boys, etc." He also worried about what might happen to old feeble slaves. He told Orville Browning, senator of Illinois, that he especially wanted to give "old Gov. Wickliffe," the seventy-three-year-old proslavery Kentucky representative, and his two sick family servants time to get out of Washington.[21] That he did.

Over the next nine months, the Board of Commissioners appointed to administer the act received 966 petitions for compensation. Rejecting Ashley's claim that Washington was swarming with secessionists, they turned down only thirty-six petitioners. They accepted 909 petitions in their entirety, twenty-one in part, from the former owners of the 2,989 men, women, and children who were set free.

The border-state men were still mourning the loss of slavery in Washington, DC, when one of the "incidents" of war that Lincoln had warned them about suddenly became newsworthy. The newsmaker was David Hunter.

A sixty-year-old major general, Hunter was anxious to make a name

Major General David Hunter. Civil War Collection,
Library of Congress (LC-DIG-cwpb-04526).

for himself. His grandfather had signed the Declaration of Independence. He had accompanied President-Elect Lincoln from Springfield, Illinois, to Washington in 1861. He had been wounded at Bull Run that July. He had been decorated. But all that wasn't enough. In January 1862, he literally begged Secretary of War Edwin Stanton to let him have his "way" on the subject of slavery. The administration, he wrote, would not be responsible for what he did. He would bear all the blame. Indeed, the administration could censure him, arrest him, dismiss him, even hang him if need be. All he wanted was the chance to make his "mark in such a way to be remembered by friend and foe."[22]

That March, Hunter was put in charge of the Department of the South, which officially consisted of all of South Carolina, Georgia, and Florida, but in reality consisted of no more than a handful of sea islands along the South Carolina and Georgia coasts. These islands had been abandoned by the planters on the coming of Union troops. Left behind were thousands of slaves without masters—men, women, and children who were now living as free people. Overnight, the islands had also become a mecca for runaway slaves. From middle South Carolina and Georgia, slaves by the thousands had set off for the Union installations, hiding during the day, making their way down the water-ways at night. Some twenty thousand had reached Hilton Head, Port Royal, and the other islands in the first nine months of Union occupa-tion. The Treasury Department had put these people to work harvest-ing cotton for sale to Northern mills, and Treasury Secretary Chase had encouraged dozens of missionaries and school teachers to go south and educate them.

Immediately after Hunter arrived, he began handing out certificates of freedom to all slaves who had once worked for the Confederate army. Then when his men captured Fort Pulaski, Georgia, he emanci-pated all the captured slaves. He then began recruiting black troops on the grounds that he had been told to organize black men and women into "squads, companies, or otherwise." Four weeks later, on May 9, he dropped a bombshell. He declared all the slaves in the Department of the South to be "free forever." He also ordered the forced enlistment of all able-bodied black men between ages eighteen and forty-five.

Lincoln knew Hunter well, but he had no idea what Hunter was doing. He learned about Hunter's actions weeks later, mainly from newspapers. Once Hunter's decrees became public knowledge, promi-nent Republicans urged Lincoln to endorse them, while border-state politicians called on the president to rescind them. The border-state men, as usual, prevailed. On May 22, Lincoln countermanded Hunter's orders.[23]

James Ashley was furious. The next day, he rose in Congress and blasted the administration's policy. Not only was it weak, but it also did "more to encourage treason than to terrify traitors."[24]

That, however, was not the end of the Hunter story. Congressman Charles A. Wickliffe of Kentucky, who had been dubbed the Duke and Pompous Charley for his arrogant ways, demanded more infor-mation. What had Hunter done regarding fugitives? Had he organized them into a black regiment? Had the War Department authorized this? Had the War Department supplied these men with arms? With military pay? Rather than respond himself, Secretary of War Stanton forwarded Wickliffe's questions to Hunter and asked for more information.[25]

On receiving the secretary's letter, Hunter was delighted. He told his adjutant general that he wouldn't part with this opportunity for "fifty thousand dollars." Then, in ironic and forceful prose, he composed an answer. He said that he had organized no "fugitive slaves." Instead, he had organized "a fine regiment of persons whose late masters are fugitive rebels — men who everywhere fly before the appearance of the National flag, leaving their servants behind them to shift, as best they can, for themselves." Moreover, the "loyal persons composing this regiment" were anxious to go after "their fugacious and traitorous proprietors," and he wished he had thousands more like them. Indeed, he apologized for having organized only one regiment, rather than "at least five or six," and he hoped by year's end to have under enlistment "48,000 to 50,000 of these hardy and devoted soldiers."

When the letter reached the House, the Speaker had the clerk, Emerson Etheridge, read it in full. Etheridge, a Tennessee unionist, had trouble keeping a straight face. Ashley and the Republican members didn't even try. They roared with laughter, hooted and hollered, and cheered the more sarcastic lines. Meanwhile, Wickliffe's Kentucky colleagues fumed. The Duke himself was absent, but another Kentuckian, George W. Dunlap, called for a resolution condemning Hunter for "discourteous" language and for "insulting" the dignity of the House. The Republicans, however, had more than enough votes to block it, and they rammed through a proposal to print Hunter's letter for distribution. Isaac N. Arnold of Illinois then moved that ten thousand additional copies be printed, while Harrison G. Blake of Ohio called for an additional hundred thousand.

Three days later, Wickliffe returned to the House. He demanded that the members revoke their decision to publish Hunter's letter. In making his case, he launched into a long attack on Hunter and the very idea of arming blacks. He dismissed as poppycock the argument that Andrew Jackson had used black troops at the Battle of New Orleans. He said that those soldiers were "quadroons," men who were three-quarters white. A true African, he contended, was "afraid, by nature or by instinct, of a gun." A true African would have to be given "a bowie-knife or a John Brown pike" if he was to be used in "a servile war, of murder, conflagration, and rapine."

Backing Wickliffe was another Kentuckian, Robert Mallory. He insisted that arming black men was uncivilized, that given the black man's "depraved nature," it was as bad as "enlisting the Indian, and arming him with the tomahawk and the scalping knife, to be let loose on our rebellious countrymen." Moreover, said Mallory, the black man would never become a good soldier. "One shot of a cannon would disperse 30,000 of them."

That opened the door for Republicans. Led by Thaddeus Stevens and Owen Lovejoy, they tore into the two Kentuckians. How, asked Stevens, could they consider blacks "a savage and barbarous race, if one gun will disperse an army of them?" Throughout history, argued Stevens, nations at war had liberated slaves and used them against their former masters, and it was about time the United States did the same thing. Freeing South Carolina slaves was essential. First, it would deprive the Confederacy of their labor, and second, it would provide reinforcements for white troops who were dying in the disease-infested South Carolina swamps. And once trained, these slaves should be given the job of "shooting their masters if they will not submit to this Government." That was the only way "of putting down this rebellion."[26]

In the end, Wickliffe's attempt to stop the House from printing General Hunter's letter failed. His motion was tabled by a 74–29 vote. Hunter, meanwhile, never got the forty-eight or fifty thousand men he wanted. The War Department refused to supply him with the weapons he needed or with money to pay his black soldiers. So on August 10, after his black soldiers had served three months without pay, he let most of them go and retained only enough men for one company.

No sooner had Hunter been put in his place than the War Department learned of another general, Brigadier General John W. Phelps, a forty-nine-year-old Vermont Yankee, who had also taken matters into his own hands. A West Point graduate who had spent much of his army life in the South, Phelps had no use for slaveholders. For years he had regarded them as deadwood, as a cancer on American society. He hated them even more than he hated slavery.

Now in southern Louisiana, just seven miles from New Orleans, Phelps's contempt for the slaveholding elite had become a constant headache for his superior, Major General Benjamin Butler, who was no longer dealing with Virginia "contraband," but trying to make peace with the Louisiana whites who dwelt in the area that Union troops had recently conquered. These white folk had not only been alarmed by Phelps's welcoming of runaway slaves into his camp, but they also accused him of having his soldiers scour the countryside and entice slaves to run away from their plantations.

Then on June 16, 1862, Phelps wrote Butler suggesting that fifty regiments of contrabands be enlisted in the Union army. It would prepare the men for freedom, argued Phelps. It would also provide Butler's army with the reinforcements that were badly needed. Butler ignored the letter. Then six weeks later, Phelps decided to create three black regiments on the grounds that he needed reinforcements, that black men were better suited than white Yankees to fight in the Louisiana bayous, and that if he didn't enlist slaves in the Union cause they might take up "robbery and plunder." Shortly thereafter, he wrote Butler that he had already organized "upwards of 300 Africans" into five companies and needed arms for "three regiments of Africans."

All this was too much for Butler. So, instead of furnishing guns, he ordered Phelps to put the fugitives to work cutting down trees around the camp and had his quartermaster send Phelps a load of axes. In response, Phelps said that he had no intention of becoming a slave driver, "having no qualification that way," and offered his resignation as of August 21. Butler refused to accept it. He also decided to bounce the Phelps's problem on to Washington, while privately telling his wife, "Phelps has gone crazy."

What would the Lincoln administration do? Would it rebuke Phelps? Would it treat him as it had Frémont and Hunter? No, it essentially tried to ignore the problem. Secretary Stanton simply told Butler to use his "accustomed skill and discretion" in handling Phelps. That didn't work either. At the end of August, Phelps returned his commission to Lincoln and headed back to Vermont.[27]

By this time, Lincoln had begun to rethink his policy. The Hunter decision had infuriated many of his Republican supporters. So, too, had the dismal failure of the Army of the Potomac.

Following the disaster at Bull Run the previous summer, Major General George B. McClellan had been installed as commander of the Army of the Potomac. He had proved to be a wizard in whipping a huge army into fighting shape but was unable or unwilling to lead his troops into battle. Months passed, and in June 1862 Lincoln all but ordered McClellan to march against the Confederate armies defending Richmond, Virginia. The Peninsula Campaign went poorly. Though McClellan had superior numbers, his army couldn't cope with the speed and aggressiveness of the Confederates, and by the end of June the campaign was over. McClellan withdrew his men south to the James River and, from there, launched a series of letters denouncing Lincoln and other politicians for mishandling the war effort.

Finally, on July 7, Lincoln decided to pay McClellan a visit at Harrison's Landing. There, to his shock, the general handed him a letter instructing him on how the war should be fought. "It should not be a war looking to the subjugation of the [Southern] people." Nor should "confiscation of property . . . or forcible abolition of slavery . . . be contemplated for a moment." It was also wrong to allow military power "to interfere with the relations of servitude." Moreover, any "declaration of radical views, especially upon slavery," would result in the rapid disintegration of the army. The tone was respectful, but the underlying message was also clear: McClellan, not Lincoln, should be commander-in-chief.[28]

Five days later, on July 12, Lincoln again invited border-state congressmen to a meeting. Two months earlier, in rebuking General Hunter, he had tried to sweet talk them into accepting his plan of gradual, compensated emancipation, with colonization of freed slaves outside the United States. They had nothing to fear, he had contended. The change "would come gently as the dews of heaven, not rending or wrecking anything. Will you not embrace it? . . . You can not if you would, be blind to the signs of the times."[29]

Now, at the July meeting, he again called their attention to the Hunter decision. It had caused him much grief, he said. It also had alienated many "whose support the country can not afford to lose." And this could not go on forever. He also warned them that if they did not act soon, slavery in their states would be "extinguished by mere friction and abrasion—by the mere incidents of the war"—and they would "have nothing valuable in lieu of it."[30]

Two days later, twenty of the twenty-nine representatives sent Lincoln a reply. They rejected his offer. Furthermore, they made no bones about having done so. While affirming their loyalty to the Union, they said that the change he proposed to the "social system" in their home states would be too radical. It would also cost too much. And it would drive "unionist slaveholders into rebellion." The next day, the president received a minority report from seven representatives who were willing to take his offer to their constituents and, in addition, a private letter of support from Horace Maynard of Tennessee.[31]

Among the eight supporters was George Fisher, who had tried and failed to get such a proposal through the Delaware legislature and had suffered politically for it. On Election Day, he was still in deep political trouble, even though he had the backing of federal troops, who harassed Democratic voters, and the support of soldiers in the field, who hadn't been able to vote in previous elections. Losing by thirty-seven votes to the moribund William Temple, who died soon after the election, Fisher blamed his defeat on Lincoln.

Also in the president's camp was John W. Noell of Missouri, who had shown signs of backing the proposal months earlier. He promised Lincoln that he and Senator John Henderson would try to make compensated emancipation a political issue that November in the Missouri elections. They did, and the proposal's supporters won six of the nine congressional seats and a majority of both houses of the state legislature.

That December, on returning to Washington, Noell and Henderson sought funding for the proposal. Opposing them were three Missouri congressmen: William A. Hall, E. H. Norton, and Thomas Price. The House took up the Missouri question in January 1863. By a 73–46 vote, it authorized $10 million for compensation but required the state to pass an act of immediate emancipation by January 1864. A month later, the Senate passed a different measure. By a 23–18 vote, it authorized up to $20 million for compensation and permitted gradual emancipation, giving Missouri until July 4, 1876, to rid itself of slavery.

To men like Ashley, the Senate proposal was absurd. The compensation package was twice that of the House. In addition, the end of slavery was too far in the future. And the bill set a bad precedent. The secessionist states, along with their Northern and border-state supporters, would clamor for the same deal. They, too, would expect to be given thirteen years to get rid of slavery and to get paid for doing so by Northern taxpayers. He wanted no part of it. Others agreed with him and the measure died in the House.[32]

Meanwhile, on the day that Lincoln received the border-state rejection, he took a step closer to the radicals. On his schedule that day was a funeral. Two days earlier, the infant son of Secretary of War Edwin Stanton had died of pneumonia. Just five months earlier, Lincoln had buried his own son, eleven-year-old Willie, after the boy contacted typhoid fever, and the death of Stanton's son had added to the president's well-known melancholy. He asked Secretary of State William H. Seward and Secretary of the Navy Gideon Welles to accompany him to the funeral.

As the presidential carriage rolled through the dusty streets of Washington and across the Potomac to Georgetown where Stanton's son was to be laid to rest, Lincoln told his two companions that he had been doing a lot of thinking, and he had "about come to the conclusion that we must free the slaves or be ourselves subdued."

The words caught Seward and Welles by surprise. Both men had heard Lincoln on many occasions emphatically reject forced emancipation. Why the sudden about-face? Lincoln explained that the matter had been on his mind "day and night" for several weeks, and he had decided that emancipation was a "military necessity," that the "slaves were undeniably an element of strength to those who had their service," and that "element" should be on the side of the Union rather than against it. Moreover, just as the commander-in-chief could order the destruction of enemy railroads, so too could he order the seizure of enemy slaves. As for the border states, he had concluded that they "would do nothing" on their own. Therefore, "the blow must fall first and foremost" on the Confederate states. And it must be decisive. If the army is "to strike more vigorous blows," the administration "must set an example, and strike at the heart of the rebellion."[33]

A few days later, Congress also made a momentous decision. For months its members had been debating Lyman Trumbull's proposal for a second confiscation act, one that authorized the seizure of the land, crops, and slaves of anyone who supported the rebellion, and not just those who hired out their slaves to work for the Confederate army.[34]

Trumbull had been careful not to link his bill with the crime of treason, which would have necessitated at least a hundred thousand individual trials. Instead, he tied his bill to international law and the war powers of Congress under the Constitution. The leading rebels, he pointed out, were "beyond the reach" of the US court system. There was no US court that presently could touch them. Thus, for all practical purposes, they were no different than belligerents who lived on foreign soil, and under the Constitution and international law Congress had the power to seize the property of such belligerents without taking them to court.

Trumbull's contention, in turn, had infuriated border-state congressmen, Northern Democrats, and a handful of conservative Republicans. They insisted that Confederate property could be seized only for treason and that federal prosecutors already had the necessary authority to initiate treason trials.

Thus it went for weeks. Then into the breach stepped three important Republican senators, John Sherman of Ohio, Henry Wilson of Massachusetts, and Daniel Clark of New Hampshire. The debate had convinced them that only a more limited bill could pass Congress. They also disagreed with Trumbull's notion that congressional confiscation was consistent with legal precedent and the Constitution. They saw more merit in the conservative view that only the courts could legitimately seize property. They also accepted the conservative argument that many Southerners were not truly disloyal, that many just lived in the wrong part of the country and had been duped into supporting the war by the slaveholding elite, and thus should not suffer the loss of their property.

With these thoughts in mind, Senator Sherman on March 12 offered an amendment to Trumbull's bill. A younger brother of the soon-to-be-famous William Tecumseh Sherman, the thirty-nine-year-old Ohio senator had entered congressional politics in 1854 determined to make sure that slave owners never profited from the repeal of the Missouri Compromise. But he had never embraced the more radical notions of men like James Ashley. Nicknamed the Ohio icicle for his lack of emotion and his focus on "cold hard facts," the tall and gaunt Ohioan was usually classified as a moderate Republican, not a radical one. Accordingly, his proposed amendment called for the confiscation of the property of only the top Confederate military and civil leaders and exempted most Confederates, including soldiers, who didn't hold leadership positions.

That was not a major blow to Trumbull's bill, however. As the factually minded Sherman pointed out, the biggest Southern landowners and slave owners were the people named in his amendment. Said Sherman: "There is no slaveholder in the ranks of the Southern army. They are all officers. It is part of the nature of the institution that the owner of a slave becomes elevated in social and political status above his neighbors." This assessment was hard to quarrel with. Trumbull and the radicals had said much the same thing on numerous occasions.[35]

More problematic was Sherman's insistence that the judiciary must have a larger role in property confiscation. His amendment, coupled with those of his colleagues, allowed the federal government to seize rebel property in the rebellious states, harvest and sell the crops, set slaves free, and use or rent the land but not transfer title until the courts reopened and so decreed. That didn't satisfy the conservatives who maintained that property could only be confiscated after an individual trial for treason. But it nonetheless led to more enforcement problems.

One problem was that the grounds for seizing rebel property permanently rested on the law of treason. That is, in taking up arms against the United States, the rebels had committed treason, and therefore their property should be seized. Ashley, among others, argued this position at length. The rebels, he contended on May 23, were traitors, and the Northern people demanded that they be punished for their crimes and made to pay for the costs of this deadly war. The soldiers also expected to see the rebels punished for their crimes. The soldiers had gone to war for principles worth dying for, said Ashley, and not for compromises worked out by politicians that would leave the rebels "in undisputed possession of all their property, and thus offer a premium to rebellion and treason." Indeed, "if this question of the confiscation of property and the liberation of slaves of rebels could be submitted to a vote of our Army . . . there would no doubt about its passage."[36]

Unfortunately, the penalty for treason under federal law was clear. And it was not the confiscation of property. It was death. In 1790, Congress had mandated that all traitors must be executed, and on this matter there could be no judicial discretion. That, in turn, led to a further problem. How, then, could rebels be coaxed back into the Union? Was the US government obliged to hang every West Pointer who had taken an oath to the Union and was now fighting for the Confederacy? Was it obligated to kill every former US congressman who now sat in the Confederate legislature? That, said many, was clearly what the 1790 law called for. With an eye on future reunion, the lawmakers decided that they needed to modify the 1790 law and establish more lenient penalties. That they did. The main penalty for treason remained death, but "at the discretion of the court" it could be modified to "not less than five years" in jail and "not less than ten thousand dollars" in fines.

The final bill thus turned out to be a mishmash. Four sections were in line with conservative thinking and provided for the seizure of property only after individual trials for treason or some analogous crime. Four sections were less strict, providing for the immediate forfeiture of the property of Confederate leaders after the law went into effect. All others were to be given a sixty-day warning to become Union supporters or suffer the consequences. Three sections were more radical, allowing, as they did, for the immediate liberation of all rebel slaves who escaped to Union lines. The latter sections of the bill also authorized the president to employ "persons of African descent" in any capacity to suppress the rebellion. Then there was another section that appealed to colonizationists. It authorized the president to colonize willing ex-slaves to "some tropical country."

This scissors-and-paste creation disgusted many radicals. They knew that it would be virtually impossible to enforce, and they suspected that Lincoln would never even try to enforce it. Only a few, however, publicly denounced it. Senator Zachary Chandler of Michigan was the most notable. He declared the bill "utterly worthless." He voted against it. So did his Michigan colleague, Jacob Howard. Also voting against it was another Republican senator, Orville H. Browning of Illinois, who thought the bill was too radical and urged his friend Lincoln to veto it.

Outside of these three men, however, the final bill had the full support of the Republican Party and passed mainly on a strict party-line vote, twenty-eight to thirteen in the Senate, eighty-four to forty-two in the House.[37] On the same day, Congress passed the Militia Act authorizing the president to employ "persons of African descent" in the army or navy.

From James Ashley's perspective, the final bill was much weaker than the original proposal. He was also troubled by the fact that sixteen of his fellow House Republicans had voted against a stronger measure, one that would have made emancipation more extensive. But all in all, progress had been made. Not only had more Republicans joined him in saying that the war should be a war to destroy slavery, but many now also agreed with him that the slave barons should be stripped of all their wealth, in land as well as in slaves.[38]

Then, to Ashley's horror, Lincoln demanded an "explanatory resolution" from Congress that furthered weakened the final bill. In their deliberations, the lawmakers had never made clear if rebel land was to be confiscated permanently or only for the lifetime of the rebellious owner. Lincoln insisted on the latter. Through Senator Daniel Clark, he called on Congress to declare that no punishment shall "be construed as to work a forfeiture of the real estate of the offender beyond his natural life." If Congress so declared, reported Senator Clark, Lincoln would sign the bill.

That was a major blow to Ashley and the other radicals. It undermined their efforts to remake the South, to break up the great Southern plantations, to provide land for poor whites and ex-slaves, and to pay for the war. What would become of the land of Jefferson Davis, Robert E. Lee, and the other Confederate leaders? Who would buy it at auction if it was to be returned to their heirs on their deaths? And how much would the land be worth? Just a fraction of its true value? And how much would that, in turn, cost the Treasury? Moreover, how much money would the Treasury have to spend just to keep track of all the heirs awaiting the return of the confiscated land?

Lincoln's mandate infuriated not only the radicals but also moderate Republicans. Nothing could be more absurd, said Preston King of New York, "than to talk about the confiscation of their estates during their lifetimes in a bill that provides for hanging them as soon as we catch them." In agreement was John Sherman. "The idea," said Sherman, "that we may draw a distinction in a military operation between a life estate and an estate in fee . . . is an absurdity."[39] Yet, rather than go back to square one, the Congress accepted Lincoln's terms. They had been in session since December. They were anxious to get out of Washington and the oppressive July heat. The resolution passed twenty-five to fifteen in the Senate, eighty-two to twenty-one in the House. The next day, July 17, Lincoln signed the Second Confiscation Act, the Militia Act, and the "explanatory resolution" into law.

In reporting the outcome, newspapers carefully covered the details, the legal loopholes, and the enforcement problems. At the same time, however, they generally highlighted the more radical sections of the Second Confiscation Act, especially section nine, the one that declared all slaves of rebel masters "forever free" as soon as they came into Union lines. The bill thus came to be widely seen as a giant step toward universal emancipation.

First Reading of the Emancipation Proclamation before the Cabinet.
Commemoration engraving, 1866, Library of Congress
(LC-DIG-pga-02502).

Five days later, on July 22, Lincoln met with his cabinet. He told them of his intention to issue a proclamation liberating rebel slaves.

The proclamation had been drafted in almost total secrecy in one of the president's favorite haunts, the telegraph office on the second floor of the War Department.[40] It also had been composed with the explicit intention of placing emancipation beyond the reach of the Supreme Court, which was still in the hands of Chief Justice Roger B. Taney, the author of the notorious *Dred Scott* opinion prohibiting Congress from banning slavery in the territories, and five other staunch Democrats who were well-known apologists for slavery. That the Taney Court would strike down emancipation if given the chance was beyond question. In fact, the chief justice had already written a preliminary opinion declaring emancipation unconstitutional.[41]

For Lincoln, the most dangerous threat to the proclamation was the Fifth Amendment's "taking clause," which prohibited the federal government from seizing property for public use without just compensation. The Fifth Amendment had provided the legal framework for

Chief Justice Taney to protect the rights of slaveholders in the territories. And it was in keeping with the spirit and letter of the Fifth Amendment that Lincoln had pushed his gradual compensated emancipation plans on Delaware and the other border states. The obvious response to this problem might have been that the Confederacy, which claimed to be a foreign nation, was no longer subject to the US constitution and thus didn't have the protection of the Fifth Amendment. Unfortunately, however, Lincoln had steadfastly denied that the eleven rebel states had any legal right to secede, and therefore he couldn't claim that they weren't part of the United States.

To make it more difficult for the Taney Court to strike down emancipation, Lincoln couched the proclamation as an exercise of his presidential war powers: "Now, therefore I, Abraham Lincoln, President of the United States, by virtue of the power in me vested as Commander-in-Chief . . . in time of actual armed rebellion against the authority and government of the United States, and as a fit and necessary war measure for suppressing said rebellion, do. . . ." Such sweeping war powers had been recognized by the Supreme Court during the War of 1812, by Justice Joseph Story in his widely used legal text, *Commentaries on the Constitution*, and by ex-President John Quincy Adams in his days as a congressman.

On learning about Lincoln's intentions, only Montgomery Blair, the postmaster general, objected. He thought the announcement would cost the Republicans too many congressional seats in the fall elections. Secretary of State Seward approved the edict but questioned the timing. Given the North's recent military defeats, counseled Seward, the whole world might view the proclamation as act of desperation—"the last measure of an exhausted government, a cry for help . . . our last shriek, on the retreat." It would be better, said Seward, to wait for some success on the battlefield before issuing the document. Lincoln thought this was good advice and, thus, put the proclamation in his desk to await a military victory.[42]

Meanwhile, Union commanders began recruiting black troops. Three weeks after turning down Phelps's request to arm three black regiments, General Butler found himself in trouble. Union soldiers were under attack at Baton Rouge, and he was short of men. Butler called on the War Department to provide him with reinforcements. He was told that none were available. Then his men at New Orleans also came under attack. On August 14, Butler wrote Stanton: "I shall call on Africa to intervene, and I do not think I shall call in vain." He expected to get a reaction from Washington. He didn't.

Eight days later, having heard nothing from Washington, Butler issued a general order to enlist free blacks "to defend the flag of their native country." Free blacks rushed to join, as did fugitive slaves, and by September 27 Butler had a new regiment, the "First Regiment of Native Guards." Their first assignment was to guard the bridges, railroads, and important bayous in the Lafourche district. They did well and thus freed up more of Butler's white troops for combat. Butler still heard nothing from Washington. That troubled him.[43]

While Butler worried about having the War Department's blessing, that was not the case with Brigadier General James H. Lane in Kansas. Lane didn't really care. Once a proslavery Democrat who had voted for Stephen A. Douglas's Kansas-Nebraska Act, the forty-seven-year-old general had become a fierce antislavery man on moving to the Kansas Territory in 1855. Over the next six years, he had led hundreds of like-minded settlers, who were soon dubbed Jayhawkers, into battle against proslavery elements. To his followers, he was a hero, the Grim Chieftain who stopped the "Slave Power" from moving into Kansas. To those who suffered from his aggression, he was a terrorist, a cold-blooded monster who encouraged his men to loot and destroy everything in sight.

In 1861, Lane had been elected to the US Senate. Immediately on reaching Washington he had organized a company to protect the president. That summer, he had returned home to Kansas and recruited his own army, Lane's Brigade. That September, he had led his men into Missouri, burning and plundering, singling out for special attention the small town of Osceola, an alleged proslavery stronghold. His men confiscated some three hundred slaves.

Lane's policy from the outset of the war was to confiscate as many slaves as possible. The very idea of returning slaves to their masters struck him as absurd, and he made certain that everyone knew it. Never, he said, would he allow his brigade to be turned into "Negro catchers." He also began recruiting into his brigade runaway slaves, mainly from Missouri and Arkansas, long before it was legal to do so. He told Secretary of War Stanton about his success on August 5, 1862. Seventeen days later, he received a carefully worded note from Stanton telling him that he couldn't recruit black troops unless the president authorized it. Lane ignored the reprimand. A month later, Stanton sent another, this one in more forceful language. Again, Lane ignored it, and by the end of the month he had enough men for two regiments. They immediately saw action at Mound Island in Bates County, Missouri, "fighting like tigers" and killing "rebel bushwhackers by the dozens."[44]

While Lane and Butler acted without authorization, Hunter's successor in South Carolina, Brigadier General Rufus Saxton, received the blessing of the War Department. On August 25, just three weeks after Hunter had been forced to disband his black troops, Stanton authorized Saxton to "arm, uniform, equip, and receive into the services of the United States such number of volunteers of African descent as you may deem expedient, not exceeding five thousand."

Why the sudden turnaround? No one knows for certain. But one of Saxton's subordinates, Lieutenant Charles Francis Adams, told his father that the War Department undoubtedly regarded Saxton as more trustworthy, more even tempered, and less likely to act impetuously just to please antislavery "fanatics."[45]

In any event, once Saxton received authorization, he immediately went to work to re-create Hunter's First South Carolina Volunteers. To command this regiment he turned to Thomas Wentworth Higginson, a well-known Massachusetts abolitionist who had openly backed the notorious John Brown in his raid on Harpers Ferry in 1859. Higginson jumped at the opportunity. "I had been an abolitionist too long, and had known and loved John Brown too well," wrote Higginson, "not to feel a thrill of joy at last on finding myself in the position where he only wished to be."

A preacher by training, but a fighter by nature, Higginson quickly put together a unit and by November 7 had more than enough men. Six days later, 240 of these men were sent on a foraging expedition to gather boards and planks. They were ambushed but successfully fought off their attackers and returned with two hundred thousand feet of lumber. They also participated in a coastal raid that liberated one hundred fifty slaves.[46]

At the same time as black men were being incorporated into the Union army, Lincoln stepped up his colonization campaign. On August 4, he appointed the Reverend James Mitchell, an enthusiastic colonizationist, as commissioner of emigration and told him that his first task was to assemble a delegation of five black men, preferably local preachers, for a meeting at the White House on August 14.[47]

It was a media event. If the five men thought they were going to a real meeting, they were sadly mistaken. When they arrived, they found that Lincoln had a reporter in the room to take stenographic notes and to relay his exact words to the nation's major newspapers. The five men were just props and treated accordingly. In essence, they were expected to just listen politely as the president lectured them on race relations in America, blamed the Civil War partly on them, and told them to their faces that the whole country would be better off if they went somewhere else. The president no longer pushed Liberia as their best option, probably because the cost of transportation across the Atlantic was too expensive and few blacks had shown any desire to go there. Instead, he touted Central America and its rich coal deposits but didn't mention by name Chiriquí, the place he clearly had in mind. There, he said, a small band of colonists, the best and brightest of their race, might succeed and set an example for the rest of their people.

A few days later, the prominent black abolitionist Frederick Douglass read about this meeting. He was not simply furious—he was stunned. Was Lincoln serious? Did he actually expect four million black people to leave the country? The reasoning was so fallacious, wrote Douglass, that anyone with "an ounce of brain in his head" knew that it was claptrap. How could anyone blame the Civil War on blacks? That was like blaming a horse for the crime of horse stealing. Worse, the president's words would have dire consequences. They would give license to "ignorant and base" racists "to commit all kinds of violence and outrage upon the colored people of the country."[48]

Lincoln paid Douglass no heed. On September 5, Lincoln received a report from the renowned scientist Joseph Henry that the coal deposits in Chiriquí were almost worthless. Nonetheless, he pressed forward and signed a contract with Ambrose Thompson, the land developer who owned the site. He then appointed as his agent for colonization Senator Samuel C. Pomeroy of Kansas.

It was a strange choice, to put it mildly. Not only had Pomeroy voted against money for colonization that April, he had also mocked colonizationists as late as that June, suggesting that their main target for expulsion should not be the nation's slaves but, rather, its slave owners, "a class whose absence would be least felt." Despite such remarks, Pomeroy accepted the job and immediately began recruiting blacks for the new colony, now dubbed "Lincolnia" by the press. Then came the news that Thompson's title to the land was shaky, that he might even be a swindler, and that two countries—Costa Rica and New Granada—also had claims to the land. Within months, the project fell apart.[49]

On September 17, the Lincoln administration finally got what looked like a major military victory. Earlier that summer, the Confederacy's top commander, General Robert E. Lee, had gone on the offensive. Routing Union forces at the second battle of Bull Run, he then struck north through western Maryland. There he divided his forces, sending Stonewall Jackson farther west to capture Harpers Ferry, Virginia. A copy of his orders fell into McClellan's hands. But instead of acting quickly, McClellan allowed Lee's depleted army to take a strong defensive position behind Antietam Creek, near Sharpsburg. Outnumbered eighty-seven thousand to fifty thousand, Lee's men fought off McClellan's attack until Jackson's troops arrived and saved them from a major defeat.

The fighting was savage. By day's end, the Confederate and Union dead numbered forty-eight hundred and the wounded eighteen thousand five hundred, of whom three thousand soon died. It was the bloodiest single day in American military history. Appalled by the growing number of Union casualties, McClellan chose not to fight Lee to the bitter end. Instead, he allowed Lee to slip back into Virginia. In private, Lincoln criticized McClellan for not crushing Lee when he had the chance. In public, however, he went along with those who claimed that the slaughter at Antietam was a great Northern victory. And, five days later, he issued the proclamation that had been sitting in his desk for over two months.

At first glance the document appeared revolutionary. It declared that as of January 1, 1863, all slaves in rebel territory "shall be then, thenceforward, and forever free; and the executive government of the United States, will, including the military and naval authorities thereof, recognize and maintain the freedom of such persons, and will do no act or acts to repress such persons, or any of them, in any efforts they make for their actual freedom."

Did that mean that slaves could rebel, take up arms against their masters, even slit their masters' throats? Critics said that it did—and accused Lincoln of inviting slave rebellions. In the fall elections, Democrats pounced on the wording, denounced the entire document, and talked incessantly about hordes of black men coming north, undercutting white workers, and molesting white women. Their appeal, coupled with how badly the Union army was doing on the battlefield, worked. That fall, Democrats did extremely well at the polls, smashing Republicans in one congressional district after another, gaining twenty-eight seats in the House, winning majorities in Pennsylvania, New York, New Jersey, Ohio, and Illinois.

In response, Lincoln decided to eliminate the controversial wording from the final document, and in its place substitute a new provision enjoining slaves "to abstain from all violence" and another new provision welcoming slaves into the Union army and navy. Also eliminated from the original document was the word "forever" in the phrase "forever free," probably because Lincoln thought the proclamation might not stand up in court.

Indeed, many in the legal community were up in arms, questioning the president's constitutional reasoning. In a hastily published pamphlet titled *Executive Power*, former Supreme Court Justice Benjamin Curtis, a bitter opponent of the secessionists and one of two justices to dissent in the *Dred Scott* case, asserted that the president possessed no authority, in wartime or otherwise, to "repeal and annul valid states laws which regulate the domestic relations of their people." Even more strident was Joel Parker, the Royall Professor at Harvard Law School. Said Parker: "There is no sound foundation on which to rest such extreme 'War Powers' as are claimed for the President." Equally harsh was Robert Winthrop, the former Speaker of the House and an old Whig like Lincoln. The proclamation, declared Winthrop, was "undoubtedly one of the most startling exercises of one-man power, which the history of human government, free or despotic, has ever witnessed."[50]

Yet, despite the outcry over its wording, the preliminary proclamation was in many respects a conservative document. The tone was legalistic, and it applied only to those Confederate states that were outside Lincoln's control. It exempted all sections of the Confederacy that on January 1 were in Union hands (Tennessee and parts of Louisiana and Virginia), as well as the four Union slave states (Missouri, Kentucky,

TABLE 2.1. Impact of Emancipation
Proclamation as per 1860 Census

State	Number of Slaves
Declared free:	
Georgia	462,232
Virginia (part)	450,437
Mississippi	436,232
Alabama	435,132
South Carolina	402,541
North Carolina	275,081
Louisiana (part)	247,734
Texas	180,692
Arkansas	111,104
Florida	61,753
Total:	3,062,938
Excluded:	
Tennessee	275,784
Kentucky	225,490
Missouri	114,465
Maryland	87,188
Louisiana (part)	85,281
Virginia (part)	29,013
West Virginia	12,761
Delaware	1,798
Total:	831,780

Delaware, and Maryland). It thus willingly left over eight hundred thousand slaves in permanent bondage.

It also gave the rebels more time to get back into the Union and avoid emancipation altogether. The Congress, in the Second Confiscation Act, had offered them a sixty-day grace period. The preliminary proclamation, as Lincoln later put it, offered them "a hundred days fair notice" to become again "good citizens of the United States." If they did, they could turn emancipation "wholly aside" and enjoy peace under the "old rules."[51]

The hundred-day delay, in Lincoln's mind, was crucial. For he had high hopes of luring various parts of the Confederacy back into the Union, maybe the Norfolk region of Virginia, perhaps segments of Ar-

LINCOLN'S LAST WARNING.
" Now, if you don't come down, I'll cut the Tree *from under you.*"

"Lincoln's Last Warning." Prints and Photographs Division,
Library of Congress (LC-USZ62–47218).

kansas and Tennessee, and especially several Louisiana parishes. He
didn't demand much out of them. He didn't expect them to go through
a half-dozen legal hoops, call a statewide convention, and get a two-
thirds majority to repeal disunion. They would not even have to repeal
disunion. Nor would they have to denounce slavery. All they would
have to do before the January 1 deadline was break ranks with the Confederacy and hold a US congressional election in which the partici-
pants no longer favored disunion. If a rebellious area of a Confederate
state met that condition, then the president would consider the area
and its people "not then in rebellion" and thus not subject to the final
Emancipation Proclamation. They could "have peace again upon the
old terms of the Constitution of the United States."

In October and November, Lincoln dispatched envoys bearing this message to "gentlemen of character" in Louisiana, Tennessee, and Arkansas. The envoys, however, could get only two Louisiana parishes to accept his offer.[52]

Yet, despite the failures, Lincoln remained persistent. He still carried the torch for gradual emancipation, compensated emancipation, and colonization long after September 22, the day he announced the preliminary Emancipation Proclamation.

That November, his friend David Davis found him totally "absorbed in his plan of remunerative emancipation." His "whole soul," said Davis, was still committed to it. A week later, on December 1, Lincoln in his annual message called on Congress to pass three constitutional amendments: one for federal compensation to states voluntarily abolishing slavery by 1900; another for federal compensation to loyal slave owners who lost their slaves during the war; and a third authorizing Congress to allocate money for the colonization of American blacks to foreign nations.[53]

These proposals so alarmed Ashley that he went to see Lincoln. What was the president up to? Surely he realized that none of the proposed amendments had a chance of getting through Congress. Was he about to renege on the Emancipation Proclamation? Did he still expect Congress to compensate the "man stealers"? After a long talk, Ashley left assured that his fears were unwarranted, that Lincoln "at heart was far in advance of his message," and that the final Emancipation Proclamation would be issued on January 1 as promised.[54]

Then on December 31, the day before the Emancipation Proclamation went into effect, Lincoln signed another contract, one that his many admirers would like to forget. This one was with the associates of Bernard Kock, an ambitious and unscrupulous con man. It provided $250,000 in federal funds to remove five thousand freedmen from the United States to the Île à Vache, a small island off the coast of Haiti. The contract had the enthusiastic support of Postmaster General Montgomery Blair and his brother Frank. The Blair brothers, both ardent colonizationists, saw it as the first step in "the 2nd great Exodus." Less impressed was another ardent colonizationist, Attorney General Edward Bates. He warned Lincoln that Kock was a "charlatan adventurer."

Bates was right. In May 1863, 453 colonists from Washington and

Hampton, Virginia, made the trip, only to discover that Kock had confiscated all their money and failed to provide them with adequate food and housing, much less the schools, church, hospital, and profit sharing he had promised. Nearly one hundred died from smallpox and starvation. The following February, Lincoln abandoned the experiment and had the survivors hauled back to the United States. So ended his dream of colonizing free blacks out of the country.[55]

Chapter Three

TO A WHITE AND BLACK MAN'S WAR

Along with the Emancipation Proclamation came the decision to arm black men. The double-barreled change in policy struck friends and foes alike as monumental. Not only would Confederate runaways be welcomed into Union camps, and not only would they be declared free, but they might even be armed and turned against their masters.

Especially delighted was James Ashley. He had never shared the fears of some of his Republican colleagues, including Lincoln, that freeing and arming runaways might prove to be disastrous, that they might even run again, this time away from the Confederate troops they were meant to be fighting, and leave their weapons behind to be used against Northern farm boys. Nor had he ever accepted the popular notion that black men "by nature" lacked the "pluck" and fortitude to be good soldiers. He knew from his own experience, helping runaways get across the Ohio River, that black men had more than enough courage to fight well, distinguish themselves on the battlefield, and thus bring the entire North one giant step closer to accepting black freedom.

Indeed, hadn't he and his fellow radicals been calling for such a policy since the first months of the war? Hadn't they been castigated for doing so? Hadn't they been right all along? Feeling vindicated, he fired off a letter to his constituents. The "Rubicon," wrote Ashley, had finally been crossed, and "thanks to the persistent demands of her earnest sons," the nation was now "irrevocably committed" to putting slavery and the slave barons on the road to extinction.[1]

At the same time, just the thought of black men bearing arms infuriated Northern Democrats and border-state unionists. Typical was

Albert G. Hodges, a Kentucky unionist and the owner and editor of the Frankfort *Tri-Weekly Commonwealth*. That the president's edict didn't apply to Kentucky was meaningless, declared Hodges. It still endangered every white family in Kentucky. It would undermine not only slavery in the Blue Grass State but white supremacy as well. It would lead to race war. The "President's nigger proclamation ought to be crammed down his throat."[2]

In the first months of the war, to Ashley's disgust, both the Lincoln administration and the free states had followed a different policy, one that was more in tune with the *Tri-Weekly Commonwealth*'s thinking. They had rejected black participation in the Union army.

Two weeks after the firing on Fort Sumter, Jacob Dobson, a janitor employed by the US Senate, wrote Secretary of War Simon Cameron that he knew of "some 300 reliable colored free citizens" who lived in the nation's capital and were anxious to defend it. He offered their help. He also pointed out that he had once been part of Frémont's military expedition exploring the Wild West, and as a result he had been "three times across the Rocky Mountains." Days later, he received a curt response. Wrote Cameron: "In reply to your letter of 23 instant, I have to say that this Department has no intention at present to call into the service of the Government any colored soldiers."[3]

Similarly, in Providence, Rhode Island, 106 black men led by Samuel Dorrer offered to march alongside the First Rhode Island Regiment as it left for the war. They were told to stay home. In Pittsburgh, Pennsylvania, the Hannibal Guards tendered their services to General James S. Negley, the militia commander of western Pennsylvania. He rejected their offer. In Albany, Ohio, the Attucks Guards offered their services. Their offer was also rejected. In Battle Creek, Michigan, a physician named G. P. Miller notified the War Department that he could raise five to ten thousand men in sixty days, and his men would take any position assigned to them, even though they preferred to be "sharpshooters." And, added Miller, if this offer was not acceptable, his men would fight as guerrillas "if armed and equipped by the national government." His offer, too, was rejected.[4]

The services of black men were not simply rejected—often, the rejections involved the threat of violence as well. In New York City, right after the fall of Fort Sumter, black men hired a public hall and began performing drills so they would be prepared for battle. As soon as the chief of police heard about this, he paid them a visit. He told them if they kept this up, they would be attacked by white mobs and there was nothing he could do to protect them. In Cincinnati, a city that had a long history of racial violence, black men formed, out of sense of patriotism, a company of Home Guards to help defend their home city if the need should arise. They, too, suddenly found the police at the door. The police demanded that they relinquish the keys to the schoolhouse where they planned to meet, forced one potential recruiter to take down the American flag that he had over his shop, and told another, "We want you damned niggers to keep out of this; this is a white man's war."[5]

That was the message in 1861 throughout the free states. From Maine to California, from Boston to San Francisco, the dominant view was the same: it was to be a "white man's war."

Black activists complained bitterly and to no avail. It was just plain stupid, said Frederick Douglass, to fight the rebels "with one hand when both were needed." And it was especially stupid to reject "the very class of men" who had "a deeper interest in the defeat and humiliation of the rebels than all others." The entire policy made no sense whatsoever, argued Douglass. The president, the governors, the Congress, and the generals were all "screaming" for volunteers. Yet at the same time they insisted on fighting "only with the white hand" and allowing "the black hand to remain tied." Hadn't black men fought with distinction under George Washington during the American Revolution and under Andrew Jackson at the Battle of New Orleans? Why couldn't they now fight under George McClellan? And Henry Halleck? "Men in earnest don't fight with one hand, when they might fight with two, and a man drowning would not refuse to be saved even by a colored hand."[6]

Agreeing with Douglass was one of his long-time associates, the wealthy New York land baron and white abolitionist Gerrit Smith. In Smith's opinion, however, the exclusion of blacks wouldn't last. "Unless the war shall be ended very soon," wrote Smith in May 1861, "black regiments will be seen marching Southward." Indeed, argued Smith, a long, bloody war would turn all Northerners into "radical, uncompromising, slave-arming, slave-freeing Abolitionists."[7]

Of the same opinion was a twenty-three-year-old Harvard dropout, Lieutenant Robert Gould Shaw of the Second Massachusetts Volun-

Frederick Douglass. National Portrait Gallery,
Smithsonian Institution.

teers. Writing in August 1861, Shaw deemed it "extraordinary" that the
government wasn't making use of Confederate slaves—"the instru-
ment that would finish the war sooner than anything else." He also
looked forward to the day that the call went out for "all blacks in the
country to come and enlist in our army." He, like many Boston aristocrats, had his prejudices. He regarded blacks as an inferior, childish
race. Yet he also reckoned that they would make "fine" soldiers and be
much easier to "discipline than our independent Yankees." At the time,
he had no idea that he would end up leading the most famous of all
black regiments, the Fifty-Fourth Massachusetts Volunteers.[8]

Black and white abolitionists also complained bitterly that the Confederacy wasn't following the same rules. Only the North was fighting
a "white man's war." The Confederacy was not. Wrote Frederick Douglass in September 1861: "It is now pretty well established that there are
at the present moment many colored men in the Confederate army

doing duty not only as cooks, servants, and laborers, but as real soldiers, having muskets on their shoulders, and bullets in their pockets, ready to shoot down loyal troops, and do all that soldiers may do to destroy the Federal Government and build up that of the traitors and rebels. . . . That the negroes are numerous in the rebel army, and do for that army its heaviest work, is beyond question."[9]

At the time, three Confederate states had already accepted black soldiers. In June 1861, the Tennessee legislature passed an act to "receive into military service of the State all male free persons of color between ages of 15 and 50." In Mobile, free blacks were also authorized to organize. And in New Orleans, free blacks were permitted to organize two regiments. Called the Native Guards, they soon had fourteen hundred members. The governor, Thomas O. Moore, formally accepted one of the two regiments into the Louisiana state militia, appointed a white colonel, Henry D. Ogden, to command it, and commissioned a handful of black men to serve as Ogden's junior officers. That November they paraded with white troops. The *New Orleans Daily Crescent* approved of the governor's action. The Native Guards, declared the *Crescent*, would "fight the Black Republicans with as much determination and gallantry as any body of white men in the service of the Confederate States."[10]

Such sentiments, however, were clearly the exception, not the rule. Most Confederate leaders in 1861 had no intention of ever arming black men. Many, to be sure, realized that black Southerners had fought with distinction during the American Revolution and at the Battle of New Orleans. But even among those who knew their military history, the thought of arming black men was repugnant. Their new government, after all, was built on the notion that Africans were an inferior race, a childish and backward people, fit only to do the most menial tasks. The Confederate Constitution said as much, and in March 1861 the vice president of Confederacy, Alexander Stephens, underlined that fact. He hailed the document for openly embracing black subordination. That, said Stephens, was the "cornerstone" of the "new" South.[11]

More important, however, was the fear that the weapons would be turned on white masters. Lurking in the background was the nightmare story of what had happened on the island of Santo Domingo in the 1790s. While few talked about it, Southern leaders knew that the French Revolution had precipitated a slave rebellion on the island.

They also knew that twelve years later, after killing some sixty thousand whites and driving others to seek refuge in Virginia and the Carolinas, the slaves had emerged victorious. While many Southerners insisted that it couldn't happen here, that American slaves were meek, docile, and loyal, the very thought of Santo Domingo sent chills of terror through the white South. In 1860, just the possibility of Lincoln being elected caused Chief Justice Roger B. Taney to worry about "the horrors of St. Domingo . . . being visited upon . . . our own Southern countrymen."[12]

Yet while most Confederate leaders in 1861 rejected blacks as combat soldiers, they never rejected them as support personnel. From the beginning, the Confederate army relied heavily on able-bodied black men to throw up breastworks and dig trenches for white troops on the front line. Also from the beginning, officers often brought a few slaves with them to serve as personal servants. And, from the beginning, slaves were used as cooks, teamsters, laundrymen, stretcher bearers, and hospital attendants. At first, the Confederate army essentially rented these men and women from willing slave owners. As the war became bloodier and the need for workers skyrocketed, however, the army often ignored the wishes of owners and impressed both free blacks and slaves, a process that led to much bitterness and legal strife.

In 1861, there was one branch of military service that did not have a rigid color line. And that was the US Navy. In 1798, when the naval department was created, the secretaries of war and navy had issued directives forbidding blacks from serving in the Marines or on warships. These directives, however, had been ignored both in the naval war with France in 1798 and the War of 1812, largely because navy captains were responsible for crewing their own ships, and most commanders were in desperate need of well-trained and disciplined seamen. Often, captains had just one choice. They could either remain stranded in port or man their crew with some black sailors. In March 1813, Congress recognized this reality and passed a law authorizing navy captains to enlist "persons of color, natives of the U. States."[13]

The US Navy was thus integrated by law, and black seamen generally constituted between 15 and 20 percent of the navy's crews. Captain Oliver H. Perry, the hero of the Battle of Lake Erie, estimated that one-fourth of his crew was black. This situation so alarmed Senator John C. Calhoun that in 1842, when the Department of the Navy was

Black Sailors aboard the USS *Miami*. US Naval
Historical Center (NH 55510).

undergoing reorganization, he proposed that blacks only be allowed
to serve in the navy as cooks, stewards, or servants. "It was wrong,"
said the South Carolinian, "to bring those who have to sustain the
honor of the country down to a footing of the negro race—to be degraded by being mingled and mixed up with that inferior race." His
proposal passed in the Senate, but died in the House. To pacify men
like Calhoun, however, the navy agreed to limit the number of black
seamen to no more than 5 percent of the ship's crew.[14]

That proved to be impossible even when the US Navy had just

forty-two active ships. With the outbreak of the Civil War, the navy expanded quickly, first to several hundred ships, finally to over six hundred. Its chronic manpower shortages became acute. So within a matter of months, Secretary of the Navy Gideon Welles not only abandoned the navy's stated policy of limiting black seamen to no more than 5 percent of the crew but also suggested that contraband slaves be recruited. In short order, the percentage of blacks in the US Navy was once again about 20 percent.

Of the contraband seamen, the most celebrated was Robert Smalls. In May 1862, along with sixteen other slaves, Smalls commandeered the *CSS Planter*, a Confederate transport steamer with four guns and two hundred pounds of ammunition, steered it out of Charleston Harbor past five heavily armed Confederate forts, and turned it over to US authorities, reportedly with the words, "I thought the *Planter* might be of use to Uncle Abe." Having gained his freedom, Smalls then joined the US Navy and piloted the *Planter*, mainly through the shallow island waters off the South Carolina and Georgia coasts. He participated in seventeen different engagements. By war's end, he was a folk hero, celebrated far and wide. After the war, he was elected to the South Carolina legislature and US House of Representatives.[15]

Apart from the navy, however, blacks in 1861 were excluded from the armed services. The Union army obtained the services of 714,231 men in the first year of the war. None, according to War Department, were black.

Meanwhile, every Union field commander faced the same problem. Thousands of slaves had essentially freed themselves and made their way to Union camps. Many were of prime fighting age. What was to be done with them? George McClellan, Don Carlos Buell, and Henry Halleck ordered their subordinates to turn them away or return them to their masters. Then, after nearly a full year of war, a handful of Northern generals—James Lane in Kansas, John Phelps and Benjamin Butler in Louisiana, David Hunter and Rufus Saxton in South Carolina—broke ranks with the status quo. Some had abolitionist leanings, some just needed more troops. All raised or attempted to raise black regiments. Only Saxton had permission from the Lincoln administration to do so.

Up until July 17, 1862, the Lincoln administration lacked the full legal authority to call up black troops. Congress in 1792 and in 1795 had excluded everyone but "able-bodied white male citizens," ages eighteen to forty-five, from serving in the state militias, and many states had written into their fundamental laws clauses that specifically barred black men from the militia. On July 17, Congress eliminated in federal law the white-only restriction. The Second Confiscation Act authorized the president as commander-in-chief "to employ as many persons of African descent as he may deem necessary and proper for the suppression of the rebellion." And the Militia Act, which was approved the same day, authorized the president "to receive into the service of the United States, for the purpose of constructing entrenchments, or performing camp service or any other labor, or any military or naval service for which they may be found competent, persons of African descent." The act also granted freedom to slaves so employed and to their families if they belonged to disloyal masters.

Leading the opposition to both of these measures were the Kentuckians. Still led by John J. Crittenden and Garrett Davis, they denounced the bills not only as gross violations of "sacred" promises that Lincoln and his party had once made. They also predicted that these measures would lead to race war, drive their fellow Kentuckians into the hands of the Confederacy, and turn more bayonets against the Union than for it. In the end, however, they just didn't have the votes. Over their objections, the Second Confiscation Act passed both the House and the Senate by roughly two-to-one margins, and the Militia Act passed by a 28–9 vote in the Senate and a voice vote in the House.

Instead of jumping at the opportunity to enlist black soldiers, however, the Lincoln administration adopted a policy that was anything but consistent. That August, General Rufus Saxton received permission to recruit black regiments. But he was the exception rather than the rule. Everyone else was left hanging or flatly turned down.

Rejected outright was an Indiana delegation that offered to recruit two black regiments. In declining the offer, Lincoln told the men that "the nation could not afford to lose Kentucky" and that "to arm the negroes would turn 50,000 bayonets from the loyal Border States against us that were for us." Six weeks later, he told a Chicago delegation that if the nation were to arm black men, he feared "that in a few weeks the arms would be in the hands of rebels" and at a time when there weren't "arms enough to equip our white troops."[16] In making these comments, he essentially repeated what the Kentucky delegation had said in the House and the Senate weeks earlier.

Lincoln still had Kentucky constantly in mind. On the day he presented his preliminary Emancipation Proclamation to his cabinet, he also tried it out on two Kentucky friends, James and Joshua Speed, who were visiting Washington. They were appalled. They told him not to issue it because it would alienate virtually everyone in their home state and drive many into joining the Confederacy. Their forecast proved to be true. Five days after Lincoln formally announced the preliminary Emancipation Proclamation, Kentucky politicians staged an anti-emancipation rally at Frankfurt. Speaker after speaker denounced the president and his "nigger" policy.

Shortly thereafter, Colonel John McHenry of the Seventeenth Kentucky Infantry took this sentiment several steps further. He flagrantly defied both Congress and the president. Instead of accepting fugitives who had run away from rebel masters, he ordered that all fugitives be returned to their masters, regardless of whether the masters were loyal or not. When pressed for an explanation, he claimed that the situation had become so bad that he once had to work with "a northern regiment with seventy or eighty stolen slaves each on a stolen horse." The army dismissed him, but Kentucky newspapers hailed him as a hero and a martyr for the Southern way of life, and the Kentucky legislature passed a resolution praising his behavior.[17]

At the other extreme was Colonel William L. Utley of the Twenty-Second Wisconsin Infantry. Stationed in central Kentucky, Utley thought much like James Ashley. He despised Kentucky unionists. He regarded most of them as traitors or cowards. He also complained bitterly about being under brigade generals who had been chosen because of "their adherence to the Kentucky policy." Partly to irritate them, he welcomed fugitives into his camp.

Among them was a young boy owned by Kentucky Supreme Court justice George Robertson. The youngster had been rented out and badly treated. Instead of returning the boy to Robertson, who under the law was clearly a "loyal" master, Utley allowed the young runaway to remain in camp. The judge then got the Fayette County grand jury to indict the colonel for violating the Kentucky Fugitive Slave Act, but the sheriff was unable to get past Utley's soldiers and serve the warrant. So the judge then wired Lincoln and asked for help. He also got John Crittenden to intercede for him. At the same time, Colonel Utley also turned to Lincoln for help, assuring the president that he had been indicted simply because he had "upheld the Constitution," obeyed "the laws of Congress" and "honored the proclamation issued on the 23d day of September."[18]

For Lincoln, this was just another Kentucky headache. To resolve it, he offered to pay the judge "any sum not exceeding five hundred dollars" if the judge would convey title of the boy to Utley so that the youngster could be set free. Judge Robertson wouldn't budge. He turned down the offer and sued Utley for damages, not once, not twice, but again and again and again, in one court after another, and finally emerged victorious in 1871. By then, slavery had been dead for nearly six years.[19]

Meanwhile, in 1862, most field commanders had no intention of following either McHenry's or Utley's examples. Courting trouble was the last thing they wanted to do. Yet at the same time, they had no idea what they were authorized to do with the half-million fugitives who had flocked to Union camps. Yes, they could put the fugitives to work. But could they arm any of them? Like General Butler in New Orleans, they never received clear instructions.

They would remain in the dark until 1863. Then some of the murkiness disappeared. On January 1, the revised wording of the Emancipation Proclamation welcomed into the Union Army all able-bodied black men with the exception of those who lived in the border states. In February, Governor John Andrew of Massachusetts received permission from the War Department to form two black regiments, the Fifty-Fourth and Fifty-Fifth Massachusetts. To recruit men, he put in charge an energetic Boston industrialist, George L. Stearns, one of the "Secret Six" who had financed John Brown's plan to seize the federal arsenal at Harpers Ferry and liberate slaves in Virginia in 1859. Stearns, in turn, established a network of prominent black and white abolitionists to do most of the recruiting.

Stearns and his associates didn't even try to put together a typical Civil War regiment in which all the men came from one state. There were just not enough black men of military age in Massachusetts to do so. The recruiters had to look elsewhere. As a result, both the Fifty-Fourth and Fifty-Fifth were Massachusetts regiments in name only. Of the 1,007 men recruited for the Fifty-Fourth, for example, only

133 were from the Bay State. More than twice that number, 294 to be exact, were from Pennsylvania. Then came New York with 183 and Ohio with 155. And of the 133 Massachusetts volunteers, only twenty-seven came from Boston, New England's largest city. Outdoing Boston was the whaling port of New Bedford, with thirty-nine men, and thanks to the efforts of the Reverend Samuel Harrison of Pittsfield, rural Berkshire County, in the far western part of the Bay State, with thirty-three men. Also contributing thirty-three men was the tiny town of Mercersburg, Pennsylvania, where three families—the Burgesses, the Christys, and the Krunkletons—sent three or more sons off to war. All told, the regiment ended up with men from fifteen free states, the four border states, five Confederate states, Canada, and the West Indies.[20]

Equally diverse was the Fifty-Fifth Massachusetts. Of 961 men who enlisted, 222 came from Ohio. That was mainly due to the efforts of John Mercer Langston, who scoured the state, looking for "colored men enthusiastic for the Union, and ready and anxious to prove their loyalty by their deeds." Pennsylvania provided the second most, 139 men, with the little town of Mercersburg contributing another eleven. Next came Virginia with 106 volunteers, Indiana with ninety-seven, Kentucky with sixty-eight, Missouri with sixty-six, and Illinois with fifty-six. The remaining 207 men came literally from "all over"—from seven free states, eleven slave states, Canada, Africa, and "places unknown." Of the total volunteers, 247 were former slaves. The commander of this unit, Lieutenant Colonel Norwood P. Hallowell, said that his regiment "contained every known variety of citizen of African descent . . . from every class and condition of colored society."[21]

Not only were the two regiments unique in their composition, but they were also unusual in their youth and physical fitness. Governor Andrew wanted them to be model regiments. With this in mind, doctors rejected about one-third of the volunteers. The result was 1,968 unusually fit warriors. The average age was just under twenty-four, roughly eighteen months younger than the average in other Union regiments. The officers, all of whom were white, came disproportionately from the first families of New England, families with distinguished pedigrees, families that could date their first American ancestor back to the early 1600s. The officers were even younger than the enlisted men. Lieutenant Edward Emerson was just seventeen, and two captains, Luis F. Emilio and Cabot Russel, were just eighteen. One commanding officer, Lieutenant Colonel Norwood Hallowell, was only twenty-four, while the other, Colonel Robert Gould Shaw, was twenty-five.[22]

Following the creation of the Fifty-Fourth and Fifty-Fifth Massachusetts, the War Department stepped up its recruitment effort. On March 25, Secretary of War Stanton ordered Lorenzo Thomas, the adjutant general of the army, out to the Mississippi Valley to recruit and organize black regiments. A career officer, Thomas had graduated from West Point in 1823 and spent most of his military career doing paper work. Blunt, arrogant, and verbose, he had irritated many of his coworkers over the years, including Secretary Stanton. Given this fact, many thought the secretary ordered Thomas to go west just to get him out of Washington. Yet, at the same time, the secretary also gave the imperious brigadier general an important job to do and more than enough power to do it.

The orders Thomas received had him starting in Cairo, Illinois, and preceding down the Mississippi, stopping at numerous posts along the way, until he reached Ulysses S. Grant's headquarters at Milliken's Bend, Louisiana. At each stop, he was to take note of what of he saw and report back to Stanton. He was also to explain the government's new policy concerning the "use of the colored population emancipated by the President's proclamation," especially their use as soldiers. Even more important, he was to combat and mitigate the fierce racism that had long plagued the Union army and at the same time work out a plan for organizing black men into military units and finding white officers to command them.

To accomplish this task, Thomas had plenty of carrots. He had the power to grant commissions on the spot—to make a sergeant into a lieutenant, a captain, a major, or even a full colonel. And since every black regiment would require at least thirty-five commissioned officers, the goal of creating at least twenty regiments meant that he had at least seven hundred commissions to hand out. As for those who persisted in their racism, he had the authority to throw them out of the army.[23]

In moving down the river, he gave the same speech at every stop. He began by telling his listeners, who usually numbered around six or seven thousand, about all the power that he had and that he could

Brigadier General Lorenzo Thomas. Prints and Photographs Division, Library of Congress (LC-DIG-cwpb-07207).

act "as if the President of the United States were himself present." He then spoke about some of the troubling reports that he had heard. Was it true that some troops had turned fugitives away from their picket lines? That sort of behavior, he said, had to stop. It would not be tolerated. Fugitives were to be received with open arms, fed, clothed, and armed. He then explained that his job was "to raise as many regiments of blacks" as he could. And for those soldiers willing to help, he was "authorized to give commissions from the highest to the lowest." Yes, with a stroke of pen, he could make a sergeant into a captain. And for those who refused to abide by the new policy, he was authorized to kick them out of the army. In fact, he would do so gladly. He would "rather do that than give commissions," for such men were "unworthy of the name of soldiers."

Whether it was the threats or the enticements, Thomas was remarkably successful. Within three weeks, he had the makings of ten regiments. He reported to Stanton that "the rush for offices in the contemplated negro regiments was great" and that he had found enough men among the "rank in file" in the "Seventh Missouri alone" to commission as officers for one regiment. Two weeks later, he mustered into service the first of the planned twenty regiments—the First Arkansas Volunteers of African Descent. By year's end, the goal of twenty regiments had been reached, and by war's end Thomas had enrolled some seventy-six thousand men into seventy regiments, roughly 40 percent of all the black regiments that were created.[24]

Thomas's success also sparked the War Department to try to standardize the entire recruitment process. In May 1863, the department created a new office under the adjutant general, the Bureau of Colored Troops, to coordinate and administer the raising of black regiments in every part of the country, to examine officer candidates for these regiments, and to assign numbers to black units. No longer would black men be recruited to fight for a particular state, and no longer would their officers be acting under the authority of a particular state. Instead, they would be fighting for the United States and led by officers under the authority of the United States. In keeping with this transformation, a number of existing regiments underwent name changes. Thomas Wentworth Higginson's First South Carolina Volunteers became the Thirty-Third US Colored Infantry, Lorenzo Thomas's First Arkansas Volunteers became the Forty-Sixth US Colored Infantry, Benjamin Butlers' First Louisiana Native Guards became the Seventy-Third, and James Lane's First Kansas Colored Volunteers became the Seventy-Ninth. Some accepted the name changes; most preferred the old designations.

Five days after the establishment of the new bureaucracy, two of the recently established black regiments experienced war at its worst. On May 27, 1863, the Louisiana Native Guards participated in the first of two all-out assaults on the last Confederate stronghold on the lower Mississippi River, at Port Hudson, seventeen miles north of Baton Rouge, Louisiana. The battle plan was typical for the time. After the Sixth Massachusetts Artillery softened up the Confederate stronghold, the guards, along with white infantry units, were expected to charge over ground covered with fallen trees against heavily fortified positions and then overwhelm the Confederate defenders. The guards

Depiction of Louisiana Native Guards' fatal charge.
From *Frank Leslie's Journal*, June 27, 1863.

made at least three charges. Some would later say that they made six—
or maybe even seven charges. In any case, it was a fool's errand.

Out of an attacking force of 1,080 men, they lost hundreds. The
exact number is uncertain. The official casualty return was forty-four
killed, 133 wounded, and three missing, for a total loss of 180. But the
official return is now regarded as a cover-up. One recent account puts
the number killed as high as 371 and wounded at 150; another puts
the total loss at four hundred men. Among those killed was Captain
Andre Cailloux, a thirty-six-year-old cigar maker who bragged about
being the "blackest man in New Orleans." His left arm was shattered
early in the battle, but he refused to leave the field. With one arm dan-
gling at his side, he waved his sword with the other and urged his men
to rush the Confederate line. He was struck dead by an artillery shell.
Also badly wounded was a sixteen-year-old black lieutenant, John H.
Crowder, who was carried from the field, only to die from his wounds
the next day. As for the Confederates, they were well entrenched and
had few casualties. They would survive a second attack on June 14 and
finally capitulate on July 9.[25]

Much was made of the bravery of the black soldiers. Even men who
expected nothing but the worst sang their praises. One white lieuten-

ant wrote an officer friend that he had once thought that the contra-bands in his unit might lack sufficient "pluck" to be real soldiers, but that was no longer the case. They had fought bravely. A white engi-neering officer said: "You have no idea how my prejudices with re-gard to negro troops have been dispelled. . . . The brigade of negroes behaved magnificently and fought splendidly; could not have done better. They are far superior in discipline than white troops, and just as brave." A white New Yorker wrote: "They charged and re-charged and didn't know what retreat meant. They lost in their two regiments some four hundred men as near as I can learn. This settles the question of niggers not fighting well." A white colonel wrote his wife that "there can be no question about the good fighting quality of negroes, here-after; that question was settled beyond a doubt yesterday." Declared the *New York Times*: "It is no longer possible to doubt the bravery and steadiness of the colored race, when rightly led."[26]

Before the news of the battle of Port Hudson reached New York, four other black regiments also experienced war at its worst. On June 7, at Milliken's Bend, Louisiana, on the Mississippi River twenty-five miles above Vicksburg, a Confederate brigade of raw Texas recruits attacked two white Iowa infantry companies and four contraband regiments. The Iowans were experienced soldiers but were few in number. The contraband regiments had no military experience whatsoever. A few weeks earlier, most of the contrabands had been Louisiana or Missis-sippi field hands. Recruited by Lorenzo Thomas, they had been mus-tered into three Louisiana regiments and one Mississippi regiment. After a little training, they had been issued old muskets, and in the case of the Mississippi regiment only on the day before the battle.

The Texans had at least three times as many men. They thus suc-ceeded in driving the Union forces back to the water's edge. At this point the battle turned into a vicious hand-to-hand brawl with bayo-nets and clubbed muskets. Then, with the arrival of a Union gunboat, the *Choctaw*, the Texans found themselves outgunned and had to re-treat.

The carnage was devastating. The four black regiments lost 35 per-cent of their men, wounded or dead. One regiment, the Ninth Louisi-ana, had 45 percent of its men killed or mortally wounded. Especially hard hit was Captain Matthew M. Miller's company. Of thirty-three soldiers, all but one were severely wounded, most two or three times, and sixteen were subsequently killed, one after receiving six wounds.

Wrote Captain Miller three days later: "I never more want to hear the expression. 'The niggers won't fight.' Come with me 100 yards from where I sit and I can show you the wounds that cover the bodies of 16 as brave, loyal, and patriotic soldiers as ever drew bead on a rebel."[27]

News of the grit and valor of these former Mississippi and Louisiana field hands traveled far and wide. Assistant Secretary of War Charles A. Dana told Secretary of War Stanton that it "revolutionized" the thinking in Grant's army. No longer did his senior officers secretly "sneer" at the idea of using black troops, reported Dana. They were "now heartily in favor of it." Rejecting the news, however, was the diarist Kate Stone, who had fled her family's Louisiana plantation Brokenburn on the approach of Grant's army. Having been around slaves since childhood, she found it impossible to believe that former field hands had "fought like mad demons" at Milliken's Bend. That just couldn't be true, she noted in her diary. Nor was it believable "that Southern soldiers—and Texans at that—have been whipped by a mongrel crew of white and black Yankees." There just had to "be some mistake," as "we know from experience they are cowards."[28]

Six weeks later, the Fifty-Fourth Massachusetts also proved their valor. On finishing military training in Readville, Massachusetts, they had been sent south to Hilton Head, South Carolina, and then on to Saint Simon's Island, Georgia. At that point, they and their commander, Colonel Shaw, had come under the command of Colonel James Montgomery, a tall, black-bearded, and beady-eyed Jayhawker who had learned to fight under James H. Lane on the Kansas-Missouri border. Montgomery had lived among slaveholders, had learned to despise them, and had come to see himself as an Old Testament warrior chosen by God to destroy the Southern way of life.

Soon after the arrival of the Fifty-Fourth, Montgomery called on Shaw to provide him with two companies for a raid on Darien, Georgia. Shaw complied. The town was deserted, and Montgomery ordered that it be stripped of everything valuable and then burned to the ground. "Southerners," said Montgomery, "must be made to feel that this is a real war, and that they are to be swept away by the hand of God like the Jews of old."[29] Shaw and his fellow officers were appalled. The men of the Fifty-Fourth had been promised "honorable" work. This wasn't it.

Indignant, Shaw fired off a string of letters, expressing his dismay.

He tried to get Montgomery dismissed. Yes, the man was "very brave and energetic," but he knew nothing except "a bushwhacking sort of war-fare." Shaw also called for "better service" for his men. He pressed hard for active combat. His men had to be given the chance to prove themselves.

On July 18, they got it. A second assault had been planned on the formidable, well-designed Battery Wagner that guarded the entrance to Charleston Harbor. The first assault, seven days earlier, had failed. The new plan called for bombarding the fort with artillery shells all day long and then at twilight sending four brigades of infantry along a narrow, three-quarter-mile spit of sand against the battered and broken earthworks. In many respects, it was a typical Civil War assault plan, one that was certain to have heavy casualties and justified only if it worked.

Shaw was offered the honor of leading the assault. Accepting it, he ordered his men to move in quick time until they were hundred yards from the fort, then double time, and then charge. The Fifty-Fourth made good progress until they were two hundred yards out, in the narrowest part of the spit, the right flank up to their knees in seawater. Then the Confederates opened fire from three sides. Against the withering fire, the Fifty-Fourth kept pressing forward, now at double time, scaled the ramparts, fought at close range with bayonets, and even occupied parts of the fort but ultimately had to retreat.

The Fifty-Fourth suffered 272 casualties. Colonel Shaw, three other officers, and twenty-nine enlisted men were killed outright; 149 men were wounded, and twenty-four later died from their wounds; fifteen were captured; and fifty-two were missing in action and never accounted for. Later, when Union men under a flag of truce tried to recover Shaw's body, they allegedly were told, "We have buried him with his niggers." That would become a rallying cry in much of the North.

The men who survived Battery Wagner would fight in three more major battles, and by the time the war was over, only 598 of the original 1,007 were left to participate in the final ceremonies on Boston Common. Of the thirty-three Mercersburg volunteers, twenty-three were killed or wounded. In New England, Shaw was virtually canonized and his likeness carved in stone, first in 1864 and again in 1897, and his men became the stuff of legend, the heroes of the 1989 movie *Glory*.[30]

For men like Ashley, all these incidents of black valor were predictable. He had always expected the best from black soldiers. He had always been certain that they would fight well and distinguish themselves on the battlefield. But would newspaper accounts of their bravery at Port Hudson, Milliken's Bend, and Battery Wagner move more white Northerners to embrace black freedom? Would more Republicans join him in pushing for the total destruction of slavery and the slave barons who profited from it? Would the Lincoln administration?

That was still uncertain. For, to Ashley's disgust, just three days before the battle at Milliken's Bend, the War Department had delivered black regiments a devastating blow. Secretary of War Stanton had announced a drastic cut in black pay—and, to make matters worse, scores of Northern newspapers had celebrated the decision.

Originally, in August 1862, the War Department had directed General Saxton to pay his black troops the same as white soldiers. Accordingly, black privates in the First South Carolina Volunteers received $13 a month plus a clothing allowance, and black sergeants $17–$21. In March 1863, Governor Andrew offered the same pay package to men who joined Fifty-Fourth and Fifty-Fifth Massachusetts. Recruiting posters in Boston, New Bedford, and elsewhere emphasized $13 in monthly pay, food and clothing, state aid for families, and a $100 bonus at the end of the tour of duty.

At the time, neither Andrew nor anyone else paid much attention to the Militia Act of 1862, which specified that black government laborers were to be paid $10 a month, out of which $3 was to be deducted for clothing. The act, as Andrew and others understood it, didn't apply to soldiers or to men who were legally free when the war began. It applied only to contraband laborers who had fled rebel masters and sought refuge in Union camps.

Then, when the War Department created the Bureau of Colored Troops, Secretary of War Stanton apparently had second thoughts. He asked the department solicitor William Whiting, a one-time Boston patent lawyer, for a legal opinion. After studying the Militia Act, Whiting concluded that black enlisted men, regardless of whether they were free men or runaway slaves, should be paid as laborers and not as soldiers. Attorney General Edward Bates agreed.

This left Stanton in a quandary. Should he reject this advice on the grounds that the government had a contractual obligation to pay these men a minimum of $13 a month plus a clothing allowance? Or should he ask Congress to correct the inequity? He decided on the latter. Meanwhile, until Congress met and made a decision, black soldiers of all ranks—privates, corporals, sergeants—were to receive no more than $7 a month. At the same time, they had to remain in the army. They didn't have the option of leaving just because the government had reneged on its promise.

That decision sparked a storm of protest from black soldiers, their white officers, and radical Republicans. On receiving the news, Colonel Shaw wrote Governor Andrew that his men "should be mustered out of the service or receive the full pay that was promised to them." Anything else would be "a great piece of injustice to them." Governor Andrew agreed and even went to Washington to plead his case. Failing there, he then turned to the Massachusetts legislature and got them to make up the difference. The men of the Fifty-Fourth and Fifty-Fifth, however, wouldn't accept it. They deemed it an insult. Did the governor actually think that it was just a matter of money? No, for them, it was a matter of principle, and until the national government treated them as being on precisely the same footing as other Massachusetts regiments, they would accept no pay whatsoever. As a result, they did not receive any pay for eighteen months, and their families suffered miserably.[31]

Also furious was Colonel Thomas Wentworth Higginson of the First South Carolina Colored Volunteers. For five months, his men had received the same pay as white soldiers. Now they were to receive just $7 per month. He fired off a series of letters to the War Department, members of Congress, and every sympathetic newspaper. The facts, he said, were clear. The secretary of war had pledged the faith of the federal government in creating his regiment. The Lincoln administration was thus duty bound to fulfill that pledge or disband the regiment. Congress was also bound, "in all decency," to make good on that pledge or disband the regiment. His men were not mercenary. They were good and brave men who would fight "barefoot and on half-rations" if the government actually needed the money. They had the same duties as white soldiers, wore the same uniform, ate the same food, fought and died just like their white counterparts. Moreover, given their color, they were at far more risk than white soldiers. How, then, could this discriminatory pay policy be justified?[32]

Frederick Douglass, in a meeting with Lincoln that August, asked basically the same question. Lincoln's response, as Douglass remem-

Lewis Martin, Twenty-Ninth US Colored Infantry,
one of many who fought at reduced pay. National Archives.

bered it years later, was that the pay policy was necessary to placate Northern racism. It was a political necessity. Just the employment of black troops, said Lincoln, "was a great gain to the colored people" that "could not have been successfully adopted at the beginning of the war," and "the wisdom of making colored men soldiers was still doubted" and "a serious offense to popular prejudice." Moreover, black men "had larger motives for being soldiers than white men" and "ought to be willing to enter the service upon any condition" and "the fact that they were not to receive the same pay as white soldiers seemed a necessary concession to smooth the way to their employment at all as soldiers, but that ultimately they would receive the same."[33]

That December, Thaddeus Stevens introduced a bill in the House of Representatives to accomplish this goal. Standing in his way were conservative Republicans, who thought much like Lincoln did, and Northern Democrats and border-state unionists, who contended that equal pay was a gross insult to all white soldiers.

Months later, Attorney General Bates was presented with a test case involving a Massachusetts chaplain who was clearly a free man when the war began. He sought full pay. Did the pay policy apply to him? On examining the Militia Act again, Bates ruled that it applied only to contraband soldiers, not to black soldiers who had been free at the start of the war. Lincoln, however, held up the decision while Congress debated the matter.

Then on June 15, 1864, Congress finally passed an equal pay bill. It embraced Bates's thinking. It distinguished between men who had been free when the war began and those who had gained their freedom during the war. The former would receive all their back pay, but ex-slaves who had gained their freedom during the war would receive back pay only to January 1, 1864. Obtaining freedom, contended the bill's supporters, was a huge step forward. It was worth far more than the $6 a month the ex-slaves were losing.[34]

The new policy, however, further infuriated Colonel Higginson. His men were former slaves. They were certain to be short-changed. He fired off another batch of letters, denouncing the government's treatment of his men. In other units, the new policy also created morale problems, as some privates were now entitled to more back pay than their squad leaders, not just their fellow privates with the same amount of service. To avoid this problem, Colonel E. N. Hallowell of the Fifty-

Fourth Massachusetts came up with a way around the new law. He had his men swear that on April 19, 1861, the day the war started, "no man had the right to demand unrequited labor of you, so help you God." A man could do this in good conscience, contended Hallowell, if he believed that the statement was true under God's law and that God's law was "higher" than the country's. This gambit was copied by other regiments and came to known as the "Quaker oath." Finally, on March 3, 1865, just weeks before the war ended, Congress passed another bill granting full retroactive pay to all black soldiers from the day they enlisted.

Oddly enough, at the same time the War Department decided to cut black wages, it also lifted the ban on recruiting black troops from the border states. From Ashley's perspective, this decision was such an obvious step in the right direction that it should have been made long ago, as it would undermine not only slavery in the border South but also the power of men like the late John Crittenden, men he regarded as "traitors," men who still counseled Lincoln against black freedom.

Indeed, with any luck, these men might be cast aside by their constituents, treated as deadwood if not as traitors, the representatives of a dying order. And with even more luck, true antislavery men might replace them. Wasn't there already a strong antislavery movement brewing in the border states? Especially in Missouri? Hadn't Frémont's ouster proved as much?

While much of this was undoubtedly wishful thinking on Ashley's part, he had no illusions whatsoever about why the Lincoln administration suddenly changed course regarding black troop recruitment. The War Department simply had no choice. The need for more fighting men had become acute. The Union army faced a huge manpower shortage in the spring of 1863. The enlistments of 120 regiments were due to expire in a matter of weeks, and the grim realities of war had led to a sharp drop in volunteers.

To stimulate volunteering, on March 3, Ashley and his fellow Republicans had passed an Enrollment Act. It declared all able-bodied men between twenty and forty-five liable to military service for three years. Under the terms of this bill, the Provost Marshall Bureau was to send provost marshals to each congressional district to sign up all potential draftees. When the president called for a draft, the district then had fifty days to fill its quota with volunteers. It could use bounties and other enticements to get men to volunteer. If it failed to get enough volunteers, then there would be a lottery, and some of the men on the district's draft list would be called to service.

The bill also included provisions that applied to the border states. Loyal owners could receive up to $300 for each slave who volunteered. And if a slave was drafted, the loyal owner would receive a $100 bounty and have to file a claim for the remaining $200. A commission would then decide if the owner was truly loyal or not.

At the time these provisions were enacted, however, the border states were still off limits to black recruiters. Slave owners in Delaware, Maryland, Kentucky, and Missouri had been exempted from Lincoln's Emancipation Proclamation. In addition, in return for their loyalty or neutrality, the Lincoln administration had ordered that black recruiters stay out of their states. For several months, able-bodied black men could only be recruited in the free states and in the rebel slave states. They could not be recruited in the border states—especially not in Kentucky.

Among those who objected to this policy was Major General Robert C. Schenck. An Ohio politician rather than a military man, Schenck had political clout. He had served with Lincoln in Congress back in the 1840s. At the time, he had been a strong antislavery Whig. He had voted to repeal the gag rule that had long been used to prevent antislavery petitions from being read on the floor of the House. He had also opposed the war with Mexico on the grounds that it was a war of aggression to promote slavery. In 1859 Schenck had been one of the first to call on the Republican Party to nominate Lincoln for president. In the 1860 election campaign, he had campaigned long and hard on Lincoln's behalf.

Mustered into the army as a brigadier general in 1861, Schenck had been badly wounded at the Second Battle of Bull Run. Deemed a war hero, he had then been chosen by the Republican Party to run against the most notorious of Ohio's antiwar Democrats, Representative Clement Vallandigham, in the 1862 congressional election. Schenck had won handily, even though his party had taken a shellacking in Ohio, losing fourteen out of nineteen House seats. But his term didn't begin until December 1863, nearly fourteen months after the election. In the interlude, he had been assigned to a desk command that included Maryland. Short of troops, Schenck pestered Lincoln and the War Department to let him enlist black men, mainly free men who had

Major General Robert C. Schenck. Matthew Brady Photograph,
Library of Congress (LC-B8172–1399).

worked on the fortifications around Baltimore. In June 1863, he finally
got the Lincoln administration's approval.[35]

To do the actual recruiting, the War Department then turned to
Colonel William Birney, the forty-four-year-old son of James G. Birney, a famous abolitionist who had run for president on the Liberty
Party ticket in both 1840 and 1844. The colonel had just successfully
recruited two black regiments in Washington, DC. His directions were
to enlist only free blacks in Maryland. This, in turn, would irritate
Maryland's nonslaveholding whites, who had long regarded the state's
large free black population as their main source of cheap labor. But it
was less likely to enrage Maryland slave owners.

With Schenck's blessing, Birney virtually ignored the War Department's instructions. He did recruit free blacks. But he also had his recruiters comb Baltimore's jails and slave pens, looking for men who

had been interred there by Washington slave owners who were trying to evade the District of Columbia's recent emancipation act. Birney then expanded the operation to cover most of Maryland. In less than seven weeks, he had enough men to form the Fourth US Colored Infantry.[36]

Slave owners were furious. They accused Birney's agents of ignoring their exclusion from the Emancipation Proclamation, running roughshod over the War Department's mandate, and sending out armed black recruiting squads to encourage slaves to run away from their masters. They succeeded in having one recruiter thrown in jail. Meanwhile, many nonslaveholding whites insisted that Birney's methods were only fair. Why, they demanded, should they bear the entire burden of losing good workers? Why shouldn't slaveholders also share some of the war's hardships? Undeterred, the representatives of the slaveholding elite descended on Washington and protested Birney's actions. Lincoln, in turn, denounced black recruiting parties. He also assured Maryland whites that no one had the authority to recruit slaves. And at the end of September, he ordered the complete suspension of black enlistments in Maryland.

Secretary of War Stanton then stepped in. Anything but a yes-man, the outspoken secretary challenged the decision and pointed out that the army was desperate, that it was in dire need of more fighting men, that it needed them now, and that the country could no longer afford to let Maryland slave owners hamper recruitment. He was also persistent. He didn't back down. He kept up the pressure, and in early October he got Lincoln to agree to a new policy. Under it, Maryland recruiters had to limit themselves, for the first thirty days, to signing up only free blacks. Then, if more soldiers were needed to meet the state's quota, recruiters could sign up slaves whose masters consented. The slaves thereby would gain their freedom, and their masters, if judged loyal by a commission, would receive $300.

Once the thirty days passed, Stanton was still up in arms. The state hadn't met its quota. The need for more men was acute. Governor Augustus W. Bradford begged Lincoln and Stanton for more time. He didn't get that time, and Birney launched another aggressive recruitment drive. Again he dispatched armed black recruiting parties across the state to entice slaves to leave their masters and exchange slavery for military service. Whites again resisted and even murdered one recruiter. But nonslaveholding whites, realizing that slave recruits re-

Major General John M. Schofield. Prints and Photographs Division,
Library of Congress (LC-DIG-cwpb 05934).

duced the state's draft quota, accepted the change in policy. Overall,
Birney and his men recruited seven regiments.

While Birney was working his magic in Maryland, Colonel William A.
Pile tried to do the same in Missouri. An antislavery radical like Birney, Pile wanted to enlist as many black men as possible. He knew
Missouri well. He had been a Methodist minister in the state before
the war. He did not, however, have the support of a compliant commanding general.

His commander was Major General John M. Schofield, a thirty-
two-year-old West Pointer who had already made a name for himself
in the battle at Wilson's Creek in 1861. Thirty-one years later, Schofield
would be awarded the Medal of Honor for that action. And a few years
after that, a military base in Honolulu would be named after him. Un-

like General Schenck in Maryland, however, General Schofield was no friend of black enlistments. Instead, he seemingly established road-blocks at every turn.[37]

Schofield took over the Department of Missouri in 1863. At the time, the state's unionists were split into warring factions. One group thought John C. Frémont had been given a raw deal. They wanted to end slavery as soon as possible. Others wanted to prop up slavery. Still others wanted slavery to die gradually and slowly, some at a snail's pace, some a little more quickly, and then disappear entirely around 1900. On taking command, Schofield sided with the more conservative wing of the gradualist movement and decided not to let any of his subordinates, especially the supporters of black recruitment, jeopardize their plans. He also tried to limit his superiors' directives. And, as Colonel Pile and Missouri radicals learned the hard way, he usually succeeded.

The first incident of this sort began in July 1863. As part of his recruitment drive throughout Mississippi Valley, Adjutant General Lorenzo Thomas authorized Pile to enlist Missouri blacks for an Arkansas regiment. Schofield then stepped in. To placate Governor Hamilton R. Gamble and other conservatives, he set strict limits on what Pile could do. Pile could not violate any state law. Nor could he recruit the slaves of loyal masters. Indeed, he had to be doubly certain that the owners were clearly disloyal. And, if there was any doubt, he was to return the men to bondage.

In practice, that meant that Pile could only recruit black men who had been free before the war, which was a tiny group in Missouri, and rebel-owned slaves who had fled to Union camps. That was hardly what Thomas wanted. So, to widen the recruitment, Thomas authorized Pile to establish a recruiting base at Keokuk, Iowa, just across the Missouri line. From there recruiting parties were sent into northern Missouri, and slaves responded in droves.

Slave owners howled in protest. In response, Schofield banned all recruitment in Missouri except for a small operation along the Kansas border. This, in turn, put him more at odds with Thomas. In October, the War Department stepped in. It ordered more black enlistments but gave Schofield a chance to modify the order. In November, Schofield called for the enlistment of all slaves regardless of the owner's loyalty or consent.

There was, however, a hitch. Schofield forbade Colonel Pile from sending out mobile recruiting squads to sign up willing slaves and provide them with protection. Instead, willing slaves had to make their way to forty-five recruiting stations. That was dangerous. It meant traveling through hostile country, avoiding slave patrols and Confederate guerrillas, and taking the chance of being kidnapped, beaten, or murdered.

At the same time, Schofield did little to stop slave owners from wreaking vengeance on the inductees' families. Masters thus stole the paychecks that black soldiers sent home, whipped and abused their wives and children, and even sold their families to Kentucky buyers. On paper, Schofield banned such sales but, according to critics, never enforced the ban. His critics eventually forced the Lincoln administration to replace Schofield with Major General William S. Rosecrans, a less distinguished officer who had just suffered a humiliating defeat at the Battle of Chickamauga.

Rosecrans adhered to much of his predecessor's policy. Like Schofield, he stopped Thomas and Pile from sending out mobile recruiting squads. Unlike Schofield, however, he appointed provost marshals who were sympathetic to black enlistment, and some of these men sent out recruiting squads on their own.

Overall, despite the roadblocks established by Schofield, thousands of Missouri slaves fled their masters to join the Union army. Many traveled at night to avoid encounters with hostile whites. Some were seized, beaten, and even killed. But more than eighty-three hundred reached their goal, enlisted in the US Colored Troops, and provided most of the manpower for five black regiments.

By the end of 1863, only Kentucky remained off limits to black recruiters. Although the state had by far the largest black population among the border states, roughly two hundred fifty thousand slaves and ten thousand free blacks, the state's proslavery unionists still had the upper hand.[38]

Unlike their counterparts in neighboring Missouri, Kentucky's leaders were not divided into warring camps. They were for the most part unified. They fought one another for political office but differed little on matters of policy. The only potential source of serious dissent was in western Kentucky, the strip of land between the Tennessee and Mississippi Rivers. There, Confederate guerrillas terrorized the population. And there, the demand for more Union troops was intense.

Might the political elite there, in response to their constituents' need for more protection, support black recruitment? That was uncertain. Elsewhere, however, the unionist leadership spoke largely with one voice and treated federal mandates regarding slavery and black troops with contempt.

Especially loathsome in their eyes was the Emancipation Proclamation. They all blamed it on "northern fanatics." They all said it was unconstitutional. And they blatantly refused to obey it. Instead of treating slaves who fled north from the Confederacy as "free," they had the runaways arrested, thrown into county jails, and then sold at auction to the highest bidder. They also allowed private slave traders to seize runaways from the Confederate states and sell them. Both practices skyrocketed in 1863. After the news of the proclamation spread to the Deep South, more and more slaves fled north and made their way into Kentucky, and many had the bad luck of being captured by Kentucky sheriffs. In turn, the jails and auction blocks of Lexington, Louisville, and Frankfort were soon filled to capacity.

Given such open defiance, the Lincoln administration again faced a dilemma. Would it buckle to Kentucky's proslavery biases or enforce the law? Nearly every observer predicted trouble if the War Department didn't give in. John Boyle, the state's adjutant general, reported that just trying to enroll slaves for a draft would be dangerous, even in western Kentucky, where the demand for more troops was high. It could only be done, said Boyle, at the point of bayonet. General Ambrose Burnside agreed. He claimed that even enrolling free blacks would do more harm than good.[39]

Others pointed to the 1863 gubernatorial election, in which the Peace Democrat Charles Wickliffe battled the Union Democrat Thomas Bramlette. Although the Lincoln administration sided with Bramlette and took steps to make sure that Wickliffe didn't win, Bramlette was anything but a Lincoln man. He was just the lesser of two evils. A vehement opponent of emancipation and black recruitment, he came close to matching Wickliffe's bombastic rhetoric. And, at every campaign stop, Bramlette assured voters that he, rather than his seventy-five-year-old opponent, had the vigor as well as the political connections that would be necessary to keep black recruiters out of the state. He won handily—by a margin of nearly four to one.

The news out of Kentucky thus further convinced the Lincoln administration that even attempting to arm black Kentuckians would be a dangerous gamble. Accordingly, in October 1863, Secretary Stanton sent out a memorandum calling for the enlistment of blacks, both slave and free, in Tennessee, Maryland, and Missouri but not in Kentucky. Two weeks later, Lincoln called on the Union states to provide him with three hundred thousand more men. Did that mean that the War Department might enlist Kentucky slaves if the state didn't meet its 12,701-man quota? Many thought it did. Bramlette wired Washington, demanding an explanation. Within a week, he received assurance from the Lincoln administration that even if Kentucky didn't meet its quota the state's blacks would not be enlisted.

Yet, despite having the whip hand, Bramlette couldn't stop black Kentuckians from joining the Union army. Unable to enlist at home, thousands ran away, made their way north across the Ohio River, and became soldiers in free state regiments. Of the 961 men who joined the Fifty-Fifth Massachusetts, for example, sixty-eight hailed from Kentucky.[40] Then, in September 1863, the Union army began recruiting black men in Clarksville, Tennessee. Out of southern Kentucky's tobacco counties came some two thousand recruits, often accompanied by their wives and children. In response, state officials and slave owners fired off scores of angry letters to Washington, demanding a stop to the Tennessee recruitment campaign.

Then in the western part of the state, Congressman Lucien Anderson openly broke ranks with his fellow Kentuckians. A tall and rawboned unionist, Anderson had won the House seat that had once been held by Henry C. Burnett, a staunch pro-Confederate Democrat who had left the district in 1861 to raise a Confederate regiment and to become a Confederate senator. However, many of Burnett's supporters still resided in the district, and some of them harbored Confederate guerrillas. The guerrillas kidnapped Anderson, held him for ransom, and then exchanged him for Trusten Polk, a former Missouri senator who had joined the Confederacy and been captured by Union forces.

After that experience, the thirty-nine-year-old Anderson became far more militant. He authorized one of the new Tennessee recruiters, Colonel Richard Cunningham, to come into his Paducah district and recruit twelve hundred black men for an artillery regiment. He even allowed Cunningham to use black troops to do the actual recruiting. The decision infuriated many of Anderson's constituents. It also enraged Governor Bramlette and the state's power elite. They screamed and hollered and pointed out correctly that Anderson didn't represent the sentiments of most Kentuckians. And they, rather than Anderson, had the ear of the Lincoln administration.[41]

When Congress met in December 1863, James Ashley and other radical Republicans had had it with Kentucky. They refused to accept the deal that the Lincoln administration had cut with Governor Bramlette. Led by Senator Henry Wilson of Massachusetts, they demanded to know why the War Department had not enrolled Kentucky slaves as the law required.

In response, Secretary Stanton pointed to certain ambiguities in the Enrollment Act. Wilson, in turn, introduced legislation to make it harder for the Lincoln administration to drag its feet and interpret the law narrowly. The new bill explicitly stated that all able-bodied black males, free or slave, between the ages of twenty and forty-five were to be registered for the draft, and, if drafted, their masters, if found to be loyal, would receive up to $300 in compensation.

Five Kentucky congressmen, led by Robert Mallory, denounced the bill. Mallory claimed that the Union only needed white men to fight the war and that the bill's only purpose was to "demoralize and destroy the institution of slavery." Moreover, argued Mallory, if the bill's supporters were allowed to continue their "reckless crusade," they would destroy the entire nation. With some misgivings, two Kentucky congressmen refused to follow Mallory's lead. One was Lucien Anderson, the kidnap victim, who had already broken ranks with the state's proslavery unionist leaders. He voted for the bill. The act passed with votes to spare in February 1864.[42]

That same month, Lincoln upped the pending national draft from three hundred to five hundred thousand men. Kentucky's new quota was no longer 12,701 men. It was now 21,185 men. Suddenly, many white Kentuckians panicked. Why should they be liable for the draft while the slaves of wealthy planters remained untouched? They demanded that the draft rolls be expanded to include black Kentuckians.

Governor Bramlette, however, refused to budge. Instead, he quietly backed Colonel Frank Wolford, a Kentucky military hero, who went on a rampage against black enrollment. Wolford said it was unconstitutional and denounced Lincoln as a tyrant. He also called on the Blue Grass State to throw all the enrolling officers in jail. And he promised to use his troops to stop black enrollment from happening in Kentucky.

In response, the War Department brought Wolford up on charges and threw him out of the army. That only increased his popularity in Kentucky. Bramlette, meanwhile, led a protest delegation to Washington and got a new deal out of the Lincoln administration. Under it, blacks would not be enlisted in any Kentucky county that met its quota through white enlistments, and if any blacks were enlisted they would not be trained in Kentucky. Thus, boasted Bramlette, no white Kentuckian would ever be offended by seeing a black man in arms.[43]

Kentucky, however, didn't meet its quota, and the Union's need for fighting men now trumped Lincoln's three-year policy of catering to the demands of the state's proslavery unionists. On April 18, 1864, the enlistment of black Kentuckians began. It was under the direction of Brigadier General Stephen G. Burbridge, who was a Kentucky slave owner as well as a Union commander. He tried to minimize the blow to his fellow slaveholders by limiting enlistment to free blacks and to slaves whose masters requested that they be inducted. Nevertheless, that put him at odds with Governor Bramlette, who fumed and hollered and eventually broke completely with the Lincoln administration—and at one point even threatened to "bloodily baptize the state into the Confederacy."

Burbridge's limited enlistment program, however, didn't provide enough troops to meet the state's quota. It was too constraining. So, after six weeks, all restrictions had to be lifted and all able-bodied black Kentuckians of military age, with or without their master's consent, allowed to join the army. To do so, however, they had to take to the road, avoid indignant and brutal white mobs, and find a provost marshal to enroll them, for Burbridge prohibited the mobile recruiting units that Colonel Birney had used so effectively in Maryland.[44]

Yet, despite the danger, more than half of the state's eligible black men risked life and limb to get to the state's eight recruiting stations. By the end of the summer, some fourteen thousand men had enlisted.[45] And by war's end, over twenty-three thousand seven hundred black Kentuckians had joined the Union army. By then, the only state that outdid Kentucky was Louisiana, which provided some twenty-four thousand black recruits to the Union war effort.[46]

Thus one of the predictions of the Frankfort *Tri-Weekly Commonwealth* came true. Its long-time owner and editor, Albert G. Hodges, had turned out to be a prophet. In September 1862, he had denounced the Emancipation Proclamation as soon as he heard about it. He had told his readers that the fact that Kentucky was exempt from Lincoln's edict was meaningless. And he had predicted that opening the Union army to black men would do much to destroy slavery in the Blue Grass State. And that it did.

Legally, however, slavery was still the law of the land in Kentucky. And under the Constitution, the residents of neighboring Ohio as well as every other free state were still obligated to return Kentucky runaways "on demand." Slavery was also the law of the land in the rest of the border South, in New Orleans and twelve other parishes in southern Louisiana, in the forty-eight counties designated as West Virginia, in seven counties and two cities in Virginia, and, if the Emancipation Proclamation failed to stand up in court, in every Confederate state as well. Nationally, moreover, only one-eighth of the country's four million slaves in 1860 had actually gained their freedom. Might they be reenslaved after the war was over? Hadn't that been the case after the American Revolution? The editor of *Tri-Weekly Commonwealth* thus called on all Kentuckians and especially Kentucky's leaders to stop men like James Ashley in their tracks, to make sure that they never succeeded.

On June 15, 1864, the Kentucky newsman seemingly got his wish. Despite eleven slave states being out of the Union, Ashley failed to get the Thirteenth Amendment through the House of Representatives. He had the support of Northern Republicans. But he failed to get enough Northern Democrats and border-state unionists to vote with him. He needed eleven more votes. Would he try again and somehow get the two-thirds majority he needed? Or would the war end and the South be restored to the Union before he and his Republican colleagues had a chance to wreak further havoc on the Blue Grass State? The Kentucky editor prayed for the latter.[47]

Chapter Four

THE ODD COUPLE

Two weeks after the Kentucky editor Albert G. Hodges and others celebrated the defeat of the Thirteenth Amendment in the House of Representatives, James Ashley started lining up support for a second vote. The problem, as he saw it, was twofold. First, he had to make sure that all the Republicans showed up to vote. And second, he had to find some way to reduce the number of nay votes. Six of the sixty-four nay votes had come from border-state representatives, and fifty-eight from Northern Democrats. In addition, seven border-state representatives and ten Northern Democrats hadn't voted. How might these men vote the second time around? Were any likely to join the opposition? Could any be persuaded to vote aye? Or miss the vote?

Ashley realized that he didn't have all the answers. While he knew some members of the opposition quite well and could guess what they might do, others were a mystery. They had voted against the amendment. But they had never said much in debate and never revealed the level of their hostility. Might four or five be persuaded to vote aye? Or miss the vote? He didn't know for certain. He needed more information on these men. And what about his own supporters? Were there any he should worry about? Again, he didn't know for certain. So he decided to seek input from four of his House colleagues, two for a list of persuadable Northern Democrats, and two for a list of likely and dependable border-state supporters.

For the border-state list, he turned to Frank Blair and Henry Winter Davis. It was an odd choice and proved once again the old adage that "politics makes strange bedfellows." For while both men were influential and diligent, and they represented congressional districts in key border states, Missouri and Maryland, they were incapable of working together. One had been raised to cherish Andrew Jackson and everything he stood for, the other to despise Jackson and what he stood for. One thought colonization was the answer to the nation's race problems, the other dismissed colonization as impractical and "crazy." One had wanted to slow down the emancipation movement in his home state, the other to speed it up. One was becoming more conservative as time passed, the other more radical. One was a strong supporter of Lincoln, the other a harsh critic. One envisioned the Republican Party going one way, the other the opposite way.

And to make matters worse, neither man was likely to give ground. Both men liked to fight, and both had a long history of going out of their way to pick fights. Noah Brooks, who covered Washington politics for the *Sacramento Union*, portrayed both men in unusually harsh terms. Brooks and his newspaper were strong supporters of the administration and its war policy, and as a result he usually gave the members of Lincoln's party favorable press. Yet, when it came to Blair and Davis, he made it clear that they were the kind of men who "seized upon every opportunity to quarrel" not just with men who disagreed with them, but with nearly everyone in sight, even their own supporters. They were both bad actors, wrote Brooks, "insatiate" in their hates, "mischievous" in their schemes, "hollow-hearted and cold-blooded."[1]

So why did James Ashley turn to these two men for help? In the case of Frank Blair, that is a tough question to answer. Back in 1856, Ashley had touted Blair as an excellent choice for vice president and Blair's father as an even better choice. The party needed energetic support from the Blair family's vast political network. It also needed someone from a slave state. It would broaden the party's appeal.[2] But, eight years later, at the time that Ashley sought Blair's help, the Blair family clearly wanted to drive men like Ashley out of the Republican Party.

The Blair family had been a major power in American politics since the 1830s.[3] The national symbol of their power, then as now, was the Blair House, the Pennsylvania Avenue mansion right across the street from the White House. The house had come into the possession of the family in 1837. Seven years earlier, in 1830, President Andrew Jackson had lured Frank's father, Francis Preston Blair Sr., out of Kentucky and made him the editor of the *Globe*, the voice of the administration in national politics. The senior Blair was just twenty-nine years old at the time, slight, stooped, and incredibly skinny, but he was a tiger with the pen, and soon his fiery editorials had an enormous following among Jacksonian Democrats and were reprinted in some four hundred newspapers. In addition to editing the *Globe*, the senior Blair also became the most influential member of Jackson's Kitchen Cabinet, the informal group of advisers that Jackson relied on.

Once Jackson left office, Frank's father remained as editor of the *Globe* and an important adviser to the new president, Martin Van Buren. In the 1840s, however, the senior Blair alienated many Southern members of the party. Although born and bred in the South, and the owner of slaves, he opposed the annexation of Texas, even though it would add thousands of square miles of slave country to the United States. He became convinced that Southern extremists led by John C. Calhoun wanted Texas "only as a bone of contention" to "separate the South from the North."[4] And like Van Buren, he believed that annexation would hurt the Northern wing of the party, cost Northern Democrats votes on Election Day, and probably bring on war with Mexico. Nonetheless, in the 1844 presidential election, he worked hard for the Democratic nominee, James K. Polk, who championed immediate annexation. He even won a $22,000 bet on Polk's election. Once the election was over, however, Polk forced him to sell the *Globe* to Thomas Ritchie, a more acceptable editor to the party's Southern wing.

No longer the voice of the Democratic Party in national politics, the senior Blair retired to his country estate in Silver Spring, Maryland, just outside the District of Columbia. He still had considerable clout, particularly with the followers of Martin Van Buren of New York and Thomas Hart Benton of Missouri, and his new home quickly became a gathering place for his old comrades. Not only did he wine and dine and counsel them. He also tried to convince them that Calhoun and his band of Southern "fanatics" were just as bad as Northern abolitionists and that slavery must not be allowed to expand into the "new country." He essentially had one foot in the Democratic Party, one foot out. In 1848, he broke with regular Democrats and strongly supported Van Buren's Free Soil presidential candidacy, but in 1852, he was back in the Democratic fold, writing pamphlets supporting the presidential candidacy of Franklin Pierce.

Then came the Kansas-Nebraska Act. When the victorious Pierce threw the full weight of the White House behind the bill, which repealed the Missouri Compromise and opened the western territories

Francis Preston Blair Sr., the old Jacksonian. Brady-Handy Collection, Library of Congress (LC-DIG-cwpbh-00036).

legally to slavery, Blair broke completely with the Democratic Party. He insisted that the old party of Andrew Jackson had been hijacked by the followers of Calhoun and other Southern extremists. He was now an ardent Free-Soiler. And in 1855, at a sumptuous Christmas dinner at his country estate, he instigated plans for the first Republican national convention that would be held in Philadelphia that summer. He chaired the convention and was instrumental in securing the nomination for John C. Frémont. He also wrote a widely distributed pamphlet titled *A Voice from the Grave of Jackson* in which he tried to convince skeptical Northern Democrats that Old Hickory, if he were still alive, would now be a zealous Republican.

In 1860, Blair initially supported Edward Bates of Missouri for the Republican presidential nomination. He contended that Bates was an ideal candidate—a well-known Whig and widely respected judge, a one-time slaveholder who had emancipated his slaves and become a Free-Soiler, a staunch colonizationist, and a border-state man opposed to both the proslavery fanatics of the South and the radical abolitionists of the North. Unfortunately, only about 10 percent of the delegates at the Republican National Convention agreed with him, and support for Bates eroded quickly. Blair then threw his considerable prestige behind Abraham Lincoln, who won on the third ballot. In the ensuing election campaign, Blair worked hard for Lincoln and became one of his closest confidantes. Lincoln liked him and repeatedly sought his advice.

In the summer of 1864, when Ashley started his hunt for votes, Lincoln also relied heavily on two of Blair's three sons.

One was Blair's oldest, Montgomery, who served as Lincoln's postmaster general. Now fifty-one years old, Montgomery Blair was a tall, lean, hatchet-faced man with noticeably small and deep-set eyes. He had graduated from West Point, but after a year's service in the Seminole War, he left the army, studied law, and began practice in Saint Louis, Missouri. After serving as US district attorney and as judge of the court of common pleas, he moved to Maryland in 1852 and practiced principally in the US Supreme Court. He was scholarly and probably the best read man in Lincoln's cabinet. He denounced all secessionists with abandon, even though he had many secessionist relatives. He hated abolitionists, even though he was a staunch Free-Soiler and had represented the nation's best-known slave, Dred Scott, before the Supreme Court. He was an unbending racist. Indeed, his racist convictions were as strong as his Unionist's convictions. And, like everyone else in his family, he was a fighter. He was once reputed to have said, "When the Blairs go in for a fight, they go in for a funeral."[5]

The other son was Frank. He was the youngest. At age forty-three, he was more rugged looking than his older brother, more athletic, but

Frank Blair, congressman from Missouri. Prints and Photographs Division, Library of Congress (LC-B8172-1704).

he walked much the same way, ramrod straight, head up, chest out. He was also the apple of his father's eye, and many thought he had been spoiled rotten as a child. He had an uncontrollable temper, drank too much, and loved to get into mischief. As a youth, he had been kicked out of several academies, Yale University, and the University of North Carolina. He somehow made it through Princeton but was not allowed to graduate with his class, thanks to a wild party he threw during the final week. He received his degree a year later. He eventually settled down, although according to his sister he never learned to control his temper. And, like his brother, he became a lawyer and practiced in Saint Louis.[6]

In 1856, Frank Blair became a hero in Free-Soil circles. After serving four years in the state legislature, he ran as a Free-Soil Democrat for the Saint Louis seat in Congress. It was a brave undertaking. He had the backing of the *Saint Louis Missouri Democrat*, edited by his cousin B. Gratz Brown. Also in his corner were many of the followers of Thomas Hart Benton but not Benton himself, and most of the city's German population. Nonetheless, challenging proslavery forces in

Saint Louis was dangerous. It led to a duel between Brown and the city's district attorney, a duel that crippled Brown and caused him to walk with a limp for the rest of his life. Blair himself was shot at twice.

Yet, in the election campaign, Blair and his followers pulled no punches. They championed "free soil" and denounced all those who wanted to turn neighboring Kansas into a slave state. They relentlessly attacked proslavery Democrats and especially the followers of the late John C. Calhoun and the Southern Rights wing of the Democratic Party. And they won. They thus refuted the popular notion that the free-soil movement had no appeal outside the North and could never gain a foothold in a slave state.

Six months later, Blair and his supporters followed up this victory with another in the city's mayoral election. Their candidate was John M. Wimer, a forty-six-year-old Virginia native who had come to Saint Louis in 1828 and opened a blacksmith shop. Wimer's platform called for gradual emancipation with compensation. It explicitly challenged the proslavery faction in the state legislature that had denounced gradual emancipation as "impracticable, impolitic, unwise, and unjust." It declared that gradual emancipation would be "neither impracticable, unwise, or unjust" if it appeared to be "for the best interests of the people."

The Wimer camp also insisted that the nation's major slave owners, the so-called Slave Power, were just like the aristocracy of Europe in that they wanted to make paupers of workingmen. This argument had wide appeal, especially with the Saint Louis Germans who had fled Europe following the collapse of the 1848 revolution. Winning by a substantial margin, Wimer attributed his victory mainly to the "free white working men of St. Louis" whose labor was "more productive than the compelled labor of slaves."

Throughout, Blair and his followers were not only antislavery but also, seemingly perversely, blatantly racist. The only people who counted, in the eyes of both Blair and Wimer, were whites. The main problem with slavery, said both men, was that it was bad for whites. It demeaned the value of white labor. It made Missouri unattractive to white immigrants. It depressed the land values of white farmers. Look, they said, at the free state of Iowa. Its population was growing seven times as fast as Missouri's. So too were its land values. Why? The state attracted more free white labor. B. Gratz Brown's *Missouri Democrat* was especially candid: "It will be asked—what will be done with the niggers? We answer that charity begins at home, that we are only interested for the whites. . . . We will, nevertheless, suggest that our colored folks might be shipped to Liberia."[7]

Actually, Liberia was not the destination that Frank Blair and his father had in mind, though they were both zealous colonizationists. Both men insisted that the only way Missouri could get rid of slavery was simultaneously to get rid of its black population. And, if that happened, hard-working whites would pour in and the state would prosper.

But rather than send blacks to Africa, they thought Central America would be a much better destination. With that in mind, Frank studied the British penal colonies in Central America and began reading every book he could find on the region. By late March 1857, he had a plan. He outlined the details for his father. He hoped to get Congress to grant Missouri all its remaining public lands within the state, some fifteen million acres, with the understanding that they would be sold and all the proceeds would go to purchase the state's slaves and transport them to Central America.

That December, Frank took his seat in Congress. In January, in the midst of a debate over the admission of Kansas as a slave state, he set forth his plan. He proposed that Congress appoint a select committee to examine the expediency of acquiring territory in Central or South America where free blacks and liberated slaves might be colonized. In making his case, he appealed to Northern racism: "Freed blacks hold a place in this country which cannot be maintained. Those who have fled to the North are most unwelcome visitors. The strong repugnance of the free white laborer to be yoked with the negro refugee, breeds an enmity between races, which must end in the repulsion of the latter."

Therefore, argued Frank, the only solution was colonization, and Central America was ideal for such an experiment. It already had a mixed blood population that had been ruled for decades by mestizo dictators. The area suffered from poverty and revolution. The British had an eye on it and would move into it if nothing was done. Not only would American blacks counter a British takeover, but they would improve the entire area as well, given the values they had learned observing American elections, going to American churches, and studying white American behavior.[8]

The resolution, however, never came up for a vote. Undeterred,

Frank and his father plunged ahead. Instead of backing off, they fleshed out their argument, and in January 1859 Frank presented it in a speech to the Boston Mercantile Library Association. The speech's overriding theme was that Missouri, the West, and indeed the entire country should be reserved for "the Anglo-Saxon race" and that blacks were "worse than useless" in this country but would prosper in the tropics, where they were naturally suited. By sending them to Central America, moreover, the United States would gain its own "India" and block Southern efforts to create a slave empire there as well as British efforts to dominate the region.

The address was a hit and became the basis for a thirty-eight-page pamphlet, *The Destiny of the Races of this Continent*. A year later, in January 1860, Frank gave roughly the same speech at the Cooper Institute in New York City. He thus became the Republican Party's leading voice for colonization, with scores of supporters, including for a brief time James Ashley.[9]

Meanwhile, Frank Blair had trouble holding onto his congressional seat. After winning it in 1856, he lost it in 1858. He then successfully contested that election and was seated just before the two years were up. He then resigned, lost a special election to fill the vacancy caused by his resignation, then won the seat back in the next general election and served until July 1862, when he resigned to become a colonel in the Union army.[10]

His up-and-down electoral career stemmed largely from two underlying problems. First, he and his followers controlled only 44 percent of the vote in Saint Louis, enough to sometimes win when there were three candidates in the race, but not enough to hold onto power. Second, by the time Blair gave his Cooper Institute address, he had alienated some of his old radical friends, including his cousin, B. Gratz Brown.

The rift grew during the Frémont episode. The Blairs were largely responsible for Frémont being appointed commander of the Western Department. Once Frémont took command, however, they didn't like the way he handled military contracts, and they opposed his decision to emancipate Missouri slaves. They bombarded the Lincoln administration with negative reports, charging Frémont with incompetence and corruption. Frémont jailed Blair twice for insubordination, but each time the War Department ordered his release. By November

1861, the Blairs seemingly got their way. The Lincoln administration sacked Frémont. But his sacking left a bitter aftertaste. Especially upset were Frank Blair's German supporters. They had idolized Frémont and had backed to the hilt his decision to emancipate slaves. They not only denounced Frémont's ouster. They blamed it on "Frank Blair's despicable intrigues."[11]

Blair thus lost most of his German base. Needing allies, he then moved more to the right and became the leading conservative emancipationist in Missouri, stressing gradual emancipation, compensation, and colonization. His followers came to be known as Claybanks in Missouri politics. Into the vacuum stepped Blair's cousin, B. Gratz Brown. He now became the leader of the more radical members of the old Blair coalition, "the truly black Republicans." They came to be known as Charcoals.

As guerrilla war tore Missouri apart, the Charcoals gained more recruits, and by 1862 they blamed slavery for the war and all the horrors that accompanied it. They also faulted Lincoln for not ripping slavery to shreds, for excluding Missouri from the Emancipation Proclamation, for treating the rebels with kid gloves. And in the 1862 election, they decided to oppose Frank Blair's reelection. They backed, instead, Samuel Knox, a forty-seven-year-old Harvard-trained lawyer.

Blair won the election by 153 votes. The Knox forces then claimed fraud, asserting that fourteen to fifteen hundred paroled prisoners had been marched to the polls to vote for Blair and that thousands of nonresidents had "voted *early and often*, to save this amphibious, hybrid, hermaphrodite faction from disgraceful defeat."[12] Months later, a Charcoal congressman accused Blair of ordering $8,651 worth of whiskey, ale, wine, and tobacco at government expense and then selling the items for an immense profit. Soon, charges of corruption and vote tampering became commonplace. Then, after the guerrilla war worsened and drove still more Missourians into the Charcoal camp, Knox called for a recount and succeeded in unseating Blair.

Meanwhile, to counter the radicals growing strength, the conservative governor Hamilton Gamble put forth a plan for gradually emancipating Missouri's slaves. Accordingly, in June 1863, a state convention dominated by Blair's Claybank followers drew up and approved an ordinance of emancipation. It would begin the process of ending slavery in Missouri on July 4, 1870. Up to that date, Missouri slaves could be sold out of state. On that date, all remaining slaves were to be indentured to their masters as servants, those over age forty for the rest of their lives, those under twelve until they reached age twenty-three, and all others until July 4, 1876.

The terms enraged not only proslavery Democrats but also the Charcoals. Holding protest meetings across the state, the Charcoals denounced the ordinance and called for immediate abolition with no strings attached. They also blamed Lincoln for thwarting the anti-slavery movement. Three times, they said, he had rebuffed the "true" friends of freedom in Missouri, first by rescinding Frémont's procla-mation, second by excepting the state from the Emancipation Procla-mation, and now by backing Frank Blair and this "bogus ordinance."[13]

That summer, Charcoal anger increased tenfold. Since the first months of the war, unionists living along the Kansas-Missouri bor-der had suffered at the hands of Confederate guerrillas. The guerrilla movement had grown rapidly, thanks to the addition of the sons of eminent Missourians who had been bankrupted by lawsuits growing out of a scheme to funnel nearly $3 million in bank deposits to rebel troops.[14] The unionists had complained bitterly. Yet nothing much had been done. Terrorists like "Bloody Bill" Anderson and his sidekick "Little Archie" Clement were still on the loose, scalping and mutilating the men they killed. Then, in late August, twenty-six-year-old William Quantrill and 450 Confederate raiders rode into Lawrence, Kansas, burned to the ground one-fourth of the buildings, looted most of the banks and stores, and killed 183 men and boys, dragging many out of their homes and murdering them before their families. Quantrill and his men then returned to Missouri and were hailed as heroes by Con-federate sympathizers.

The news sent shock waves across much of the country. So out-raged was the area's Union commander, Brigadier General Thomas Ewing Jr., the foster brother of the more famous William Tecumseh Sherman, that he immediately ordered his men to rid the four western Missouri counties of all suspected collaborators, by which he meant all inhabitants except those whose loyalty to the Union was beyond question. His troops carried out his order with a passion, driving some ten thousand men, women, and children onto the roads and burning the homes they left behind.

Ten days after Quantrill's raid, some seven hundred Charcoal radi-cals gathered for a statewide convention in Jefferson City, Missouri.

They, too, were furious. They blamed Quantrill and all the horrors they faced on Governor Gamble, General Schofield, and the Lincoln administration. Why had Gamble failed to crack down on Confederate sympathizers? Why did he oppose bringing in federal troops to maintain order? Why did he insist that the state militia could provide all the protection that was needed? The whole Gamble program was ridiculous, declared the Charcoals. Yet it had the backing of General Schofield and Lincoln. Why was that? Why did they back Gamble's ludicrous policies? The convention then called for Gamble's resignation and Schofield's removal and dispatched a seventy-man delegation to see Lincoln. The hullabaloo eventually caused the federal government to move against Quantrill, who was forced to flee to Texas.

In the midst of the radical furor, Frank Blair stepped in. He had been out of town, making a name for himself as a general, fighting under William Tecumseh Sherman in the Vicksburg campaign, and earning respect from friend and foe alike for his reckless bravery on the battlefield. Now back home on a short leave, he delivered a blistering speech to an overflowing crowd at Mercantile Library Hall in Saint Louis. He denounced every one of the radicals' ideas. He condemned the Charcoals for calling for the immediate emancipation of Missouri slaves, insisting that no action should be taken until the war was won. He accused them of exaggerating the danger posed by Quantrill and other Confederate marauders. He said that if the radicals gained control, the country would "degenerate into a revolution like that which afflicted France," that the radicals would set themselves up as "judges, witnesses, and executioners alike," that they would send to the guillotine "men who come back grimed all over with powder from our battle fields."

He then made it clear that he was proud to be one of those grimy warriors, and, unlike the radicals, he would soon return to the battlefield. Two days later, he left Saint Louis and rejoined Sherman's army.[15]

The next day, in a small town in Maryland, more than a thousand miles away, Frank's older brother Montgomery launched an equally savage attack on the radicals. Some would later say it was a coincidence, but no one thought so at the time. The Blairs had a reputation of sticking together, coordinating their punches, piling on. "Warfare with them is open, bold, and unsparing," noted Navy Secretary Gideon Welles in his diary. The Blair family, Lincoln once said, had "to an unusual degree the spirit of a clan. . . . They have a way of going with a rush for anything they undertake."[16]

Montgomery Blair's attack occurred at an Unconditional Union Meeting in Rockville, Maryland. The audience was a mixed group, with some moderates and some radicals, as well as Blair supporters. Nonetheless, Montgomery Blair pulled no punches. He told the crowd that "loyal unionists" were not just menaced by secessionists and their Northern sympathizers. They were also

> menaced by the ambition of the ultra-Abolitionists, which is equally despotic in its tendencies, and which, if successful, could not fail to be alike fatal to republican institutions. The Slavocrats of the South would found an oligarchy—a sort of feudal power imposing its yoke over all who tilled the earth over which they reigned as masters. The Abolition party whilst pronouncing philippics against slavery, seek to make a caste of another color by amalgamating the black element with the free white labor of our land, and so to expand far beyond the present confines of slavery the evil which makes it obnoxious to republican statesmen. And now, when the strength of the traitors who attempted to embody a power out of the interests of slavery to overthrow the Government is seen to fail, they would make the manumission of the slaves the means of infusing their blood into our whole system by blending with it *amalgamation, equality*, and *fraternity.*"

And on he went, one awkward paragraph following another, insisting that the radicals were as bad as the secessionists. Not only were the radicals prolonging the war, said Blair, by trying to impose racial "amalgamation, equality, and fraternity" on "the free white labor of our land." They were also undermining the president and his Reconstruction program. They were thus endangering the future of the entire nation. To prove his case, he then cited the *Missouri Democrat*, the *Washington Chronicle*, and an article by Senator Charles Sumner in the *Atlantic Monthly*.

He thus expanded on his brother's attack and went after the entire radical wing of the Republican Party, including cabinet members like Salmon P. Chase, senators like Charles Sumner, and congressmen like James Ashley. Indeed, he saved his sharpest barbs for the radical wing, equating them with Southern nullifiers in one sentence, Southern secessionists in another, Southern traitors in still another. And he made it sound as if he was speaking for the president.[17]

Blair then had the Rockville speech circulated as a pamphlet. It was a bombshell. On the title page, he made it clear that he was the post-master general and that the speech was in "Defence of the Policy of the President." Many thus assumed that he was speaking for the White House. Could that be true? Was that really the case? Did Lincoln really want to get rid of the radical wing of his party? Democratic newsmen couldn't believe the bonanza they had been handed. They printed the speech in full and used it to attack Republican candidates in the fall elections.

The damage was unbelievable, said Governor Andrew Curtin of Pennsylvania. He estimated that Blair's speech cost the Republican Party twenty thousand votes in his state alone. Even more irate was Curtin's fellow Pennsylvanian, Congressman Thaddeus Stevens. The Rockville speech, said Stevens, was "much more infamous than any speech made by a Copperhead orator. I know of no rebel sympathizer who has charged such disgusting principles and designs on the republican party as this apostate. It has and will do us more harm . . . than all the efforts of the Opposition. If these are the principles of the Administration no earnest Anti-Slavery man will wish it to be sustained. If such men are to be retained in Mr. Lincoln's Cabinet, it is time we were consulting about his successor."[18]

Fifty congressmen agreed with Stevens. They petitioned Lincoln to remove Blair from his cabinet. Among them was James Ashley.

The Blair brothers, in the fall of 1863, thus delivered what amounted to a one-two punch. They tried to knock out the radicals by discrediting them and then drive them out of the Republican Party.

In Missouri, however, their coordinated attack didn't work. It failed to slow down the radicals. The Charcoals forged ahead, almost at breakneck speed. They kept up the agitation for immediate emancipation. They continued to denounce the Blairs, Gamble, Lincoln, and anyone else who opposed them. They also established the Radical Union Party, which called for immediate emancipation, a new state constitution, and the disfranchisement of Southern sympathizers. They put up candidates for the state supreme court and came within two thousand votes of winning. They did even better in the state legislature. They cobbled together enough votes to get their man, B. Gratz

Brown, elected to the US Senate. The vote was sixty to fifty-one. The news struck William Lloyd Garrison, the nation's most famous abolitionist, as unbelievable: "Whoever dreamed that Missouri would elect him, a thoroughgoing Abolitionist, to the Senate of the United States."[19]

Following Brown's election, the Charcoals went after Lincoln with a vengeance. In January 1864, all but three radicals in the state assembly opposed a motion calling for Lincoln's renomination. As a result, the Blair men didn't have the votes to get it passed, and the motion was tabled, forty-six to thirty-seven, with thirty-nine not voting. Then in May, a large contingent of Charcoals, led by Brown, journeyed to Cleveland to attend the Radical Democratic Convention, a gathering chiefly of disenchanted radical Republicans, to choose a "genuine" antislavery man to run for president.[20]

The delegates unanimously backed a platform that called for three constitutional amendments: one limiting the presidency to one term; another providing for the popular election of presidents and vice presidents; and finally, another that embraced Charles Sumner's proposal in the Senate to not only outlaw slavery but also secure for all men absolute equality before the law. The majority also backed a plank that called for "the confiscation of the lands of the rebels and their distribution among soldiers and actual settlers." They then nominated for president their old hero, John C. Frémont.

The following week, another Charcoal contingent also expressed hostility toward Lincoln. Sent as delegates to the Republican National Convention in Baltimore, they first had to fight to get seated at the convention. Opposing them were the Blair supporters, who claimed that they, rather than the Charcoals, were the rightful representatives of the Missouri Republican Party. The Charcoals won the battle. And, on the first ballot, they carried out the wishes of their fellow radicals back home. They voted for Ulysses S. Grant rather than for Lincoln. Their votes were the only anti-Lincoln votes cast. Once Lincoln was nominated, they changed their votes to make the nomination unanimous. But back home, most of their fellow radicals stuck with Frémont until the Frémont movement finally collapsed. Only then did they join the Lincoln camp.

Not only did the Charcoals go after Lincoln following Brown's election. They also went after slavery in Missouri. By February 1864, they had enough strength in the legislature to push through a bill calling for a statewide referendum in the fall election, whereby the people of Missouri would decide whether there should be a convention to amend the state constitution and, at the same time, choose delegates to the convention. In May, Blair and his Claybank supporters met in Saint Louis and chose a slate of "moderates" to run against the Charcoal candidates. They also called for an amendment to the Constitution that would eventually abolish slavery but also support colonization. And, above all, they denounced the Charcoals as "amalgamators" and "nigger lovers." The Charcoals struck back, castigating Blair and his men as "proslavery copperheads."

Meanwhile, the Charcoals solidified their base, and by election time they had dozens of campaign workers in all nine congressional districts. They also had a candidate for governor, Colonel Thomas C. Fletcher, a brigade commander in Sherman's army. Opposing him was General Thomas L. Price, a wealthy landowner who had commanded troops during the Mexican War.

That November, when Missourians went to the polls, the Charcoals had an easy time of it not only because they were better organized than their opponents but also because the usual number of Confederate sympathizers failed to show up. Thousands refused to take the oath of allegiance and many were intimidated by Union troops, while others had run off and joined an invading Confederate army. The proposed convention thus passed easily, and the Charcoals won three-fourths of the seats. Fletcher also won easily, beating Price by roughly forty thousand votes, as did seven of the nine Charcoal congressional candidates. One radical congressional candidate, Henry T. Blow, won 90 percent of the vote, while another, Benjamin F. Loan, won 86 percent.

On January 6, 1865, the recently elected convention delegates assembled at the Mercantile Library Hall in Saint Louis. Five days later, they passed a motion to outlaw slavery in Missouri immediately and without compensation. The vote was sixty to four. Later that day, when word of the vote reached the capitol in Jefferson City, Governor Fletcher, with great fanfare, proclaimed the end of slavery in Missouri. "Henceforth and forever," declared the governor, "no person within the jurisdiction of this state shall . . . know any master but God."

Thus the Charcoals, despite the Blairs' opposition, triumphed. But then they overreached. With the Charcoals' backing, the dominant figure at the convention, Charles D. Drake, pushed through a number

Salmon P. Chase, secretary of the Treasury. Matthew Brady Collection, Library of Congress (LC-DIG-cwpb-05620).

of measures not only to oust Confederate sympathizers from office but also to disfranchise them and to make it difficult for Democrats to govern should they ever get back into power. These controversial clauses, in turn, enabled Frank Blair and his followers to rally conservative opposition throughout Missouri. And when the new constitution was finally submitted to the people for ratification on July 1, it passed by a mere 1,862 votes out of 85,478 cast. The civilian population turned it down by 965 votes, but the state's Union soldiers supported it by 2,827 votes.[21]

In attacking the Charcoals and other radicals, the Blairs also went after Ashley's friend, Salmon P. Chase, the Treasury secretary, fully aware that the radicals preferred him over Lincoln.

In Ashley's case, that was definitely true. While Ashley no longer had any love for Frémont, whom he had come to regard as an "ass," he had been touting Chase for president since 1855.[22] He had worked hard on Chase's behalf both in 1856 and in 1860, only to see the nomination go to someone else, first Frémont, then Lincoln. Probably no one in the Republican Party, except Chase himself, was more supportive of Chase than Ashley.

Chase, to be sure, had plenty of other backers in the party. To some, the fifty-five-year-old former governor of Ohio looked just like a president should. He was over six feet tall, had broad shoulders and a massive chest, dressed meticulously, and always stood out in a crowd. Others marveled at his self-discipline. He kept to a rigid schedule, never came late to a meeting, never came unprepared, never let his office get cluttered with unfinished business. His desk was always neat, with every piece of paper and every pen in its proper place. Not everyone agreed with Ashley, however. To some party members, Chase was a self-righteous, pompous prig. To others, he was dangerous abolitionist.[23]

In the battle against slavery, Chase had long been a leader. A New Englander by birth and a lawyer by training, he had moved to Cincinnati in 1830, where runaway slaves from nearby Kentucky were almost a commonplace. Working initially with the American Sunday School Union, he volunteered to defend them in court. He eventually defended so many that he was dubbed the Attorney General for Fugitive Slaves. He also defended white men like Ashley, who helped runaways. He took the celebrated case of John Van Zandt, a farmer who got caught harboring fugitive slaves in his basement, all the way to the US Supreme Court. He tried to convince the courts that slavery was a local institution, not a national one, and therefore it could exist only by virtue of positive state law. He also argued that the federal government was not empowered by the Constitution to create slavery anywhere, and thus when a slave left the jurisdiction of a state where slavery was legal, he ceased to be a slave. Hence Van Zandt, as well as others who harbored runaways in the free state of Ohio, had violated no law. The argument didn't work. The court upheld Van Zandt's conviction. But in antislavery circles, Chase's battles in behalf of hapless black men and women resonated, and he soon added to that record by providing the intellectual basis for the Free-Soil movement and becoming one of its stars.

In 1863, when the Blairs went on the warpath, men like Ashley still hoped to make Chase president. B. Gratz Brown, the Charcoal leader, also thought highly of Chase. Frank Blair knew that, and in his speech to the packed hall at the Saint Louis Mercantile Library he singled out the Treasury secretary for abuse. The man was no better than Jefferson Davis, said Blair. The Treasury secretary was a scoundrel, a blackguard, a rogue. He was misusing his office. He was manipulating the Treasury regulations that governed the cotton trade between North and South to benefit his radical friends at the expense of the honest conservative merchants who had saved Missouri from going over to the Confederacy and "who were among the first men to come forward and clothe and arm the troops." And, on top of all that, he was scheming to get "Lincoln's seat."

At the time, the Chase enthusiasts had not yet made plans for the upcoming 1864 presidential election. Within a matter of weeks, they did. On December 9, Ashley met with another Ohio congressman, an Ohio army paymaster, and Whitelaw Reid of the *Cincinnati Gazette* to formulate a plan. Listed on their Advisory Committee were some of most powerful men in Washington, including Massachusetts senator Henry Wilson and Vice President Hannibal Hamlin. Shortly thereafter, Senator John Sherman of Ohio, Congressman James Garfield of Ohio, and Senator Samuel C. Pomeroy of Kansas joined the group. The expanded group, according to the Washington correspondent of the *Cincinnati Daily Enquirer*, included twenty-seven senators.

In February, Ashley and the other Chase men put together a "private" pamphlet titled *The Next Presidential Election*. It deplored the renomination of Lincoln. It spoke of his "vacillation," his "indecision," and his "feebleness of will." And, without mentioning Chase's name, it called for a "more advanced thinker." Ashley circulated the pamphlet under his frank. So did Sherman. A few days later, the Chase contingent cobbled together a second "private" circular that declared that the election of Lincoln was "frankly impossible." This time they mentioned Chase by name. The circular went out under the signature of Senator Pomeroy and was sent to Republicans throughout the North.[24]

The Lincoln supporters then went into action. They got party regulars in Chase's home state of Ohio, mainly state legislators, to call unanimously for Lincoln's renomination. That stopped the Chase movement in its tracks. Then Frank Blair stepped in. In the House, he again accused the Treasury Department of being hopelessly corrupt and blamed the corruption on Chase. Never "under any government" in history, said Blair, had there been a "more profligate administration" than Chase's. He called for a full-scale investigation.[25]

Then on March 9, Chase made it clear to all that he was not about to challenge Lincoln's renomination. That, however, did not stop Frank Blair, who in late April, in the House, launched still another savage attack on the Treasury secretary. With his father and sister in the gallery cheering him on, he began by saying that Chase was out to get him, that Chase was behind the false reports that he, Blair, had swindled the government out of $8,651 in liquor and tobacco. Then, getting angrier by the minute, he accused Chase of corruption, of lacking patriotism, of treasonous behavior, and of sordidly hankering for Lincoln's office.[26] The speech lasted about an hour. After delivering it, Blair immediately headed to the White House, where he was given the stars of a major general and dispatched again to the battlefield.

James Garfield, who heard the speech, was appalled. He thought Blair was doing Lincoln's bidding, that he was Lincoln's "creature," that he had been sent by Lincoln to the House for the "special purpose" of destroying the Treasury secretary's reputation. Even worse, he also thought that Lincoln was "bound hand and foot by the Blairs" and that they were "dragging him and the country down the chasm." The Treasury secretary, with whom Garfield regularly met for a chess match, initially agreed with this assessment.

What did the secretary's old friend and long-time supporter James Ashley think? No one knows for certain. But the Ohio congressional delegation sent Rufus Paine Spaulding to see Lincoln and find out what was going on, and Lincoln reportedly disavowed any connection with the Blair attack. Ashley went to see Lincoln a few days later, and he probably got the same assurance.[27]

In any event, in June 1864, James Ashley and Frank Blair were hardly in the same political camp. To a casual observer, they probably seemed far more likely to meet on the dueling ground than in a conference room. Yet, despite all the harsh words and despite fighting one battle after another with the Blairs, James Ashley decided that to get the Thirteenth Amendment passed he had to have Frank Blair in his corner. So he turned to him for assistance.

At the same time Ashley turned to Blair, he also sought the help of someone who hated the Blairs even more than his friend Chase did.

Henry Winter Davis, congressman from Maryland.
Reprinted from *McClee's Gallery of Photographic Portraits of the
Thirty-Fifth Congress* (Washington, DC: McClees & Beck, 1859), 121.

That was Henry Winter Davis, the pride of the Maryland radicals. By
the time Ashley sought his help, Davis had become the primary target
of Montgomery Blair.

Davis represented Maryland's Fourth Congressional District, the
upper twelve wards of Baltimore, the entire city west of Jones Falls.
It was a tough district, the scene of many Election Day brawls, and at
first glance Davis had nothing in common with the roughnecks he represented. A slim six-footer, with sandy hair and a matching mustache,
he looked more like a prep school teacher than a fighter, and from a
distance he appeared to be much younger than his forty-seven years.

Yet, when he rose to speak, no one paid attention to his boyish good
looks. Instead, both friends and foes alike marveled at his brilliance,
his razor-sharp mind, his oratorical skills, his sarcastic tongue, and
his vindictiveness. He had learned to read before he turned four and
seemingly remembered everything he had read. James Garfield said

that he possessed an eloquence that was "clear and cold, like starlight."
His friend Peter G. Sauerwein said that he was "our greatest man in
power and ability by long odds: but no constituency ever had so much
trouble with their pet," for he was not only extremely proud and intol-
erant, perverse and hardheaded, but also a born agitator and "never
comfortable unless fighting somebody."[28]

The somebodies were usually Democrats. Over the years, Davis
changed parties on numerous occasions, moving from Whig to Know-
Nothing to Union to Republican, but his party affiliation seemed to
depend almost entirely on which party had the best chance of beating
the Democrats on Election Day. Besides hating Democrats, he also
hated the Catholic Church, deemed it the worst oppressor on earth,
and accused it of joining the Democratic Party in pouring money and
illegal voters into his district to defeat him. To keep his enemies in
check, he did what other Baltimore politicians did. He relied on street
gangs to watch the polls and harass the opposition. In the 1850s, the
notorious Plug Uglies, a gang that was involved in several Baltimore
shootings and assassinations, provided him with Election Day muscle.
His excuse for using them was that the other side had the support of an
even bigger and nastier gang, the New Market Fire Company.[29]

Davis had been raised to hate Democrats. His father, the Reverend Henry Lyon Davis, was an Episcopal clergyman and for several
years the president of Saint John's College in Annapolis. He was also
an ardent Federalist and, because of his politics, he ran afoul of the
Democrats on the College Board of Trustees. They sacked him in 1824
and replaced him with an "Irish Democrat," William Rafferty. Young
Henry, who was just seven years old at the time, had to go and live
with his aunt until his father got resettled in Wilmington, Delaware.
Years later, when young Henry was away in Ohio, studying at Kenyon
College, his father gave him a piece of advice: *My son, beware of the
follies of Jacksonism!*[30]

Davis never forgot his father's advice. Nor did he ever learn to completely trust a former Democrat. In his eyes, any man who had once
been a follower of Andrew Jackson was suspect, and men like the
Blairs who had worshiped Old Hickory and his policies were simply
beyond redemption. They might now call themselves "Unionists" or
"Republicans," but he never did. He always referred to them as "former
Locofocos" or "old Locofocos."

His hatred of Democrats ran so deep that it had once cost him his seat in Congress. In 1859, he had won his district easily, with 78 percent of the vote, but then when Congress convened that December he became the key player in a long and bitter dispute over who should become Speaker of the House. On the early ballots, he cast his vote for a Southern Whig, John A. Gilmer of North Carolina. Then, rather than see the gavel go to a Northern Democrat, John McClernand of Illinois, he cast what turned out to be the decisive vote for William Pennington, a New Jersey Republican and, thus, made him Speaker. Horrified, the Maryland House of Delegates, by a margin of sixty-two to one, condemned Davis for voting "for the candidate of the Black Republicans," and the Baltimore County representative charged him with being a traitor to the South and proposed that $500 be appropriated to send him to Liberia. In the subsequent election, Davis received just 42 percent of the vote.[31]

Davis, however, didn't adhere to everything his father taught him. The Reverend Davis, besides being a zealous Jackson hater, was also a slave-owning colonizationist. And in 1828, four years after he lost the Saint John's presidency, he came up with a plan to liberate his slaves. First, teach them to read. Then when they reached age twenty-five, emancipate them and send them to Liberia.

Young Henry, who was just eleven years old at the time, and his sister Jane, who was seven, were given the task of teaching the slaves to read. That they did, and most of the slaves "learned to read well." The problem, however, was "none of them could be induced to take their freedom on condition of going to Liberia." So the plan didn't work, and all the slaves remained slaves until the Reverend Davis died in 1836. At that time, Henry and his sister set them free.[32]

On reaching adulthood, Davis had no use either for colonization or for men like Blair and Lincoln who embraced it. And, as usual, he didn't bother to hide his contempt. In 1863, he told a Philadelphia audience that colonization was "simple craziness" and anyone who thought it was the answer to the nation's race problems was a blathering idiot. "Expel four millions of people? Where are the ships? Where is the land that will receive them? Where are the people who will pay taxes to remove them? Who will cultivate the deserted regions that they leave?"

Five months later, he told another audience, this time the members of Congress, that black people were here to stay and everyone better get used to it. "The folly of our ancestors and the wisdom of the Almighty, in its inscrutable purposes, having allowed them to come here . . . , they have a right to remain here. . . . And whether they become our equals or our superiors, whether they blend or remain a distinct race, your posterity will know. . . . These are things which we cannot control. Laws do not make, laws cannot unmake them."[33]

The question of when Davis became an antislavery man is open to debate. Before the Civil War, he seemed to be far less radical than the Blairs. He never was a Free-Soil hero like Frank Blair. He never even ran for office as a Free-Soiler. Instead, he spoke out against agitating the slavery issue and worked to keep it out of politics. And in the 1860 presidential election, he supported John Bell of Tennessee, the choice of John Crittenden and other border-state "moderates," rather than Lincoln, the choice of the Blairs and other Free-Soilers.

Yet, as early as 1854, his Democratic opponents had little trouble convincing their followers that he was really an "abolitionist" in disguise. Initially, in making their case, they pointed to two public letters that he had written defending the constitutionality of the Wilmot Proviso, the notion that Congress had the power to prohibit slavery in the land taken from Mexico. Would a true Southern man do that? Never, said the Democrats. Instead, a true Southern man would follow the lead of the great Calhoun and proclaim that Congress lacked the authority to bar slavery from the territories. Then, after John Brown tried to seize the federal arsenal at Harpers Ferry and launch a slave rebellion, they upped their attack and somehow managed to convince many that Davis was responsible. Finally, after he cast the decisive vote for Pennington, they delivered the killing blow. No one except a "Black Republican" and a "traitor to the South," they said, would cast such a vote. With this argument, they drove Davis out of office and elected a Peace Democrat, Henry May, to take his place.

With the beginning of the Civil War, Davis quickly gave up any pretense of being a moderate. Denouncing Maryland secessionists with abandon, he became one of the leading voices of the new Union party. The Unionists soon gained control over much of the state, thanks partly to some twenty thousand Maryland men going south and fighting for the Confederacy and others being jailed or intimidated by the Lincoln administration. And by 1862, the Unionists controlled sixty-eight of seventy-four seats in the Maryland House of Delegates.

Not all the Unionists, however, marched to the same drummer. The more conservative members followed Montgomery Blair, the more radical Davis. Although both factions thought slavery was a dying institution, the Blair contingent favored compensated emancipation along the lines that Lincoln proposed, opposed black soldiers, and sought to win Democratic support, while Davis and his followers pushed for immediate and uncompensated emancipation, black enlistments in the Union army, and a strict loyalty test to weaken the Democratic Party.

Hopelessly at odds with one another, the two Union factions in June 1863 held separate conventions and nominated separate slates of candidates for the fall elections. The Blair men ran as Conservative Unionists, the Davis men as Unconditional Unionists. That October, when Blair delivered his Rockville speech, he singled out Davis and his supporters for special abuse. He blasted Davis's interpretation of the Constitution. He accused Davis and his followers of wanting to disrupt the balance in federal relations. He said it was part of their scheme to promote racial "*amalgamation, equality, and fraternity.*"

Davis gave as good as he got. Not only did he attack Blair personally, referring to him as a "rattlesnake," a "muttonhead," and a "fool," he also ripped into Blair's program of gradual, compensated emancipation. It was too slow and too costly. Immediate abolition, said Davis, would transform Maryland quickly into a prosperous free labor society and destroy the long-time domination that "aristocratic" planters had over yeoman farmers and urban workers. As for compensation, said Davis, the planters had already been compensated in "the cleared lands of all Southern Maryland, where everything that smiles and blossoms is the work of the negro that they tore from Africa." [34]

In the November election, Davis and the Unconditionals triumphed. Like their counterparts in Missouri, they scored a decisive victory over the Blair family as well as the conservative Democrats, winning four out of the five congressional seats, fifty-two out of seventy-four assembly seats, and the only statewide race, the race for controller, with 69 percent of the vote. Among the formidable conservative Democrats they whipped were John W. Crisfield, who was beaten by John A. J. Creswell, and Thomas Swann, who was beaten by Davis. The losers blamed their losses on Major General Robert C. Schenck. His men, they said, had intimidated their supporters and kept them from voting. Was that the case? Without question, Schenck favored Davis and his followers, but whether that was decisive is a matter of dispute, with one Maryland historian essentially saying yes, another no.[35]

Once the election was over, Montgomery Blair refused to accept his diminished status. Instead, he made plans for the next battle. His goal now was to build a new national coalition with amenable Democrats and at the same time drive men like Davis out of the Republican Party. How might that be done? In December 1863, he contacted Samuel L. M. Barlow, the Democratic Party manager and part owner of the *New York World*, Manhattan's leading Democratic newspaper, and laid out his strategy. He told Barlow that Democrats had to give up the past, consider slavery to be extinct, and focus on what was surely to be the next item on the abolitionist agenda, "the Negro equality question." That, he insisted, would be the undoing of men like Davis. For once they embraced black equality, said Blair, they would be scorned by the people and left powerless against a new coalition of Democrats and conservative Republicans.[36]

While Blair was laying out plans for a new coalition, Davis and the Unconditional Unionists set about to destroy slavery and its supporters in Maryland. Now in control of the state legislature, they rammed through a bill calling for a statewide referendum in April 1864. At that time, the people of Maryland would decide whether there should be a convention to amend the state constitution and, at the same time, choose delegates to the convention.

By April, the emancipationists had all the votes they needed. And this time, when the people went to the polls, there was not even a hint of military intimidation. The army was nowhere to be seen. The call for a convention passed decisively, 31,953 to 19,524, with sixty-one convention seats going to the emancipationists, thirty-five to proslavery Democrats. The northwestern counties and Baltimore backed the convention by more than three to one, the southern tidewater counties opposed it by two to one. The outcome thus underscored what everyone knew. The state, just like the nation, was divided, north versus south.[37]

The delegates convened on April 27. Davis wasn't there, but to his delight his followers clobbered his Locofoco enemies. The thirty-five Democrats, representing mainly southern Maryland, fought first to retain slavery, then to get state compensation, then federal compensation, and then an apprenticeship system. They lost on every issue. On June 24 came the crucial vote. By a 54–29 margin, the delegates outlawed slavery and declared all Maryland slaves free. Then, by a 42–13 vote, they imposed a fine of between $500 and $5,000 and imprisonment up to five years for anyone who violated the emancipation provision. All the aye votes came from Unconditional Unionists, all the nays from Democrats.[38]

The Unconditional majority then went on to strike a series of blows against the "Slave Power." They disfranchised all Marylanders who had left the state to fight for or live in the Confederacy. In addition, they also disfranchised all those who had given the Confederacy "any aid, comfort, countenance, or support," made it difficult for them to regain full rights of citizenship, and required officeholders to take a new oath of allegiance to support the state and the Union and to repudiate the rebellion. Then, while restricting the franchise to "white" males, the majority also reapportioned the general assembly so that it was based on white inhabitants, thus reducing the influence of small counties that historically had the largest slave populations. At the same time, they voted to give the ballot to one group never entitled to it before—soldiers in the field.

The last measure turned out to be crucial. When the delegates submitted the new constitution to the people for ratification on October 13, those casting ballots at the usual voting places opposed it, 27,541 to 29,536, but soldiers in the field favored it, 2,633 to 263. So the new constitution, along with the decision to outlaw slavery, passed by a razor thin margin of 375 votes, 30,174 to 29,799.

While Davis's followers were busy turning Maryland into a free state, Davis himself became a major player in Congress. On returning to the House in 1863, he was made chairman of the committee that handled Lincoln's Ten Percent Plan.

The president, in his annual message, had proposed that the rebellious states be brought back into the Union as rapidly and painlessly as possible. In keeping with this, he had offered a full pardon to all rebels except high Confederate officials and their accomplices and promised executive recognition to any rebel state when 10 percent of its 1860 voters took an oath of loyalty to the federal government. At that time, the state could write a new constitution and rejoin the Union. It would have to comply with the Confiscation Acts and recognize the Emancipation Proclamation, but otherwise it would be free to make laws governing its former slaves that were "consistent, as a temporary arrangement, with their present condition as a laboring, landless, and homeless class."

What did that mean? Was the president sanctioning temporary peonage? Did he plan to leave freed blacks just one step above slavery? Did his plan guarantee the return of the old Southern ruling class to power? No one was certain, but many members of Lincoln's party feared the worst.

Then, on December 24, Lincoln ordered Major General Nathaniel P. Banks, Commander of the Department of the Gulf, to set up a free state in Louisiana. Banks had taken over from Benjamin Butler, and like his predecessor he was a Massachusetts politician who had been appointed to the high rank of major general mainly because of his political connections. He differed from Butler, however, in that he had never been a proslavery Democrat and he never became a radical Republican. Instead, he started out as an antislavery Democrat, became a Know-Nothing, and then a conservative Republican. He also had been far more successful in politics than Butler. He had been the Speaker of the House of Representatives for two years and the governor of Massachusetts for three terms.

Yet, despite his political skills, Banks had already alienated many in Lincoln's party. He had installed a labor system in Louisiana that recognized the freedom of former slaves but also forced them to work on plantations whether they liked it or not. Contending that the former slaves would become idle layabouts if allowed to choose for themselves, he had the army "induce" them to enter yearly contracts with plantation owners. Once hired, the former slaves were entitled to 5 percent of the proceeds of the year's crop or a wage of $3 per month along with room and board. But they couldn't leave the plantation without the master's consent. If they did, the army would hunt them down and bring them back. They would also be punished for violating the law. Some fifty thousand former slaves had been "hired" under this system. To Banks, it was the "first step in the transition from slave to free labor." But to antislavery radicals like Ashley, it was despicable, just a cynical device to provide the plantation aristocracy with a well-disciplined labor force.[39]

On receiving Lincoln's order to turn Louisiana quickly into a free state, Banks realized immediately that he had a problem. Free blacks

in New Orleans demanded the right to vote, while the vast majority of
Louisiana's white residents vehemently opposed giving any black man
the right to vote. In carrying out the president's order, Banks decided
that alienating the white population would be disastrous. Accordingly,
he held elections for officials under the old state constitution, which
recognized slavery and severely restricted the rights of the free black
population. The campaign for governor made matters worse. It pitted
Michael Hahn, a Bavarian immigrant, against Benjamin Flanders, a
New Hampshire–born teacher and newspaperman. Hahn ran a blatantly racist campaign and won.

The news from Louisiana, in turn, undermined what little support
Lincoln's Ten Percent Plan had in Congress. That Banks had given in
to white racism angered Senator Charles Sumner of Massachusetts
and several other members. That Banks had acted without congressional authorization infuriated many more, including James Ashley
and Henry Winter Davis. Where, they asked, did Banks get the power
to hold elections for state officials under the old Louisiana constitution? From Lincoln? The president didn't have that power to grant.
Only Congress had it, and Congress hadn't granted it. Thus Banks's
action was unauthorized. It was unconstitutional. It was "a most wanton and defenseless assumption of military power."[40]

To Davis, especially, the Ten Percent Plan was an abomination. It both
usurped the authority of Congress and was too lenient on the insur-
gents. And it came from a man that Davis didn't respect. Never a Lincoln man, Davis had been sour on the president ever since he took
office. Many had pushed Davis for a cabinet post, but to Davis's dismay
Lincoln had chosen the Locofoco Montgomery Blair instead.

In addition, Davis had begun the war as a critic of the Lincoln's administration abuse of the civil liberties of suspected traitors. In Maryland, said Davis, the president had been too quick to resort to martial
law, to make arbitrary arrests, and to deny free speech. He had acted
like a "tyrant." Where did he get the authority to suspend the writ of
habeas corpus? To lock up hundreds of his fellow citizens without a
trial? Without even filing charges? And where did he get the power,
a year later, to issue the Emancipation Proclamation? Wasn't emancipation a congressional prerogative? And what good would Lincoln's
proclamation do? Not only did it fail to guarantee the rights of freedmen, but it wouldn't stand up in court either.

To no one's surprise, then, Davis introduced a bill on February 15 that directly challenged the president's plan. While retaining the 10 percent feature, the bill added an extra or "ironclad oath." Just swearing future loyalty to the federal government was not enough. Those who wanted to vote for delegates to a constitutional convention had to swear that they had neither held office in any rebel government nor voluntarily borne arms against the Union.

The bill was also more severe than Lincoln's plan when it came to emancipation. In Lincoln's plan, emancipation would come from new state constitutions. In Davis's proposal, it would come from federal statute. In Lincoln's plan, freed people had only the rights that states granted them. In Davis's bill, they had federal habeas corpus rights, and former masters who violated their rights would be subject to federal fines and imprisonment.

Debate on the Davis bill began on March 22. The 10 percent provision didn't stand a chance of surviving. It was absurd, said one House Republican after another. It enabled nine-tenths of the rebels to remain "openly disloyal." Hence, with Davis's enthusiastic support, the 10 percent clause was dropped and replaced by one requiring a majority of the 1860 voters to take a loyalty oath before Reconstruction could begin. Further, the House insisted on disfranchisement of Confederate leaders. All but six Republicans supported the amended measure, and it passed the House on May 4 by a 73–49 vote. It then went to the Senate, where Benjamin Wade took charge. With the support of all but five Republicans, he pushed the House bill through the Senate on July 2 by an eighteen-to-fourteen vote.

The outcome dismayed Lincoln. The Wade-Davis Bill was widely regarded as a reprimand of him personally, and, what's more, it would interrupt the process of Reconstruction in Louisiana and Arkansas that he had already begun. In addition, he did not want to be committed to so rigid a plan and he disliked the ironclad oath with its demand of past loyalty. Thus Lincoln sided with the opposition—which included fifty-two Democrats and just eleven members of his own party—and pocket vetoed the bill. His decision infuriated the radicals. Charles Sumner told Chase that there was "intense indignation" against the president.

In Davis's case, that was a gross understatement. Davis's fury was boundless, and along with James Ashley and other radicals he began a movement to replace Lincoln on the Republican presidential ticket.

He also put pen to paper and wrote what came to be known as the Wade-Davis Manifesto. It was harsh and brutal. It berated Lincoln for defying "the exercise of an authority exclusively vested in Congress by the Constitution" and accused him of using Reconstruction to secure electors in the South who would "be at the dictation of his personal ambition."

Elsewhere, Davis also accused Lincoln of meaning to leave slavery "exactly where it was by law at the outbreak of the Rebellion." The Emancipation Proclamation, contended Davis, didn't destroy slavery. It "merely professed to free certain slaves while it recognized the institution." Indeed, under Lincoln's plan "every Constitution of the Rebel States at the outbreak of the Rebellion may be adopted without the change of a letter."[41]

Pundits immediately denounced the manifesto, and many commentators would later say that the manifesto backfired, that it hurt Davis and Wade far more than it hurt Lincoln. But at the time, its impact was anything but certain. Albert G. Riddle, one of Ashley's Ohio colleagues, reckoned that Lincoln had the solid support of only two Republicans in the House. Carl Schurz thought the president had "only one steadfast friend in the lower House . . . and a few more in the Senate." Thaddeus Stevens said he knew of only one true supporter, Representative Isaac N. Arnold of Chicago. And George Julian estimated that only one in ten Republican members sided with the president.

Exaggerations? Maybe. Yet, whatever the real level of support, Lincoln knew that he had to make peace with the radicals, and in September he agreed to get rid of the man who most angered them, his postmaster general, Montgomery Blair. And with that, the movement to replace Lincoln at the head of the ticket collapsed, and even Henry Winter Davis grudgingly threw his support behind Lincoln in the fall election.[42]

So, in seeking help in the summer of 1864, Ashley turned to two men who were at war with one another. He didn't expect them to work together. That was clearly impossible, and Ashley was not a foolish man. He just wanted a list of names, just a list of border-state men who could be counted on to support the Thirteenth Amendment, plus a handful who might be won over to the cause.

He got nineteen names. On the list were twelve men who had voted aye the first time around, five who had missed the vote, and two who had voted nay. One of the nonvoters was Henry Winter Davis, who had been sick in bed when the June vote was cast. In truth, Davis hadn't expected the amendment to pass and had told his friend Wade as much. In his mind, his own creation, the Wade-Davis Bill, was "the *only* practical measure of emancipation *proposed* in this Congress."[43] Whether Ashley knew Davis's true sentiments is uncertain.

Also uncertain is who, exactly, provided what name. But, if one assumes that the Maryland names came primarily from Davis, and the Missouri names from Blair, then Blair was the more valuable source. The Maryland names were predictable. They were all men with radical credentials. The same was true of the one Delaware representative who made the list, the three West Virginians, and three of the four Kentuckians. But of the Missourians who ended up on Ashley's list, there were two men, Austin A. King and James S. Rollins, who appeared at first glance to be long shots. Both had voted against the amendment, both were slave owners, and both represented districts in "Little Dixie," the area in Missouri with the heaviest concentration of slaves and the fewest Charcoals.[44]

King especially was unique. He was the only border-state man on Ashley's list who still ran for office as a regular Democrat, which usually was a strong signal to voters that the candidate favored slavery. Some of the others, including Frank Blair, had once been staunch Jackson men, but they now presented themselves to the voters as Unionists, Unconditional Unionists, Conservative Unionists, or Republicans. Not King. He still presented himself as an old-fashioned Jacksonian Democrat. Now sixty-two years old, he had been doing so all his adult life, first in Tennessee, where he was from, and then Missouri, where he had lived for the past thirty-four years. In 1834, four years after he arrived in Missouri, he had won a seat in the state legislature. Subsequently, he had been a circuit court judge for eleven years and then the governor for five years. He was, in short, an old hand in Missouri politics.

Throughout his thirty years in Missouri politics, King had sided with proslavery men more often than he had opposed them. In 1849, as governor, he had signed the controversial Jackson Resolutions that instructed Missouri's long-time US senator, Thomas Hart Benton, to act in "hearty cooperation" with John C. Calhoun and his proslavery followers "against the encroachments of Northern fanaticism." Six years later, in 1855, King had attended the Missouri Slave Owners Con-

Austin A. King, congressman from Missouri. Brady-Handy Collection,
Library of Congress (LC-DIG-cwpbh-01331).

vention in Lexington, Missouri, which had encouraged Senator David
Atchinson and his "border ruffians" in their crusade to turn neighboring Kansas into a slave state. Later, however, he had opposed Atchinson's plan of having Missourians cross over the state line to cast illegal
ballots for the proslavery Kansas Lecompton Constitution. In 1860,
King had been a delegate to the Democratic National Convention and
had campaigned for the choice of Northern Democrats, Stephen A.
Douglas. And in 1862, he had run for Congress as a regular Democrat
and won.

King represented the sixth district. Located in northwest Missouri
and bisected by the Missouri River, the district had the highest percentage of slaves in the state. Roughly one-fifth of the population was
in bondage, and in Saline and Lafayette counties, roughly one-third.
In winning the district, King had polled 45 percent of the vote in a
four-man race. Of his three rivals, only one had called for emancipa-

tion. That was Henry B. Bouton, the Charcoal candidate. Bouton had finished dead last, winning under 7 percent of the vote, the poorest showing by far of any of the Charcoal congressional contenders that year. King had denounced Bouton as an abolitionist. He had also voted against emancipation when it came up before the House in June 1864. Yet he made it on Ashley's list.

The other long shot on Ashley's list was James S. Rollins. He represented the ninth district, some 136,000 people living directly east of King's district, and just north of the Missouri River. The ninth also included several counties with heavy slave concentrations. One was Rollins's home county, Boone, where roughly one-fourth of the population was in bondage. Of its 885 slave owners, Rollins ranked near the top.

Ten years younger than King, Rollins was a native of Kentucky who, like King, had migrated west to Missouri in the 1830s. Unlike King, he was not a Jacksonian Democrat. As a young man, he had been a Whig and had even run against King for governor in 1848. He lost that race, but over the years he had been elected to the state legislature on numerous occasions. When the Whig party fell apart in the 1850s, he began flirting with alternatives to the Jacksonians. In 1860, he presented himself to the electorate as a Constitutional Unionist and was elected to Congress. Two years later, he ran as a Unionist and won again, this time defeating the Charcoal candidate, Arnold Krekel, by a whopping three-to-one margin.

Rollins remained a Unionist throughout the war, and voted for most war measures, but he had never shown any signs of becoming an emancipationist. His stands on slavery and black rights were much more like John Crittenden's than like James Ashley's. He was one of the twenty border-state congressmen who rejected Lincoln's program of gradual compensated emancipation. He voted against a measure that would have allowed blacks and Indians to enlist in the war, on the grounds that such a policy would offend Southerners. He also stated that the Emancipation Proclamation was legally void and only defensible as a military necessity. And in 1863, he joined Frank Blair in vehemently attacking the Charcoals. Not only did he characterize his Charcoal opponent Krekel as a "dangerous abolitionist," but he also blamed virtually every problem in Missouri on "these political Ishmaelites, known as Radicals" and called on Lincoln to "settle the hash" of men like Krekel and B. Gratz Brown.[45]

James S. Rollins, congressman from Missouri.
Reprinted from North Todd Gentry, *The Bench and Bar of Boone County, Missouri* (Columbia, MO: The Author, 1916).

So, given their pasts and the people they represented, both King and Rollins were long shots. Yet, they made it to Ashley's border-state list.

Was it just wishful thinking on Ashley's part? On Frank Blair's part? No, they weren't alone in thinking that these two men could be persuaded to vote for the amendment. Over the next several months, Abel Rathbone Corbin, a New York City financier and Republican moneyman, came to the same conclusion. In December 1864, he told Lincoln that it would be easy to get the support of both Missourians. All Lincoln had to do was dangle before their eyes the opportunity for them to have a say in the appointment of a federal judge.[46]

In any event, when it came time to vote in January 1865, both King and Rollins voted for the amendment. By then, they were both lame ducks, no longer answerable to the people back home. And that, perhaps, was the telling fact. For when the votes were finally tallied, the only names on Ashley's border-state list that truly mattered were those of six lame ducks, King and Rollins and four other men who were serving out their last few months in Congress. All the other men on the list, besides the lame ducks, had supported the amendment the first time around. They didn't need to be persuaded. They had already committed themselves. The six lame ducks, however, had not. None of them had cast aye votes in June 1864. King and Rollins had voted nay. The other four had missed the vote. In the end, when the final vote was taken in January 1865, five of the six supported the amendment. They were the only border-state representatives to change their votes.

The only lame duck who didn't come through for Ashley was Brutus J. Clay. A Kentucky Unionist who had missed the first vote in June 1864, he voted nay the second time around. Otherwise, Ashley got the support of eighteen of the nineteen men that Blair and Davis helped him line up. Had three of those men voted no, the amendment would have gone down to defeat.

Chapter Five

HOSTILITY OF THE NORTHERN DEMOCRACY

At the same time that Ashley turned to Frank Blair and Henry Winter Davis for a list of potential border-state supporters, he also sought a list of Northern Democrats who might vote for the Thirteenth Amendment. In June, when the amendment went down to defeat, he had the backing of only four Northern Democrats. Ten had missed the roll call, and fifty-eight had voted against the amendment. Getting a dozen or so to switch their votes was thus crucial. For help, he turned to two New York Republicans, Reuben E. Fenton and Augustus Frank.

Unlike Blair and Davis, the two New Yorkers were compatible. Still, they were an odd choice. Their outreach, at first glance, was too narrow. Both were radical Republicans. And both hailed from western New York, the part of the state where the Democracy was weak. For years, the strength of the New York Democracy had been in Manhattan, Brooklyn, and the old Dutch counties along the Hudson River. Neither Fenton nor Frank had ever been in a position to master the intricacies of any of these districts, much less to develop the expertise needed to deal with Tammany Hall, Mozart Hall, and the other political factions that fought for patronage in the heavily populated southeastern quarter of the state. Both men had lived their entire lives hundreds of miles away from these Democratic strongholds, in two congressional districts that touched one another, Fenton in the southwest corner of the state, Frank slightly to the north and east, in that part of New York that historians often refer to as the "burned over district."

The region got its name because in the early nineteenth century it experienced one religious revival after another, so many that the great evangelist Charles Grandison Finney referred to it as the "burnt district," an area that had been so heavily evangelized that it no longer had any "fuel" left to "burn," or, more precisely, anyone left for men like Finney to convert. Not only had the region been repeatedly "burned over" by religious revivals, it also had been the hotbed of scores of social movements, including temperance, women's rights, and abolition. In Chautauqua County, where Fenton grew up, sixteen different antislavery societies had been formed by the time he celebrated his seventeenth birthday. In nearby Genesee County, where Frank spent his boyhood, there were thirty. Only one county in the entire state had more.[1]

Especially active in the antislavery movement was Frank's hometown of Warsaw. The town had no more than twelve hundred residents. Yet during Frank's boyhood, it had an antislavery newspaper, the *American Citizen*, along with two antislavery societies, one a men's group, the other a women's group. There were also six families in town that openly sheltered runaway slaves, and a resident ex-congressman, Seth Gates, with a price on his head because of his antislavery activities. In 1840 he had used his congressional frank to mail antislavery literature. He had also defied the House gag order prohibiting members from mentioning slavery in debate. A group in Savannah, Georgia, in turn, had offered $500 for Gates, dead or alive.[2]

Frank and Fenton were not only from roughly the same social background but, in addition, neither was running for reelection when Ashley sought their help.

In Fenton's case, he had been approached by the Republican Party to run for governor of New York against the Democratic incumbent Horatio Seymour. The party leadership thought Fenton had the command presence that a governor should have. Tall and well built, with a full head of graying wavy hair, he was widely regarded to be one of the "best looking" men in Congress. He was also an old hand in Republican politics even though he was just forty-five years old.[3]

Like Ashley, Fenton had originally been a Jacksonian Democrat. Elected to Congress in 1852 as a Democrat, he had vehemently denounced the Kansas-Nebraska Act of 1854 and unsuccessfully tried to persuade President Franklin Pierce and Secretary of State William L. Marcy to oppose it. Defeated for reelection that year, Fenton became one of the founders of the New York Republican Party, organizing and

Reuben E. Fenton, congressman from New York.
Brady-Handy Collection, Library of Congress (LC-BH824-4722).

presiding over its first convention in 1855. Then, in 1856, he ran again for his old House seat, against the same opponent who had whipped him in 1854, and won by eight thousand votes. Subsequently, he was reelected three times, winning his last election with over 63 percent of the vote. In Congress, he never gave set speeches but was an important figure on the Ways and Means Committee. He also was known as "the friend of the soldier" and a fierce opponent of the Fugitive Slave Act.[4]

Fenton had been approached to run for governor in 1862 but had declined the offer. This time, he accepted. In the election campaign, he was no match for Seymour when it came to stump speaking. He lacked the incumbent governor's magnetism, his dramatic gestures, his way with words. But Fenton was a vote getter and he proved it once again. Not only did he beat Seymour on Election Day, he also outpolled Lincoln in New York by more than fifteen hundred votes. Unfortunately for Ashley, however, Fenton's victory cost the emancipation movement an aye vote, as the newly elected governor had to resign from Congress before the amendment came up for reconsideration.

Ashley's other source, Augustus Frank, had strong roots both in antislavery circles and in politics. When he was a child growing up in Warsaw, his father, Dr. Augustus Frank, was the leading figure in the town's antislavery movement. A delegate to the conventions that had formed the American Anti-Slavery Society in Philadelphia in 1833 and the New York Anti-Slavery Society in Utica in 1835, Dr. Frank had been attacked by antiabolitionist mobs on several occasions. He had also been a "station master" on the Underground Railroad and a consistent breaker of the Fugitive Slave Law. Young Frank also had contact with several well-connected politicians as a child. That was mainly because of his mother. Two of her brothers, William Patterson and George Washington Patterson, were congressmen, and one, George, became the lieutenant governor of New York.[5]

On leaving home, Frank had first tried his hand at various mercantile pursuits. He then got involved in railroads, the hot new industry of the age, and soon was the director and vice president of the Buffalo & New York City Railroad Company. Following the Kansas-Nebraska Act, he immediately affiliated with the new Republican Party and was a delegate to its first national convention in 1856. He was elected to Congress in 1858, beating two rivals in a three-man race with over 56 percent of the vote. He was then reelected in 1860 with over 67 percent of the vote, and again in 1862 with just over 52 percent of the vote. Though the 1862 election was much closer than the previous contests, he had what everyone deemed to be a "safe" seat. Nevertheless, at age thirty-eight and after six years in the House, he decided not to run again and became, instead, the director of the Wyoming County National Bank.

So Ashley, in his search for potential Democratic supporters, turned to two lame duck Republicans from western New York. What did he hope to accomplish? Perhaps his intent was to get them to concentrate on New York while he tended to the Ohio Valley. If so, the choice made some sense. For while the Democratic Party as a whole was hostile to emancipation, there were men in the old Van Buren wing of the New York party who had been mavericks in the past.

Getting their support, however, was certain to be an uphill battle.

Augustus Frank, congressman from New York. Brady-Handy Collection, Library of Congress (LC-DIG-cwpbh-03452).

For the Democratic Party was not simply hostile to emancipation— it had a history of punishing party members who broke ranks and showed signs of supporting black freedom. Since the 1820s, the party had been the home of most Northerners who favored the harsher forms of white supremacy. Not every Northern racist, to be sure, became a Jacksonian Democrat. Their opponents—first the Whigs and then the

Republicans—also included plenty of men who played the race card. One of them, as many historians have pointed out, was Abraham Lincoln. Yet Lincoln, even on his worst days, was never as hostile to blacks as Stephen A. Douglas and the leaders of the Democracy. And some of Lincoln's Whig and Republican colleagues clearly sympathized with the plight of blacks, while others were too busy denouncing the Irish and the Catholic Church to have any time for race baiting. The Jacksonians, by and large, took the opposite tack, defending the Irish on the one hand, while appealing to the worst strains in white racism on the other. That had long been the stock-in-trade of one Jacksonian politician after another.

Besides being hard on blacks, Northern Democrats also tended to be soft on the slavery question. That, too, had been true for decades. Between 1836 and 1844, the key votes to stop antislavery petitions from being read in Congress had come mainly from free-state Democrats. They also provided the votes that were key to enabling Southern planters to obtain the lands of the Cherokees, the Creeks, the Chickasaws, the Choctaws, and the Seminoles in the 1830s and to allowing Texas to come into the Union in 1845 as a slave state with the right to divide into as many as five states. They also had provided the key votes to defeat the Wilmot Proviso in 1847 and to enact the Fugitive Slave Law of 1850 and the Kansas-Nebraska Act of 1854.[6]

The Civil War accentuated these tendencies. The party, to be sure, included some War Democrats, men who wholeheartedly supported the war effort. They received a lot of attention from the press, and the Lincoln administration made much of them, mainly to prove that one measure or another had bipartisan support. And at times, given the amount of attention War Democrats received, it seemed as if they were a major force within the Democratic Party, that the party was evenly divided, half War Democrat, half Peace Democrat. But that was never the case. The War Democrats were never numerous enough to threaten the party regulars. Nor did they ever enjoy much voter support among hard-core Democrats. Moreover, once the war became a war to end slavery, much of the support they had evaporated.

The regulars, in short, were in charge. And, at first glance, they were in rough shape when the war began. Not only did Lincoln win the presidency in 1860, but the Republicans won 108 out of 152 Northern House seats as well. And in two states, Massachusetts and Vermont, Republicans won so easily that regular Democrats might as well not have been on the ballot. Yet, even though Northern Democrats came out of the election with only forty-four House seats, party regulars looked at the numbers and realized that their losses weren't as bad as the pundits said. Indeed, outside of Vermont and Massachusetts, the regulars had put up a good fight in most of the districts they lost. They were a "respectable minority," within five or six percentage points of capturing the district.

So when the war began, the regulars didn't change their tune. They had always denounced their opponents as Black Republicans. They had always accused Republicans of having "nigger on the brain," shilling for the "abolitionists," and promoting "amalgamation." They continued to do so as the war progressed. In addition, they charged the Lincoln administration with incompetence as one Union general after another botched an assignment and as the Union war dead mounted, first to a thousand, then ten thousand, then a hundred thousand, finally 340,000. They also portrayed Lincoln as a tyrant when he suspended the writ of habeas corpus and locked up citizens by the thousands, beginning with Maryland in April 1861, then across much of the North in 1862. They lambasted the Lincoln administration as well for the draft, for rising inflation, for high new taxes, and for corruption. They even blamed the Lincoln administration for the Confederacy's closing of the Mississippi River and the subsequent hard times that befell much of the Midwest.

Yet nothing infuriated Northern Democrats more than the Republicans' racial policies. Only wild-eyed "abolitionists," they said, would support the recognition of the black republic of Haiti, the abolition of slavery in the District of Columbia, the repeal of the Fugitive Slave Act, and the use of black troops. All of these measures were not only barbarous, said Democrats, but many were also unconstitutional. The federal government had no right to tamper with slavery. It was a local institution and guaranteed by the Constitution as such. And relying on black troops? Nothing, said Democrats, could be further from what the Founding Fathers intended.[7]

Then in September 1862 came the preliminary Emancipation Proclamation, followed two days later by another proclamation suspending habeas corpus across the North. Democrats went ballistic. Freeing rebel slaves, said one pundit after another, would destroy white America. Soon, Illinois, Indiana, Ohio, Pennsylvania, and other North-

ern states would be overrun by hundreds of thousands of black vaga-
bonds and paupers. Shiftless "niggers" would be everywhere, pushing
up the urban crime rate, stripping poor white workers of their jobs,
molesting white women and children. The proclamation even invited
"niggers" to cut their masters' throats.

Alarmists soon had a field day. What was Lincoln thinking? What
would Republicans do next? What should Democrats do in retaliation? The editor of the *Circleville (OH) Watchman* called for hanging
all abolitionists "till the flesh rot off their bones." A Cincinnati newsman proposed changing the Democratic Party's slogan to read "The
Constitution as it is, the Union as it was, and the Niggers where they
are."[8]

In the Empire State, the home base of Fenton and Frank, the loudest
denunciations came from Peace Democrats led by New York City's ex-
mayor Fernando Wood. Just sixteen months earlier, when the country
was falling apart, Wood had recommended that the city join the secessionists and become an independent republic, a duty-free port, free
of meddling upstate lawmakers as well as free of federally mandated
tariffs. Now he was back, running for Congress, denouncing the Lincoln administration as "fanatical, imbecile, and corrupt" and openly
urging New Yorkers to resist emancipation, before it flooded the city
with cheap black labor, led to integrated schools, and, if Republicans
had their way, "amalgamation." At the state level, the more moderate
Democrat Horatio Seymour, running for governor, adopted the same
stance. He assailed emancipation as "a proposal for the butchery of
women and children, for scenes of lust and rapine, for arson and murder unparalleled in the history of the world."[9]

That fall, as elections approached, Wood, Seymour, and other
Democratic leaders sensed victory. They thought that they now had
the smoking gun. With the Emancipation Proclamation, they could
now prove to voters that the Black Republicans had no intention
of just restoring the Union. No, they said, the Republican goal was
clearly black equality. And with that argument, Democrats ran vigorous campaigns, especially in the lower North. Outside of Vermont and
Massachusetts, where they got crushed as usual, their efforts paid off
on Election Day. They won the gubernatorial races in New York and
New Jersey, statewide races in Illinois and Indiana, and twenty-three
Republican-held House seats. In New York City, Fernando Wood ran

away with the election, winning every precinct, capturing over 70 percent of the vote.

Yes, Democrats suffered a few losses. In Ohio, the chief spokesman of the Peace Democrats, Clement Vallandigham, lost his district, but even that could be explained away. The district, Democratic pundits noted, had been gerrymandered by the Republican-controlled state legislature. One county had been taken away, another added. Yet Vallandigham still had the support of his base, namely, Irish Catholics, German Catholics, and transplanted Southerners.[10]

More typical, noted the pundits, was what happened in Ohio's eleventh district. Located in southeast Ohio, along the Ohio River, it had been the scene of a nail-biting contest back in 1860. Both candidates had polled over eleven thousand votes, and the Republican winner, Valentine B. Horton, had a victory margin of just 3 percent. Now in 1862, the Democracy enlisted Wells A. Hutchins to run against another Republican, H. S. Bundy. Hutchins brought up the preliminary Emancipation Proclamation at every opportunity and won the district by more than 12 percent. The proclamation, everyone agreed, was decisive. It appeared just in time to defeat Bundy and other Ohio Republicans. "I thought until this year the cry of 'nigger' & 'abolitionism' were played out," moaned Bundy, "but they never had as much power & effect in this part of the state as at the recent elections."[11]

In licking their wounds, many Republicans agreed with Bundy, but a few did not. Ashley, who won a tough three-man race by some eleven hundred votes, blamed his party's losses on conservatives. They had failed to embrace emancipation. Many of them, in fact, had run away from it. The conservatives, in turn, blamed radicals like Ashley for pushing black freedom too hard, for getting too far ahead of the electorate. Meanwhile, both the *Chicago Tribune* and the *New York Times* blamed the party's losses on the low Republican turn-out on Election Day. Too many Republican patriots, said the *Times*, had "disfranchised themselves by entering the army for the defense of the Union." Had they been able to vote, the outcome would have been different. Only a few contests, noted the *Times*, resulted in landslides like Wood's. Most were close, decided by no more than a few thousand votes.[12]

The Democracy didn't just go after Republicans in the 1862 election. The party regulars also made War Democrats pay for collaborating with Republicans. Singled out for reprisals were William E. Lehman of Pennsylvania, George T. Cobb of New Jersey, and Edward Haight of New York.

All three had committed the same "sins." They had voted for compensated emancipation in the District of Columbia. They had also supported Lincoln's plan of compensated emancipation in the border states. In Lehman's case, the regulars in Philadelphia simply denied him renomination. In New Jersey's fourth district, the regulars, led by Andrew J. Rogers, drove Cobb off the ticket by demanding that he endorse a revised district platform, written secretly by Rogers, that denounced emancipation as inexpedient and unconstitutional. Cobb refused and hence was denied renomination.[13] In New York's tenth district, the regulars first tried to stop Haight from running again. Failing in that effort, they ran a regular Democrat, William Radford, against him in the general election and thus turned the contest into a three-man race. Haight then sought and received Republican help. Yet, even with Republican backing, he had three thousand fewer supporters than he had in 1860. He lost to Radford by nearly a thousand votes.

So the regulars not only gained twenty-eight seats in Congress, twenty-three at the expense of the Republican Party and five at the expense of the Unionists, they also purged their party of some dissident members. In the place of the dissidents, they could now point to three dependable regulars—Samuel J. Randall of Philadelphia, Andrew J. Rogers of New Jersey, and William Radford of New York. In June 1864, all three toed the party line. They all voted against the Thirteenth Amendment.

After the election of 1862, regular Democrats stepped up their assault on emancipation. Taking the lead was the party's national chairman and its leading financier, August Belmont.

Now in his early fifties, the German-born Belmont had been one of the country's richest men since the day he became a naturalized citizen in 1844. Thanks partly to his role as the American agent for the Rothschild interests, he had risen quickly on Wall Street, had acquired his own bank, and had made huge profits from foreign exchange transactions, corporate real estate, railroad investments, and a host of other enterprises. He was also famous for his stable of thoroughbred horses, his promotion of horse racing, his support of the opera, his collection of fine paintings, and his lavish dinner parties. He walked with a limp, a souvenir of a duel he had fought in 1841 in defense of a married

August Belmont, head of the Democratic Party. Brady-Handy Collection,
Library of Congress (LC-DIG-cwpbh-02771).

woman's honor. That, in turn, had only added to his stature as an aris-
tocrat, as one of the pillars of high society, and as the "king of Fifth
Avenue."[14]

In 1860, Belmont had been chosen by Stephen A. Douglas to run his
presidential campaign. After Douglas's defeat in November and death
the following June, Belmont took over as the head of the Democratic
Party and remained in that position for the next twelve years. Even
though Douglas lost the 1860 election, the contest had proved to Belmont once again the value of playing the race card. While Lincoln captured over 53 percent of the New York vote, further down on the New
York ballot was the old issue of whether the state's black population
should have the same voting rights as its white population. Since 1821,
the state had a property restriction on suffrage that applied only to
black males. To vote they had to own a $250 freehold. Should that re-
striction be lifted? Or retained?

Reformers had tried to repeal the restriction in 1846 and failed. In
1860 they tried again. They mounted a full-scale campaign, sent out
speakers, held a statewide convention, and formed hundreds of free
suffrage clubs, including forty-eight in New York City alone. While
many Republican spokesmen tried vainly to duck the question, Belmont and his fellow Democrats jumped on it and used it to hammer
their Republican opponents. If all black males got the vote, said Democrats, then blacks would soon take jobs and political power away from
deserving whites and, even worse, "negroes of Five Points" (the most
notorious New York City slum at the time) would be "privileged to
take on their arms the palefaced beauties of the Caucasian race." On
Election Day, Belmont and his fellow Democrats won easily. More
than 63 percent of the voters, including at least 16 percent of Lincoln's
backers, still supported their ongoing crusade to deny black men full
voting rights.[15]

Not only were Belmont and his well-heeled associates old hands in
playing the race card. They also coupled it with their larger economic
agenda. For over a decade, they had envisioned New York City as the
free-trade capital of the world. They hoped to create a free-trade empire, free of all tariff barriers, in which steamers coming out of New
York carried not only Southern cotton and western wheat to England
but also California gold and the "treasures" of China, India, and Japan
to all parts of the world. They also wanted the United States to ac-

quire more territory, namely, Cuba and Nicaragua, and perhaps some islands in the Pacific. In these efforts, too, they were zealous supporters of white supremacy. The free-trade empire they envisioned would be totally dominated by white men. The "lesser" races would have no say in its governance. Nor would they have any influence over its culture.[16]

For years, the Belmont circle's commitment to a free-trade empire and white supremacy had made it easy for them to work with the Southern wing of the Democratic Party. Both had the same goals. Both pushed for low tariffs. Both wanted to acquire slaveholding Cuba. The bombardment of Fort Sumter, however, changed everything. Eight days after the fort fell, Belmont and his circle of rich Democrats threw their support behind a huge rally in behalf of the Union. And for the first sixteen months of the war, many of them served on New York's National War Committee, an organization that had been established by antislavery Republicans to encourage voluntary enlistments and thus avoid a state draft.[17]

With the preliminary Emancipation Proclamation, however, that, too, came to an end. Belmont reclaimed his latest $1,000 donation to the recruitment fund, and several of his friends resigned from the committee. Then in February 1863, at Delmonico's Restaurant in New York City, Belmont and the party's other leading moneymen launched the Society for the Diffusion of Political Knowledge. Chosen to be titular head, the president of the society, was the famous inventor and well-known racist, Samuel F. B. Morse. The society was to be an adjunct of the Democratic Party, a think tank, waging war against Republican policies, especially emancipation.

The society turned out pamphlets by the dozen, defending slavery, defending white supremacy. The tone was highbrow, the message racist. Pamphlet 5, for example, contended that emancipation would bring "ruin" to the entire country, North and South, just as it had to Jamaica and New Granada, but if slavery were left intact, all would be well. The "MUSCLES" of the black man and the "INTELLECT" of the white man would enrich everyone, including those who lived on the "rocky island" of Manhattan, and "line our streets with marble palaces."[18]

Belmont and his rich Democratic friends also promoted the same ideas in the *New York World*, a newspaper edited by twenty-seven-year-old Manton Marble, which they had saved from financial ruin just before the 1862 election.[19] Together, Belmont and Marble turned the struggling daily into the nation's leading Democratic organ. The message was constant. While supporting victory over the Confederacy and praising General George B. McClellan to the hilt, the paper denounced the Lincoln administration at every opportunity, especially for its arbitrary arrests of political dissidents and, above all, for its emancipation policy.

Then in March 1863, Lincoln and his party provided the *World* and its friends with a new issue. In response to heavy losses on the battlefield, soaring desertion rates, and dwindling recruitment, Republicans in Congress passed the National Conscription Act. The bill authorized government agents to go house to house, enrolling single men from age twenty up to age forty-five and married men up to age thirty-five, and then hold a lottery to choose draftees from this pool if the congressional district didn't meet its quota. The law also stated that a draftee could provide a substitute to fight in his place or pay $300 — a prohibitive sum for a workingman — for the government to use as a recruitment bounty.

Attacking the law, and especially its blatant class bias, was easy pickings, and the *World* joined other Democratic newspapers in making the most of it. The paper denounced the law as unjust and called on Governor Seymour to protect New Yorkers from the latest madness of the Lincoln administration. The governor, in turn, vowed to take the law to court and have it declared unconstitutional. Until then, he promised to protect New Yorkers from the draft. He also pointed out that the Republicans had set unfairly high quotas for heavily Democratic New York City. Singing his praises, the *World* portrayed him as the protector of the New York working class. It also endorsed a mass protest meeting held on July 4 at the Academy of Music. Other papers went further. The editor of the *Catholic Metropolitan Record*, John Mullaly, called for armed resistance if the governor failed in his mission to stop the draft.

The governor failed, and on Saturday morning, July 11, the drawing of names began. The timing was bad. The city was without military protection as most of the troops had been sent to Gettysburg to fight Robert E. Lee's invading army. Anticipating trouble, the authorities decided to hold the drawing at an office on the city's outskirts, at Third Avenue and Forty-Seventh Street, an area of vacant lots and few buildings. In hopes of convincing onlookers that the drawing would be fair, they placed a rolling drum before an open window and had a blindfolded clerk reach in and pick out the slip of paper on which the draftee's name had been written. A major then announced the name and address to the crowd: "William Jones, 49th Street near Tenth Avenue."

The crowd at first greeted every name with a groan or a hiss. But that soon gave way to making fun of the draftee. "Goodbye, Patrick!" "Goodbye, James!" "What's the matter, Connolly? Couldn't you come up with the $300 to buy your way out?" "Good for you, Brady! You finally got yourself a job." "Hey, O'Connell! Wouldn't your wife give you the money? Maybe she [*sic*] saving it to buy herself a nigger!" "And you, Jones! What kind of soldier are you going to be? What's old Abe going to do with you? You aren't even worth $300." Then, periodically, someone in the crowd would chant: "Three hundred dollars! That's all you're worth! Just three hundred dollars, when a nigger goes for a thousand!"

After 1,236 names had been called, the provost marshal decided that it was getting too late in the day to finish the drawing and that the remainder of the two thousand–man quota would be drawn on Monday. The news spread far and wide. On hearing it, some voluntary fireman, members of the Black Joke Engine Company No. 33, decided not only to stop the draft but also to destroy all evidence that men in their unit had been drafted. Accordingly, on Monday, they dressed in their full regalia, in their red shirts and shiny black suspenders and black pants and black helmets, and raced pell-mell down the street, pulling one of their fire trucks behind them and elbowing aside scores of other New Yorkers on their way to the Third Avenue drawing site. Then, when the selection process began again, they drove off the police, stormed the building, spread turpentine throughout, and set fire to the structure. So began the New York Draft Riot, the worst riot in the city's history.[20]

Shouting, "Down with the rich men," some rioters focused their attention on well-known Republicans, especially the owners of fancy mansions on Fifth Avenue. More vicious yet were attacks against blacks. At Fifth Avenue and Forty-Third Street, rioters stormed the Colored Orphan Asylum, screaming, "Burn the niggers' nest." That night and the next day, gangs attacked bars, brothels, and boarding-houses that catered to blacks. Up and down Sixth Avenue, black homes were burned, black men hanged, drowned, and mutilated. Singled out

Burning of the Colored Orphan Asylum. Reprinted from
The Illustrated London News, August 15, 1863.

especially were blacks and whites who mingled and/or lived as interracial couples and, thus, dared to defy taboos on "amalgamation."

On Tuesday morning, while the atrocities mounted, Governor Seymour tried to placate the rioters. With the leaders of Tammany Hall
at his side, he met with a large group at City Hall Park. Addressing
them as "my friends," he called on them to maintain law and order,
telling them their "salvation" depended on it and that "anarchy" would
ruin them. He also assured them that he understood their grievances,
that he would work hard in their behalf, first to get the draft law declared unconstitutional, and then if that failed to make "it bear pro-
portionately on the rich and poor."[21] By this time, some of the rioters
had already concluded that the protests had gone too far. The Black
Joke firemen, among others, were now defending their neighborhoods
against riot and arson. They would later be hailed as heroes for protecting the West Side.

After a third day of atrocities, troops from Pennsylvania arrived
and began battling the rioters. By the next night, it was all over. Some

six thousand soldiers were now in the city. The authorities again took charge. Many insisted that at least twelve hundred people had been killed, although only 119 deaths could be verified. Republicans called for retribution, but Democrats had the upper hand. And while William Marcy Tweed and his Tammany Hall compatriots talked tough, denounced the transgressors, and called for law and order, they also succeeded in keeping federal prosecutors away from their constituents. Instead, two of their stalwarts, District Attorney A. Oakley Hall and Recorder John T. Hoffman, brought scores of rioters up on charges. But, in the end, only sixty-seven were convicted, and only a handful got prison terms of more than six months.[22]

The *New York World*, like all the city's newspapers, had much to say about the riots. Who was at fault? While deploring the violence, its editor, Manton Marble, pinned most of the blame on Lincoln. "Will the insensate men in Washington now at length listen to our voice? Will they now give ear to our warnings and adjurations? Will they now believe that Defiance of the Law in rulers breeds Defiance of Law in the people." And what did the defiant people want? They wanted a war for "the Union and the constitution"—not one for abolition. Two years earlier, they had thronged Union Square in support of the war. And what did Lincoln do? He ignored them. Yes, these "are the very men whom his imbecility, his wanton exercise of arbitrary power, his stretches of engrafted authority have transformed into a mob."[23]

That fall, the managing editor of the *World*, thirty-two-year-old David Croly, and one of his reporters, twenty-two-year-old George Wakeman, decided to exploit one of the rioters' biggest fears, the old saw that emancipation would inevitably lead to "amalgamation." Since the founding of American Antislavery Society in 1833, white and black abolitionists had been attacked time and again by men screaming "Amalgamators, amalgamators, amalgamators." No charge had been more effective in stirring up the rancor and brutality of mobs. It had generated violence everywhere, in small towns like Canterbury, Connecticut, and Alton, Illinois, as well as in big cities like New York and Philadelphia.[24] It had always been explosive, and it had been explosive once again in the draft riots that summer.

To take advantage of its explosiveness, Croly and Wakeman concocted a seventy-two-page pamphlet titled *Miscegenation: The Theory of the Blending of the Races, Applied to the American White Man and*

Negro.[25] They wrote the pamphlet in the voice of an abolitionist with a scientific bent and never let on that they were the authors. Only a few insiders knew about their involvement. That would remain the case until 1870, when the readers of Wakeman's obituary learned of his participation. Then, many years later, Croly's widow fully disclosed their authorship.

Throughout the pamphlet, Croly and Wakeman had their anonymous abolitionist promoting amalgamation at every turn, pushing the "superiority" of mixed races in one chapter, the "blending" of mixed bloods in another, the "Love of the Blond for the Black" in still another. And then in a chapter titled the "Irish and the Negro," they went hog wild. They had their anonymous abolitionist arguing that the "blending of the Irish in this country with the negro" would be a "positive gain" for the Irish, for the Irish were "a more brutal race and lower in civilization than the negro," and "with education and an intermingling with the superior black, the Irish may be lifted up to something like the dignity of their ancestors, like Milesians." Finally, in the concluding chapter, they had the author calling on Lincoln and his fellow Republicans to add a miscegenation plank to the 1864 Republican Party platform and to proclaim that "the solution of the negro problem will not have been reached in this country until public opinion sanctions a union of the two races . . . that in the millennial future, the most perfect and highest type of manhood will not be white or black but brown, or colored, and that whoever helps to unite the various races of man, helps to make the human family the sooner realize its great destiny."[26]

Throughout, Croly and Wakeman also had their imaginary author using new "scientific" words like "melaleukation" and "melamigleukation" and "miscegenation." These Greek and Latin-based words were supposedly more accurate and less racially biased than "amalgamation" when referring to interracial couples and their offspring. The only one that caught on was "miscegenation," which soon found its way into Webster's Dictionary. It was formed from two Latin words, *miscere* ("to mix") and *genus* ("race"). But Croly and Wakeman obviously weren't trying to coin new words. Their intent was to portray their make-believe author as a crazy scientist, a weird antislavery Republican zealot, who liked to use big words to convince everyone that miscegenation was the foundation of human progress, and that the war's "final fruit" would be the "blending of the white and black."

Finishing their handiwork just before Christmas, 1863, Croly and Wakeman then tried to trick some well-known abolitionists and Republicans into endorsing it. As bait they sent out complimentary copies and asked for the recipient's reaction. The responses were to be sent to an anonymous post office box in New York City. Within weeks, they received letters from Lucretia Mott, Sarah and Angelina Grimke, Albert Brisbane, Parker Pillsbury, and Dr. James McCune Smith. Most of the responses were guarded, praising the author for his sincerity and his good intentions, but also urging him to be more cautious. Only Dr. Smith, the editor of the *Anglo-African Review*, gave Croly and Wakeman much to work with. Smith indicated that making miscegenation a political issue might be a good move for the Republican Party. The others obviously thought it was a horrible idea.

Croly and Wakeman then fed the information they received to a Democratic congressman from Ohio, Samuel Sullivan Cox. Now in his fourth term in the House, the thirty-nine-year-old Cox had just been through a tough election, winning by just 272 votes, by less than 1 percent of the 20,472 votes cast. Nevertheless, he was a party leader. He was also known to be a great speaker, so verbally gifted that he was certain to get the press's attention. He had once described a sunset in such memorable detail that he had been nicknamed "Sunset" Cox.

On February 17, the silver-tongued orator took the House floor and launched a tirade against "the detestable doctrine of Miscegenation." He quoted at length from the letters sent by Dr. Smith and the other abolitionists who had reviewed the pamphlet. Exaggerating what they said, he heaped scorn on their "positive" reaction. He also insisted that his Republican colleagues were just agents of the abolitionists and thus certain to embrace miscegenation. As anticipated, the speech got enormous attention from the press.[27]

The impact of Cox's speech, in turn, prompted Horace Greeley, the arch Republican and the editor of the New York *Tribune*, to respond. In an editorial on March 16, Greeley declared that while he did not want to promote interracial marriage, he felt it was really no one's business but the marrying couple's themselves. The comment did his party more harm than good. Democratic newspapers jumped on it and wildly exaggerated what Greeley actually said. The *World* told its readers that Greeley's editorial proved that the "leading Republican newspaper in the nation" was an "unblushing advocate of 'miscegenation.'"[28]

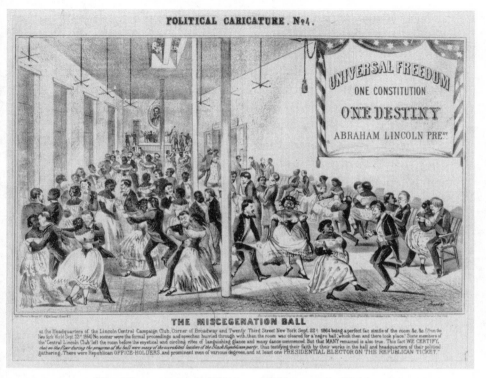

"The Miscegenation Ball." Prints and Photographs Division,
Library of Congress (LC-USZ62–14828).

Thus by March, 1864, Croly and Wakeman had sparked a huge political debate. Charges and countercharges now flew back and forth in
the press. One wild story followed another. Especially vile was John
Van Evrie, the editor of probably the most racist newspaper in the
country, the *New York Weekly Day Book*. He had a field day. He published anonymous pamphlets, a book that went through several print-
ings, and scores of newspaper articles attacking Republicans for allegedly endorsing miscegenation. The *New Hampshire Patriot* claimed
that sixty-four abolitionist Yankee schoolmistresses had given birth to
sixty-four mulatto babies. Van Evrie spread the story far and wide. His
goal had always been "the utter rout, overthrow, and extermination of
Abolitionism from American soil." He now thought he had a chance
of achieving it.[29]

Besides underwriting the *World* and the Society for the Diffusion of
Political Knowledge, the Belmont circle also simultaneously launched

the presidential candidacy of General George B. McClellan. In November 1862, when the Lincoln administration sacked McClellan, the War Department essentially left him in limbo. He was the senior general in the Union army, but they didn't give him anything to do. Instead, Secretary of War Stanton just directed him to go to Trenton, New Jersey. McClellan stayed there for less than a week and then took up residence in New York City in a Fifth Avenue hotel.

With no one to command and nothing to do, McClellan began writing a report vindicating his fifteen months as commander of the Army of the Potomac. He also helped Governor Seymour organize a militia call-up in New York State. Otherwise, he just waited to be recalled. That didn't happen, even though his old army suffered one defeat after another, first under Ambrose Burnside at Fredericksburg, and then under "Fighting Joe" Hooker at Chancellorsville.

Though the Lincoln administration no longer had any use for McClellan, the Belmont group welcomed him wholeheartedly. To them, he was a valuable asset. Ever since he had won the first Union battles of the war, in the hills of West Virginia in the early summer of 1861, he had been hailed as the Little Napoleon. He was now the highest-ranking general in the Union army, even though he was only thirty-seven years old. He was also a solid Democrat. Yes, he was at odds with the party's "peace" faction in that he insisted that the war must be fought vigorously until the Union was restored. But he had no quarrel with their slogan, "The Constitution as it is, the Union as it was." Like them, he was vehemently opposed to emancipation. He had indicated repeatedly that the war should be fought only for the restoration of the Union, not for the destruction of slavery and the remaking of the South.

McClellan also had the credibility that the Belmont circle lacked. While many questioned his competence as a general, only a few questioned his loyalty to the Union. That was not the case with Belmont and his friends. Even some Democrats doubted their loyalty. They were "known to be ultra democrats . . . as near secessionists as they dare to be," declared the father-in-law of McClellan's brother.[30] While not everyone agreed with this sentiment, many did, and McClellan was warned repeatedly to keep his distance. He clearly ignored this advice. He had known two members of the Belmont circle, Samuel Barlow and William Aspinwall, for years, and another, John Jacob Astor,

McClellan and Lincoln as portrayed by the *New York World*.
J. W. Howard cartoon, *New York World*, 1864. Library of Congress
(LC-USZ62–10356).

had been a volunteer on his staff during the Peninsula campaign. He trusted them. He also agreed with their views.

The Belmont circle began showering favors on McClellan as soon as he arrived in New York. That November, Belmont himself squired the general and his wife around Manhattan, taking them to numerous dinner parties, the opera, and the theater. Belmont also threw a huge masquerade ball at his Fifth Avenue mansion in McClellan's honor. Barlow, meanwhile, began raising money to buy the general a four-story brick house in one of the city's toniest neighborhoods, on West Thirty-First Street, just off Fifth Avenue. By December he had the donations he needed. Barlow and the other donors then made sure that the house was fully furnished before they gave it to the McClellans. They also paid the insurance on it.

By the following winter, Belmont began putting together a plan to get McClellan elected president. He first sought the advice of the New York congressional delegation. They advised him to hold the nominating convention in Cincinnati in May. He thought that was too early. It would be better, especially for McClellan, to wait a few months and take advantage of all the bad news that seemed likely to develop—the additional battles lost, the rising death toll, the need for heavier taxes, the need for more draftees.

In mid-January 1864, Belmont held a meeting of the Democratic National Committee at his Fifth Avenue mansion. They agreed with him that time was on their side and decided to hold the convention on July 4. They also overruled the New York congressmen on place, choosing Chicago over Cincinnati, in memory of Stephen A. Douglas. On one matter, however, Belmont didn't get his way. He wanted to tie the hands of the Chicago convention by having the National Committee take a position on the major issues of the day and essentially tell the people what the party stood for. That was too daring for the majority on the committee. They insisted that deciding policy matters should remain a function of the national convention.[31]

Belmont then tried to tie the hands of the New York delegation that would be sent to Chicago. He wanted the entire delegation committed in advance to vote for McClellan. With that as his primary goal, he made his way up the Hudson River to attend the February meeting of Democratic State Convention at Albany's Tweddle Hall.

Again, he failed to get his way completely. The state convention denounced emancipation and chose him to be one of the state's four delegates at large at the Chicago convention. It also agreed to vote as a unit at the Chicago convention. But the Peace Democrats didn't want a general at the head of the national ticket, and some of the others preferred Governor Seymour or wanted to be in a position to negotiate with other delegations once they got to Chicago. The state convention thus refused to commit the New York delegation in advance to McClellan.[32]

Disappointed by the outcome at Tweddle Hall, Belmont and his political cohorts still had high hopes. The news was on their side. In the spring and early summer of 1864, everything seemed to be going wrong for Lincoln and his party. His generals suffered still more military setbacks. In May, Republican dissidents met in Cleveland and nominated Frémont to run against him. Then on the last day of June, Secretary Chase resigned from the cabinet, causing many Republicans, including James Ashley, to start mumbling again about making him Lincoln's replacement. A short time later, Lincoln pocket vetoed the Wade-Davis Bill. That, in turn, infuriated many of the bill's ninety-one Republican supporters, and in retaliation its two Republican sponsors issued a scathing denunciation of the president whom they had just helped to renominate.

The news was so good that Belmont in mid-June began toying with the idea of postponing the Democratic National Convention. Maybe more Republican chaos and more defeats on the battlefield would swing more support for McClellan. After testing the waters, getting McClellan's approval, and meeting briefly with six other national committeemen, Belmont concluded that delaying the convention for another eight weeks was a smart move. He pushed through the delay. Instead of opening on July 4, the convention would begin on August 29. He also felt certain that by this date his man, George B. McClellan, would have the votes needed to be chosen the party's nominee on the first ballot and that the party would take a stand against the Thirteenth Amendment.[33]

Again, Belmont had to overcome some major roadblocks. Standing in his way were the Peace Democrats, especially their handsome leader, Clement L. Vallandigham. Although Vallandigham and the Peace Democrats lacked a presidential candidate to rally behind, they had close to half of the delegates at the Chicago convention. Some of them took comfort in the fact that McClellan in 1863 had supported George W. Woodward, a Vallandigham ally and staunch proslavery man, for governor of Pennsylvania. Most of them, however, still had doubts about McClellan's peace credentials. Wasn't the general a War Democrat? Hadn't he just sanctioned the war in a speech to a West Point audience?

The doubters at Chicago tried to tie McClellan's hands. They nominated him, but on a peace platform and gave him as a running mate Congressman George H. Pendleton, a close ally of Vallandigham. For the most part, the platform had full party support. It denounced the Lincoln administration for its "arbitrary arrests" and "suppression of freedom of speech and of the press." It also promised to preserve the "rights of the States unimpaired," which were code words for not imposing emancipation on any of the states. But one plank, drafted by Vallandigham, was divisive. It deemed the war a "failure" and called for its "immediate" cessation.

What exactly did that mean? Did it mean that peace should be obtained at all cost? That obtaining peace was even more important than preserving the Union? Many thought it did, including Alexander Stephens, the vice president of the Confederacy. In Stephen's eyes, the controversial peace plank presented the "first ray of real light" since the war began. Of the same opinion was Clement C. Clay, the Confederate secret agent in Canada.[34]

Yet along with the rest of platform, the peace plank received the endorsement of the Chicago convention. It passed almost unanimously. Adding to its significance was the party's choice of Congressman George Pendleton of Ohio as McClellan's running mate. Like Vallandigham, Pendleton had opposed the war from the start, voted against war supplies, and frequently expressed sympathy for the Confederacy. His nomination thus underscored the importance of the peace plank.

That left Belmont with a problem. For if McClellan endorsed the platform, or simply said nothing about it, he would be committed to it. And Vallandigham was putting pressure on McClellan to do just that. "Do not listen to your Eastern friends," Vallandigham counseled the general. For if "in an evil hour" they were to "advise you to *insinuate* even a little war into your letter" accepting the Democratic nomination, that would be disastrous. It would alienate two hundred thousand western men. Did the general dare to take that chance?

McClellan hesitated. He tried to find words that would give him some wiggle room. He drafted one acceptance letter after another. The early ones would have satisfied Vallandigham. They endorsed an armistice with a proviso that if the armistice didn't lead to reunion the war could be renewed.[35]

Adding to Belmont's woes was the news from the front lines. As his party met in Chicago and declared the war a dismal failure, Northern soldiers under General William Tecumseh Sherman were about to score a major victory. For months, they had been fighting their way to Atlanta. On September 1, they forced Confederate General John B. Hood to abandon the city, and with bands blaring Union songs they marched into the city and raised the stars and stripes over city hall. "Atlanta is ours, and fairly won," wired Sherman to his superiors in Washington. The next day, the breaking news had enormous impact. Talk of the war being a complete failure suddenly vanished, cannons boomed hundred-gun salutes in Northern cities, and one newspaper after another hailed Sherman as the greatest general since Napoleon.

Belmont, at this point, stepped in. On September 3, he essentially told McClellan that his wishy-washy attempt to appease Vallandigham and the Peace Democrats made no sense—indeed, that it was foolish to think that the war, if once stopped, could be started again or that an armistice without conditions would result in anything other than the triumph of the Confederacy. The general, therefore, should reject Vallandigham's "four years of failure plank" and make it clear that there would be no laying down of Union arms until the Confederate states agreed to reenter the Union. At the same time, he should also make it clear that emancipation would not be a condition for reunion.

McClellan, in turn, reversed his stand. Adopting Belmont's position as his own, he issued a letter of acceptance on September 8 that came to be seen as virtual repudiation of Vallandigham's peace plank.

But there was more to his letter than that. What many commentators later failed to mention was that McClellan also clearly rejected emancipation as a condition for reunion. Instead, he promised any rebel state "willing to return to the Union" that it would be "received at once, with a full guaranty of all its constitutional rights."[36]

At the time this decision was made, the Thirteenth Amendment was still anathema as far as Northern Democrats were concerned. In June, in the House of Representatives, fifty-eight members of Belmont's party had voted against it.

Only four had had the nerve to break ranks and vote with the Republican majority. Two of the mavericks were New Yorkers, Moses Odell of Brooklyn and John A. Griswold of Rensselaer County. The other two were Joseph Bailey of Pennsylvania and Ezra Wheeler of Wisconsin. What was to be done with them? Were they to be purged from the party? That, indeed, was the case.

Of the four mavericks, the one who irritated Belmont the most was Moses Odell. In most respects, the forty-six-year-old Brooklyn representative was a hard-core Democrat like Belmont. Since his early twenties, Odell had been a Tammany Hall regular who had worked the streets of New York to get James K. Polk, Franklin Pierce, and other Democrats elected to office. And for his efforts, he had been rewarded with various patronage jobs, first as a clerk in the New York Custom House in 1845, later as a public appraiser. In 1860, he had been a staunch supporter of Stephen A. Douglas. In that year, he had also run for Congress and won easily. In 1862, he ran again and again won easily. The district he represented was 46 percent foreign-born, and

Moses F. Odell, congressman from New York. Matthew Brady photograph, Library of Congress (LC-MSS-44297-33-097).

nearly two-thirds of the foreign-born were Irish Catholics. It was a Democratic stronghold.

For the most part, Odell also had the same core beliefs as Belmont and other Douglas Democrats. He, too, sang the praises of strict construction of the Constitution, states' rights, and white supremacy. And like his fellow Democrats in Congress, Odell could be counted on to vote against most of the Republican agenda. Yet, unlike many House Democrats, he didn't blame the war entirely on Northern abolitionists. He didn't claim that their fanaticism drove the South to secession and the bombardment of Fort Sumter. Instead, he blamed the secessionists. He also told a large gathering of soldiers in Brooklyn that his only loyalty was to the US government and that although he had been a Democrat his entire life he would support the Lincoln administration in its efforts to subdue the rebellion.

On taking a seat in Congress in December 1861, Odell had been appointed to the powerful and controversial Joint Committee on the

Conduct of the War. He was the token House Democrat on the committee, a lonely voice on a committee that was dominated by radical Republicans who were determined to push an antislavery agenda. Some thought that the Speaker of the House, Galusha Grow, another radical Republican, had put him on the committee simply because he was an obscure Democrat, a freshman congressman with no national standing, a nobody that the press would never bother to quote. Others said it was because of Odell's strong support of the Northern war effort. Whatever the reason, Odell turned out to be one of the committee's hardest-working members and its toughest questioner.

At first, Odell's actions on the committee had pleased his fellow Democrats. In the committee's investigation of John C. Frémont's handling of the Missouri campaign, he had taken the Republican members to task. They clearly had been on the Pathfinder's side. They had treated him as a Republican hero. They also had tried to portray him as an antislavery martyr who had been wrongly sacked by the Lincoln administration for emancipating slaves in Missouri and thus irritating proslavery Kentuckians. Odell had refused to go along. He had ripped into Frémont, questioned his military decisions, portrayed him as an incompetent general. Odell's questioning, in fact, was so harsh that Frémont's wife added him to her hate list and singled him out for revenge.[37]

But Frémont was not the only general whose actions displeased Odell. A year later, the committee investigated Belmont's favorite, George B. McClellan, and his handling of the Army of the Potomac. This time the Republican members had no intention of whitewashing a general. They were out to get him. And so was Odell. He had visited McClellan's headquarters on numerous occasions and didn't like what he saw and heard. Not only did the general offer one excuse after another for not engaging the enemy in battle but he also met daily with the leaders of the peace wing of the Democratic Party. These gatherings, concluded Odell, were a "continuing caucus for the consideration of plans of resistance to all measures which proposed to strengthen the army or the navy . . . and to devise means of embarrassing the government by constitutional quibbles and legal subtleties." Odell was so upset by McClellan's inactivity and dubious friends that he called on Lincoln to get rid of the general long before Lincoln did so. Thus, when the Republican majority on the committee put together a report that essentially branded McClellan as "an imbecile if not a traitor," Odell didn't quarrel with it. He signed the report. Indignant Brooklyn Democrats, in turn, read him out of the party.[38]

Although disowned by his party, Odell still had nearly a year and a half to serve before his term expired in March 1865. On most issues, he remained a good party man, and in February 1864, when the Thirteenth Amendment came up for a test vote, he followed the dictates of his party and voted against it. But after the amendment passed the Senate in April, he threw his support behind it and voted for it in June. He also made it clear that he intended to vote for the amendment again if Ashley brought it up for reconsideration before the March deadline. That outraged Belmont and other New York Democrats, and they made sure that Odell didn't get renominated for the 1864 fall election. In his place, the party chose Thomas H. Faron, a Peace Democrat, who in a close contest lost the district to James Humphrey, a Republican whom Odell had beaten easily in 1862 by some fourteen hundred votes.

Also on the New York party's hit list was John A. Griswold, the representative of two Hudson Valley counties, Rensselaer and Washington. The forty-two-year-old Griswold had lived there his entire life. He had grown up in Rensselaer County, in the village of Nassau, roughly fifteen miles east of the state capitol in Albany. At age seventeen, he had left home to work in an iron foundry and hardware store in nearby Troy. He had married one of the bosses' daughters and soon made the most of his good connections, becoming one of the wealthiest men in town, with substantial holdings in iron manufacturing, banking, and railroads.

At age thirty-five, Griswold got into politics. He became the mayor of Troy, which had grown quickly into a city of some thirty-five thousand residents, well known for both steel making and the manufacture of collared shirts. Seven years later, in 1862, he ran for Congress on the Democratic ticket and won easily, polling 52.8 percent of the vote. He was given the minority position on the House Committee of Naval Affairs. As a man of means as well as an ironmonger, he had already agreed to finance the building of an ironclad, which, as luck would have it, turned out to be the one destined to become the Union's most famous warship, the *USS Monitor*.

The success of the *Monitor*, and the hundreds of stories about its battle with the *Merrimac*, added much to Griswold's reputation and made him unbeatable in Hudson Valley politics. Nonetheless, after

Griswold voted for the Thirteenth Amendment, the Democratic Party dropped him from the 1864 ticket and ran William A. Van Alstyne, a prominent member of one of the Hudson Valley's old Dutch families, in his place.

No longer welcome in the Democratic Party, Griswold went over to the Republicans, who were eager to win the district. Running on the Republican-Union ticket Griswold was reelected, polling 54.1 percent of the vote, the largest majority ever given to a candidate in his district. He would serve as a Republican two more terms until 1869. The Republicans would also put him up for governor in 1868. He lost that election.[39]

Also going over to the opposition was Joseph Bailey. The representative of a district in southern Pennsylvania just north of the Maryland border, through which Robert E. Lee's Confederate troops had marched on their way to Gettysburg in 1863, Bailey had been solid member of the Democratic Party for most of his fifty-four years. Originally a hatter by trade, he had first been elected as a Democrat to the Pennsylvania assembly back in 1840. He had subsequently been elected to the state senate and then state treasurer. He then studied law and was admitted to the bar in 1860. In that year, his fellow Pennsylvania Democrats chose him to run against Benjamin F. Junkin, a Republican who had won the district in 1858 by a mere forty-six votes.

In 1860, Bailey beat Junkin by 357 votes. He then made a name for himself as a War Democrat. That, in turn, alienated the Peace Democrats in his district. So when he came up for reelection in 1862, they challenged his nomination and eventually ran their own candidate, Adam J. Glossbrenner, against him. Bailey, however, still had the backing of most regular Democrats. And, with the help of Republicans, who offered no candidate of their own, he whipped Glossbrenner easily, winning over 55 percent of the vote.

Then came the Thirteenth Amendment. Bailey was the only Democrat to vote for it when it came up for a test vote in February 1864. He also voted for it in June. With that, regular Democrats in his district decided to drive him out of the party. Throwing their support behind Glossbrenner in the 1864 election, they forced Bailey to run on the Republican ticket and beat him badly, limiting him to just 44 percent of the vote.

The fourth Democrat to be purged from the party in 1864 was Ezra Wheeler of Wisconsin. Compared to Bailey, the forty-four-year-old

Wheeler was a relative newcomer to Democratic politics. A New York by birth and a graduate of Union College, he had moved to Wisconsin in 1849, where he made a name for himself first as a lawyer, then as a judge. In 1862, when Wisconsin—thanks to the 1860 census—got three additional seats in Congress, the state Democratic Party chose him to run for one of the newly created seats. He won handily with over 52 percent of the vote.

Unlike Bailey, Wheeler initially opposed the Thirteenth Amendment, and when it came up for a test vote in February 1864, he voted against it. In June, however, he changed his mind. The day before the June vote, he got the Speaker's attention and addressed the House. To the surprise of his fellow Democrats, he called on them to back the amendment on conservative grounds. He insisted that the amendment didn't violate the intentions of the "framers" of the Constitution and that it would stop radical Republicans from promoting even more radical programs.[40]

The speech cost Wheeler dearly. For openly supporting the amendment, the Wisconsin state party denied him renomination in 1864 and ran Gabriel Bouck in his place. Bouck, a War Democrat who had raised troops for the Union army, supported the war but opposed the amendment. He got trounced in the fall election. He did much worse than Wheeler had two years earlier, losing the seat by 13 percentage points. But unlike Wheeler, the party never abandoned him. Instead, they ran him for Congress again and again and succeeded in getting him elected in 1876 and 1878.

The Democracy in 1864 thus sent a message to all House Democrats. There would be a price to be paid if they dared break ranks with the party and support the Thirteenth Amendment. They would be replaced by "true" Democrats. And unless they had the good fortune of Griswold, of being embraced by the Republicans and elected on the Republican ticket, that would be the end of their political careers.

This was well understood by Ashley. While he had a hard time understanding why the party of his youth was still committed to protecting slavery at all costs, he had no doubt that any Democrat who dared to break ranks and vote with him was, in effect, committing "political suicide." He said so repeatedly. Thus he and his two New York associates, Fenton and Frank, had a tough task before them. They had to find not only a dozen or so Democrats who "were naturally inclined to favor the amendment" but also a dozen or so who were "strong enough to meet and repel the fierce partisan attack which were certain to be made upon them."[41]

Who might these dozen or so men be? In the end, Fenton, Frank, and Ashley came up with seventeen possibilities. All but a handful were backbenchers who no longer had much to gain from toeing the Democratic party line. One, John Griswold, had already gone over to the Republicans, and twelve were lame ducks with only a few more months to serve in Congress. Eight of the seventeen represented New York districts, five Ohio, two Pennsylvania, one Connecticut, and one Michigan. Two of the seventeen, Odell and Griswold, had already voted with Ashley. Of the remaining fifteen, two had missed the vote the first time around, and thirteen had voted no.

Targeting these seventeen men undoubtedly paid off. Twelve would support the amendment when Ashley finally brought it up for a second vote in January 1865, two would conveniently miss the vote, and three would vote no. Had three more voted no, the amendment would have failed.[42]

Chapter Six

THE LAME DUCKS OF 1864

When Congress reconvened on December 5, 1864, Ashley had his two lists. On them were thirty-six names. Half of the men listed had voted for the amendment the previous June, but at some political risk. More critical were the eighteen who had not voted for the amendment. Five had been selected by Frank Blair and Henry Winter Davis, the rest by Reuben Fenton and Augustus Frank. Eleven of the eighteen had voted no in June. Seven had missed the vote. But one fact, more than any other, soon caught the attention of Washington insiders. Fourteen of the eighteen were definitely lame ducks, men who were serving out their final few weeks in the nation's capitol, and still another was a likely lame duck as he had lost a contested election.

Why so many lame ducks? Why had fourteen—and perhaps fifteen—ended up on Ashley's two lists? And why did the two lists include only three House members who had clearly won reelection, men who would have at least two additional years to serve in Congress? Did Ashley and his advisers decide to concentrate mainly on lame ducks, men whose political careers were all but over? Was that their strategy from the beginning?

Ashley never admitted as much, but that question immediately arose in Washington, and soon talk of backroom deals, political corruption, and outright bribery ran rampant. For nearly everyone in the nation's capital believed that lame ducks were corruptible, and none of the fifteen had shown even the slightest bit of support for the proposed amendment back in June. On the contrary, most of them had denounced it as "unconstitutional" and a gross violation of "states' rights." And during the fall elections, all but one had endorsed the Democratic Party's pledge to uphold the rights of the states against the Black Republicans. Why the sudden change in values? What made them decide to buck the will of their party? Had they been bought? Had they sold their votes for political gain?

Ashley never addressed this question. Instead, he claimed that the men who came over to his side were just braver, more patriotic than their colleagues.[1] Democrats, however, tried to find a smoking gun, absolute proof that corruption was involved. They never succeeded in their efforts. But that didn't stop the talk. Nearly every insider thought the worst. And, in the end, all but a handful agreed with Thaddeus Stevens, the most powerful Republican in the House—namely, that the "greatest measure of the nineteenth century" had been "passed by corruption" and that the corruption had been "aided and abetted" by Lincoln.[2]

Of the 186 House members who met that December, only ninety-five would be back for the next session that began in December 1865. The other ninety-one were lame ducks. They either had not run for reelection that fall or had been defeated. They had only four more months to serve and would finish their terms in March. Most would never return to Washington.[3]

That nearly half the House members were lame ducks was not unusual. By 1864, lame duck congressmen had been a key feature in the nation's political fabric since the earliest days of the Republic. Every Congress had been loaded with them. And it had always occurred at the same time, in the second session, the one that began in December in an even-numbered year.

For decades, the turnover rate in the House had been over 40 percent. The old notion that the House was filled with party hacks, men who served year after year, simply is not true. Those House members who served for long stretches, men like Henry Clay and ex-president John Quincy Adams, were actually the exceptions, not the rule. In 1831, for example, when Adams first joined the House, he was just the best known of eighty-nine newcomers in a House of 213 members. Of his fellow freshman, only forty-six would return for a second term, and only twenty-six for a third. In 1833, thanks partly to a new apportionment decreed by the census, the former president found that he had

152 new names to learn in a larger House of 240 members. In 1835, he had still another 115 new names to learn. And so it went, Congress after Congress, until he died in 1848, the seventeenth year of his service.[4]

The newcomers whose names Adams had to learn always had at least one thing in common. They never took office until months after they were elected. The time lapse varied, depending largely on what state the man represented. The Constitution required each new Congress to meet on the first Monday of December in odd-numbered years, but allowed the states to set the time and place of congressional elections. And with each state establishing its own rules, the dates of election ranged from sixteen months to one month before the December meeting. The norm was thirteen months, as many states opted to hold their congressional elections in November in even-numbered years. A man elected in November of an even-numbered year, however, wouldn't be sworn in until December of the next odd-numbered year.

The dictates of the Constitution and the congressional calendar thus guaranteed that in every even-numbered year Congress would be literally half-full of lame ducks. The basic story was always the same. Some of the members had just gotten tired of living away from home, traveling to and from Washington, and coping with its boarding-houses, its stench, and its politics. Others had come from districts where party members literally took turns, with one man representing the district for two years, then another man, then still another. Some incumbents had lost their bids for reelection.

And some had dropped completely out of politics. They had no intention of running for elected office again and thus were in the unusual political position of not facing the consequences of their actions in a subsequent election. Did that give them greater freedom to go their own way, to make unpopular decisions, to buck the will of their party and their constituents? Many thought it did. And until March, when their terms finally expired, they still had all the powers and privileges of a congressman. They were still the nation's lawmakers. Their votes still counted. Thus, in the eyes of many, they were potentially dangerous men.

Most, in fact, were not. Most just did their jobs and went home in March. But nearly every Washington newsman could name a dozen or more defeated lame duck congressmen who, knowing they would not have jobs in the next Congress, had just gone "through the motions" while debating and voting on important legislation, and even worse, some who had vented their frustration by deliberately sabotaging the legislative process, delaying the passage of good bills and singing the praises of bad ones. By the same token, every newsman could also name a few lame duck congressmen who had sold their votes for soft political jobs back home.

By 1864, all of this was old hat, anything but headline news. Moreover, the only lame duck Congress that had been truly memorable was just a distant memory.

That was the Congress that had met in December 1800. It had flouted the will of the electorate. Most of its sitting members had been Federalists who had taken a beating in the general election earlier that year. Their candidate for president, John Adams, had lost the presidency to Thomas Jefferson, and their party had lost seven seats in the Senate and twenty-two in the House. As a result, they had gone from being a majority of twelve in the Senate to a minority of two, and a majority of fourteen in the House to a minority of thirty.[5] Yet, when Congress met in December 1800, they still had all the seats that they once held, thanks to the lame-duck rule. And they had made the most of it.

Before their political enemies took over, they turned the federal court system, which had jailed several of Jefferson's followers for violating the Alien and Sedition Acts, into a much bigger and more intrusive Federalist bastion. That January, in the Judiciary Act of 1801, they increased the power of the federal courts at the expense of states, reduced the size of the Supreme Court from six judges to five, but at the same time added six new federal circuits with sixteen new judges and created five new district judge positions. Then in February, to provide even more jobs for party members, they authorized the outgoing president to appoint as many justices of the peace as he saw fit for the District of Columbia.

The outgoing president, John Adams, then went to work. He received the Judiciary Act first and signed it into law on February 13, nineteen days before the end of his term. Then, with the consent of the outgoing Federalist Senate, he stacked the new courts with his own people. He also got his secretary of state, John Marshall, confirmed as the next Chief Justice of the Supreme Court. Then the District of Columbia bill reached his desk. And on March 2, two days before he left office, he nominated forty-two Federalists to be justices of the peace for the District of Columbia, got them confirmed on his last day in office, and had Marshall stay up late into the night recording and sealing the commissions. The entire list, along with all the other last minute appointments, came to be known as the "midnight appointees."

Jefferson and his followers, once in power, quickly repealed the 1801 Judiciary Act, thus restoring the jurisdictional authority of the federal courts to what it had been before the lame duck Congress. But removing all the midnight appointees proved to be trickier. The Constitution provided that federal judges were to hold office for as long as they demonstrated good behavior—in effect, until the day they died. So, try as he might, Jefferson never completely destroyed all his opponents' handiwork. On learning that John Marshall, who was his second cousin, had neglected to deliver all the commissions that he had signed on the last night of Federalist power, Jefferson made sure that twenty-two of the forty-two justices of the peace never got their appointments. This, in turn, led to the famous Supreme Court case of *Marbury v. Madison.* But many of the last minute appointments, including the one making Jefferson's forgetful cousin Chief Justice of the United States, remained in place. And Marshall, along with other Federalist jurists, remained a thorn in Jefferson's side for years to come.[6]

Yet, while the Federalists had proved that a lame duck Congress could thwart the will of the majority, there had been nothing so egregious for sixty years. Instead, the biggest fear in the 1860s was that the president and other members of the majority party might buy the votes of lame duck members of the minority party, especially the members who had no intention of running for political office again. The temptation, everyone agreed, was great. Knowing that they would not be facing the electorate again, lame ducks could vote with an eye more on their own personal gain and interests than on the concerns of their party or the needs of their constituents. Talk of backroom deals and vote buying was thus commonplace.

Reformers, to be sure, had demanded that something be done. But the reformers had gotten nowhere in their call for change. That would remain the case until 1933, when another generation of reformers finally succeeded in getting Congress and the states to adopt the Twentieth Amendment, which moved the date on which a new Congress regularly convened from the first Monday in December—

thirteen months removed from the previous November election—to January 3, just two months after the election.

When Congress met in December 1864, most of the lame duck members were Democrats. They outnumbered their Republican counterparts by more than three to one. Fifty-six of the seventy-four House Democrats were lame ducks, seventeen of the eighty-five Republicans, both of the two independent Republicans, eleven of the seventeen Unconditional Unionists, and five of the seven Unionists. In addition, the Democrats had lost one member, John Griswold, to the Republicans.

The huge disparity was mainly due to the election of 1864. The Democratic Party had done much worse than political pundits had anticipated. Back in August, just before the Democratic convention in Chicago, August Belmont had been upbeat. He thought that the future for his party looked bright. The war seemed to be going badly. All the news from the front line was depressing. The death toll at Cold Harbor, in particular, had horrified the entire nation. That Grant had lost seven thousand men in less than thirty minutes was beyond comprehension. And then Lincoln had called for five hundred thousand more troops, and another draft in September for districts that didn't meet their quota. Surely, thought Belmont, this was good news for his candidate, General McClellan, and every other Democrat.

And, at that time, many Republicans had seen the political world just as Belmont did. Particularly despondent had been Horace Greeley, the editor of the party's leading newspaper, the *New York Tribune*. He told Lincoln that the country was already "bleeding, bankrupt, and almost dying," and that the people had had it with the war. They longed "for peace" and shuddered "at the prospect of fresh conscriptions, of further wholesale devastations, and new rivers of human blood." Moreover, if Lincoln didn't do something quickly to meet their longings and counteract their fears, the Republican Party would be "beaten out of sight" in November.[7]

Lincoln had basically agreed. In fact, on August 23, he had made plans for what he would do once he was defeated. Wrote Lincoln: "This morning, as for some days past, it seems exceedingly probable that this Administration will not be re-elected. Then it will be my duty to cooperate with the President elect, as to save the Union between the election and the inauguration: as he will have secured his election

McClellan tries to ride two horses. National Union Party
Election Cartoon, 1864, Library of Congress.

on such ground that he cannot possibly save it afterwards." Lincoln
had then asked his cabinet members to endorse the memorandum,
sight unseen, and put it away in his desk. He had planned to hold them
to it once his defeat became a reality.[8]

Yet, just in a matter of weeks, everything had changed. Sherman
had scored a stunning victory at Atlanta, and in Chicago the Democrats had tried to bridge the gap in their party by nominating McClellan for president but allowing the Peace Democrats to write the platform and name the vice presidential candidate. It hadn't worked. In
the weeks that followed, the Peace Democrats emphasized the platform while Belmont and the War Democrats tried to pretend that it
didn't exist. Instead, they sang the praises of McClellan's acceptance
letter, which allegedly had turned the platform on its head. Republican orators, in turn, had a field day. What was the Democratic Party
for? Peace? Or war? The answer, said one wag after another, was both.
They were for "peace with the rebels but war against their own government."[9]

The Chicago convention also helped unite Republicans. Up against a party that was half against the war and totally against emancipation, even men like James Ashley had second thoughts. In August, after Lincoln vetoed the Wade-Davis Bill, Ashley had been determined to drive Lincoln from the Republican ticket. This time, he had tried to get his friend Benjamin Butler to run in Lincoln's place. It was an act of desperation, and nothing had come of it.[10] Now, with McClellan's nomination, Ashley's mood changed. Yes, the president was a disappointment. Yes, the president's support of emancipation was slow in coming. Yes, he was still way too soft on the South and its treasonous leaders. And yes, he should have sacked Montgomery Blair months ago. But he was no McClellan. He had no intention of turning back the clock, of letting the slave states remain slave states, and of putting millions of men, women, and children back in bondage.

So Ashley, along with scores of other Lincoln detractors, had taken to the stump in Lincoln's behalf, first in Ohio, then after winning his own reelection to Congress on October 11 in New York and Michigan.

The combination of forces, in turn, had led to a huge Democratic rout in the fall elections. McClellan won just 45 percent of the popular vote and carried only three states—New Jersey, Delaware, and Kentucky—and thus ended up with twenty-one electoral votes to Lincoln's 212. The Democrats also lost every gubernatorial race in every free state except New Jersey. They also lost all the state legislatures that they had taken away from the Republicans in 1862. And they especially got clobbered in the House races, entering the contest with seventy-two seats, leaving with just thirty-eight. Meanwhile, their Republican rivals picked up House seats not only from Democrats but from all the other contenders as well, thereby increasing the Republican total by a whopping fifty-one seats.[11]

The triumphant Republicans, many noted, could now wait thirteen months, until December 1865 when they would have a three-quarters majority in the House, to push through the Thirteenth Amendment. If they did, the nation's slaves would also have to wait for their freedom, at least one more year, maybe more. But Lincoln in his annual message on December 6, 1864, indicated that time was of the essence. He called on the lame duck Congress to reconsider the defeated amendment and pass it. He even threatened to call a special session in March if necessary.

In licking their wounds, Belmont and other Democrats pointed to two developments that had hurt them badly. One concerned primarily the border states, where many of their supporters had trouble voting on Election Day. Four years earlier, Southerners of all stripes, including outspoken secessionists, had voted. In 1864, that was not the case. Thousands of border-state men had taken off for the Confederacy, and thousands more had been locked up by the Lincoln administration. Nationwide, some eighteen thousand citizens had been arrested for disloyalty, and most of these arrests had taken place in the border states. Were these people truly disloyal? Or were they just critical of Lincoln, the Emancipation Proclamation, and the arming of black men? Democrats claimed the latter. They also insisted that the Union army, and especially the New England units, had intimidated many potential McClellan voters and kept them away from the polls on Election Day.

The other Democratic complaint concerned the soldier vote. When the war began, most soldiers didn't have the right to vote unless they were home on leave. Only Pennsylvania had allowed soldiers to vote outside their election districts. By 1864, nineteen states had changed their laws to allow soldiers in the field to vote. Republicans had led the way, largely because they believed the soldier vote would add to their numbers on Election Day. In states that Republicans controlled, the new laws had passed easily, but in New Jersey, Indiana, and Illinois, where Republicans were in the minority, Democrats had succeeded in blocking their attempts to change the law. And in New York, the state with the largest number of potential voters, the Democratic governor, Horatio Seymour, had stood in their way.

Seymour undoubtedly had a good reason to fear the soldier vote. In 1862, he had won the governorship by a mere 10,752 votes in a race where over six hundred thousand ballots had been cast. The outcome, said his opponents, would have been different if soldiers in the field had been allowed to vote. Republicans thus set about to change the law. To slow them down, Seymour pointed to a clause in the New York constitution that forbade proxy voting and promised to veto any proxy law that made it to his desk. In response, Republicans in the state legislature launched a two-pronged attack, passing a proxy law in 1863, and at the same time, crafting a constitutional amendment allowing proxy voting. As expected, Seymour vetoed the proxy law, but the electorate endorsed the amendment by a five-to-one margin and, thus, left the governor with no constitutional grounds to deny soldiers in the field the right to vote. The legislature in 1864 then passed another proxy law, and Seymour signed it.[12]

Both Seymour and his Republican opponents obviously knew what they were doing. In 1864, the Republicans chose Reuben Fenton to run against Seymour. Fenton not only was Ashley's friend but was also known in Congress as "the friend of the soldier," and his Republican backers capitalized on this fact. The election was close, even closer than the one that had taken place two years earlier. It was also marred by all sorts of voter fraud, and when the votes were finally counted, many believed that Seymour and his operatives had stolen some thirty thousand votes. At the same time, however, nearly everyone also believed that it was votes from soldiers in the field that cost Seymour the election and made Fenton the victor by 7,293 votes. Yet no one could prove it, as New York was one of the seven states that did not count the soldier vote separately.

There were, however, twelve states that did count the soldier vote separately. And in these states, with the notable exception of Kentucky, the Democratic candidates paid a heavy price because of the soldier vote. McClellan won 47 percent of the civilian vote, but just 22 percent of the soldier vote. Even soldiers in his old unit, the Army of the Potomac, voted heavily against him, giving him 5,491 votes to Lincoln's 13,704. As one Maine private put it, they had "worshipped" him as a commanding officer, but they clearly didn't support his bid for the presidency. Indeed, noted the private, it was "cruel" of McClellan to even ask them to vote for him, as that was the equivalent of asking them "to vote" that their campaigns "had all been failures" and that their "comrades had died in vain."[13]

The votes of the Maine private and his fellow soldiers, however, didn't cause McClellan's defeat. He would have lost had they not voted. But the soldier vote was decisive when it came to other elections. As we have already noted, neither the Maryland nor the Missouri constitutions, which outlawed slavery, would have passed without the soldier vote. In both states, the civilian population voted them down, by nearly two thousand votes in Maryland and one thousand in Missouri. But soldiers in the field approved them overwhelmingly, by a nine-to-one margin in Maryland and four-to-one margin in Missouri.[14]

And without the soldier vote, nine additional Democrats, and maybe as many as twelve, would have been elected to Congress in 1864.[15] One was James Ashley's opponent, Colonel Americus V. Rice.

The twenty-eight-year-old colonel had enlisted as a private in the first month of the war, recruited a regiment of Ohio farm boys for the Union cause, and risen quickly up the ranks. He had fought at Shiloh and Vicksburg, and he had been a part of Sherman's march toward Atlanta. In a frontal assault at Little Kennesaw, he had been wounded three times, and to save him the doctors had cut off his right leg above the knee. Returning home as a one-legged war hero, he had been immediately recruited by the Democrats in the Toledo district to run against Ashley. Although he ran as a War Democrat opposed to emancipation, he refused to endorse McClellan. He backed Lincoln instead and thereby gained the support of a number of conservative Republicans in the district, including Ashley's old nemesis, Clark Waggoner, the editor of the *Toledo Blade*. Rice did well with the local voters, and on Election Day, October 11, he led by 930 votes. Then the soldier vote came in, and it went overwhelmingly for Ashley. Rice thus lost the election by 827 votes.[16]

The soldier vote also cost the Democrats another House seat in Ohio, a seat that they had won easily by over three thousand votes in 1862, a year in which Ohio soldiers had not been able to vote. The winner of that election had been John O'Neill, a Peace Democrat. After a year in Washington, O'Neill had decided to resume his Zanesville law practice rather than run for a second term. In his place, the party chose Charles Follett, another Peace Democrat, to run against Columbus Delano, a former Whig and staunch Lincoln supporter. The race was tight, so tight that no one knew who won until weeks after the election. Had only the civilians been allowed to vote, Follett would have won comfortably. But the soldier vote went against him by roughly four to one, and thus he lost the election by 225 votes.

Follett contested the election. Among other things, he claimed that he had been a victim of the "bayonet vote." By this, he meant that the men in the field had been forced by their commanding officers, literally at the point of bayonet, to vote against him. This argument had become old hat in Ohio by 1864. It had been used many times the year before to explain the poor showing of Clement Vallandigham, the hero of the Peace Democrats, in the 1863 Ohio gubernatorial election. Since then, it had become a standard Democratic refrain, dragged out in every contest. It didn't work for Follett. Congress, in solid Republican hands, ruled against him.[17]

"How Free Ballot Is Protected!" Democratic View of "Bayonet Vote."
Democratic election cartoon, 1864, Library of Congress (LC-USZ-89606).

Meanwhile, in December 1864, Follett's fellow Peace Democrat, John O'Neill, returned to Washington. A lame duck by choice, he now held a seat that had just been lost to the opposition party. Yet, until December 1865, when his successor would be sworn in, O'Neill was still the official voice of his district. His vote still counted. He had used it to defeat the Thirteenth Amendment in June. He would try to do the same in the coming session. He was not one of the fifteen lame duck Democrats who bucked the will of his party. He, along with forty other lame duck Democrats, would follow the party line to the bitter end.

Ashley undoubtedly knew this. He never tried to get O'Neill's vote. He didn't bother to put O'Neill on his list. He concentrated instead on thirteen other lame duck Democrats, and in the end he got all but two.

The more prominent of the two was still another Ohio Democrat, Samuel "Sunset" Cox, the silver-tongued orator who had accused the Republicans in the spring of 1864 of promoting miscegenation. Cox

Samuel S. Cox, congressman from Ohio. Brady-Handy Collection, Library of Congress (LC-DIG-cwpbh-04916).

voted against the amendment, and in addition, years later, he also accused Ashley and his associates of resorting to bribery and corruption to get the amendment passed.

Ashley probably realized from the outset that he never had Cox's full support. For, more than most Democrats, Cox had a history of following the dictates of Belmont and the party leadership to the hilt. In instances where the party leadership did not offer a directive, he had a tendency to jump about, siding sometimes with the War Democrats, sometimes with the Peace Democrats, never committing himself fully or for long to one camp or the other. As a result, historians have had a hard time labeling him. In one book, he is a War Democrat, in another a Peace Democrat, in yet another conditional War Democrat, and in still another moderate Peace Democrat.[18] And at one time or another, he probably fit neatly into each one of these categories.

From Ashley's perspective, however, Cox was just the most articulate of the Ohio Democrats who had supported the war until it became a war to end slavery. Then, along with many other Ohio Democrats, he became a vehement opponent of emancipation and the draft. In addition, he was also a close friend of Clement Vallandigham, the most notorious of the state's Peace Democrats, and for a while worked closely with the peace faction. Then in 1864 he broke with the peace faction and joined Belmont and the Democratic leadership in backing McClellan's nomination.

The key question, then, was whether Cox would buck Belmont and the party leadership and vote for an amendment that they opposed. And that was doubtful. For Cox, like Ashley, was in politics for the long haul and enjoyed being in the Washington spotlight. Unlike Ashley, moreover, Cox had already achieved star status. First elected to Congress in 1856, two years before Ashley, he had risen fast in the Democratic Party and become a floor leader in the House. He was the party's choice for Speaker of the House in 1863. As a result, most newsmen and Washington insiders saw him as a political heavyweight destined for higher office once the Democrats gained control of the national government, maybe a cabinet post, maybe even the vice presidency.

Unfortunately, Cox also shared another similarity with Ashley, one that hurt him badly. Like Ashley, he didn't represent a "safe" district, one that was easy to win on Election Day. On the contrary, he had nearly as many opponents within his district as he had supporters, and thus even in 1862, a good year for Ohio Democrats, he barely held onto his congressional seat, beating his Republican challenger, Samuel Shellabarger, by only 272 votes.

Following that election, Cox attributed his victory and that of other Democrats to Lincoln's "unwise, ill-timed and seditious proclamation" emancipating rebel slaves. He also claimed that the voters had handed down a new commandment, "Thou shall not degrade the white race by such intermixtures as emancipation would bring."[19] Then, a year later, Cox doubled down on his reputation as an opponent of emancipation. First, he delivered his famous antimiscegenation speech in Congress. Then, he denounced the Thirteenth Amendment. Both these actions got extensive press coverage. As always, he was quotable. Newsmen loved him. Then, unfortunately, Cox had to run for office again in a slightly different district, one of the many in Ohio that had been altered because of the 1860 census. This time, Shellabarger whipped him by more than three thousand votes.

Defeated for reelection, Cox returned to Washington in December 1864 to finish out the last four months of his term. But, unlike many of his fellow lame ducks, he had no intention of dropping out of politics. Instead, as soon as his term was up, he planned to move to New York City, open a law practice there, work closely with Belmont and the party leadership, obtain the backing of Tammany Hall, and within a year or two run for Congress again, this time representing a district in New York. That he did, and thus he would serve in Congress for many more years, until his death in 1889.

Following his defeat in 1864, Cox also had second thoughts about his fervent opposition to emancipation. What good had it done him in the 1864 election? What good had it done his party? And what good would it do him and his party in the future? In December, he went to New York and "around a table at Delmonico's" discussed the matter at length with three key members of the Belmont circle, Samuel Barlow, Samuel J. Tilden, and Manton Marble. His main concern, he later wrote Marble, was the future of the party. And with that in mind, he had concluded that opposing emancipation would now be a mistake. Yes, it would undoubtedly please the party's extreme peace wing. But in the long run, it would only keep the party "in the minority and on the defensive." So, why not strengthen the party "for the future, by throwing off the proslavery odium?"[20]

That winter Cox also received news that Jefferson Davis, the president of the Confederacy, intended to free all slaves that joined the Confederate army and that Davis already had five black regiments in Richmond ready to be activated. If that was indeed true, Cox wrote Marble, then it put all Northern Democrats in an impossible position. How could they be against freeing the slaves when Jefferson Davis was "at work freeing them?" How could they now justify voting against the Thirteenth Amendment? What would their grounds be? States' rights? Peace? And "looking to the near future, as well as the remote," what would they gain "in being tied to the body of Death?" It obviously wouldn't lead to "Democratic ascendancy."[21]

Had these thoughts come to the attention of Ashley and other Republicans? Did they know that Cox was trying to get Marble and the Belmont circle to reconsider their opposition to emancipation? That is uncertain. But by the time Cox wrote about Jefferson Davis, Ashley felt he had Cox's vote, as did Secretary of State William H. Seward and one of Seward's chief operatives, Robert W. Latham. And on January 12, the day before Cox wrote the Davis letter, he got up on the House floor and undermined one of the standard Democratic arguments. The amendment, he said, might be inexpedient, but it was definitely not unconstitutional, despite what many of his colleagues had been saying for months.

Rumor also had it that Cox had invited fellow Democrats over to his boardinghouse and asked them to absent themselves from voting. Eight Democrats missed the vote, including Andrew J. Rogers of New Jersey, a vehement opponent of emancipation. Was Cox responsible? Some thought so. And two ardent Peace Democrats, James Brooks of New York and Alexander Long of Ohio, later denounced Cox as a traitor to the Democratic cause for allegedly talking James E. English of Connecticut, one of the lame ducks on Ashley's list, into voting for the amendment. Years later, Seward, a close friend of Cox, would claim that Cox "more than any other member" had contributed to the amendment's passing.[22]

Yet, what did Cox do when it came time to vote? He surprised his friend Seward and voted nay. Why? As Cox later told the story, he had prepared a speech in favor of the amendment and "fully intended" to cast an aye vote when he set off for the Capitol at noon on the day of the vote. Then, on arriving at the House chamber a half hour later, he learned that Confederate peace commissioners were waiting to be conducted over the Union lines to General Grant's headquarters. He asked Ashley if this were true. Ashley, in turn, contacted Lincoln's private secretary, "who declared that he knew of no such commission." Cox then "begged" Ashley to have a note that Cox had written taken directly to the president, and about an hour later Lincoln responded that he "knew of no such commission or negotiation." Then Cox made "further inquiries" and learned that either Lincoln was "mistaken" or "ignorant" of what was happening. And on the basis of this information, he decided to vote against the amendment rather than jeopardize the peace process.[23]

By the time Cox wrote this account, he knew for certain that Lincoln and Ashley had resorted to an act of deception.

There was indeed a peace commission waiting in the wings. It had grown out of a hare-brained scheme that the old Jacksonian newsman Francis Preston Blair had to end the war. Blair thought he could reunite North and South by proposing a joint military campaign to drive the French out of Mexico. Lincoln undoubtedly regarded the proposal as absurd, but he gave Blair permission to go to Richmond and try it out on Jefferson Davis and see what came of it. The Confederate leader also thought the proposal was absurd, but he saw a way to take advantage of Blair's peace mission and to prove to his critics that the North had no intention of offering the Confederacy "honorable" peace terms. So, after Blair's second visit, he agreed to send a three-man delegation to confer with Lincoln. The three men were on their way, but they weren't about to enter the nation's capital as the rumor had it. They were south of the city, and Lincoln and Seward would meet with them two days later at Hampton Roads.[24]

The rumor, however, was being used against Ashley in his attempt to get the amendment passed. So he turned to Lincoln and asked for a statement to contradict it. Lincoln promptly replied in a single sentence that was both factually accurate and totally deceptive. "So far as I know," wrote Lincoln, "there are no peace commissioners in the city, or likely to be in it." Ashley then used Lincoln's statement to silence the peace rumors.[25]

In his first book on his congressional career, published in 1865, Cox left no doubt that Lincoln and Ashley were guilty of duplicity. And, at the same time, he also made it clear to his readers that he was just too smart to be hoodwinked by the tricky president and his deceitful underling.

But Cox said nothing about corruption. He didn't even back up his fellow Ohio Democrats who insisted that key votes had been bought and that "upwards of $50,000" had been authorized in bribes. What deterred him? No one knows for certain, but maybe it was the source of these charges. Some had come from the lips and the pen of Cox's harshest critic, Alexander Long, a notorious Peace Democrat from Cincinnati who had supported Confederate independence and had been censured by the Congress the previous spring for "treasonable utterances."[26]

In any event, it wasn't until many years later that Cox joined Long and others in charging corruption. In a speech on the House floor and in another book on his congressional career published in 1885, he indicated that he had first learned that money had been used to get the amendment passed when he returned home to his boardinghouse shortly after the vote. His landlord, "a radical Republican who had been on General Frémont's staff," went berserk. He screamed and hollered, jumped up and down, and screamed some more. The man, explained Cox, had been promised "ten thousand dollars from New-York parties" for "influencing" Cox to vote for the amendment, and now he was to get nothing. Cox then did some detective work and eventually found out who had put up the money "for corrupting members."

Who were these villains? Cox didn't identify them. Instead, he left his readers with this question: "Can anything be conceived more monstrous than this attempt to amend the Constitution upon such a humane and glorious theme, by the aid of the lucre of office-holders?"[27]

By the time Cox wrote these words, all the principals knew that he was one of the lame duck Democrats on Ashley's list to vote against the amendment. Ashley hadn't hid that fact.

So what was Cox up to? Was he simply justifying his own behavior, portraying himself as an honest man, while implying that some fellow lame ducks probably had been bribed? That is obviously one way to look at his second account. Another way would be to give Cox the benefit of the doubt and say that he was simply laying out the facts as they happened. That, of course, means that Ashley and his associates resorted to bribery to get the votes they needed.

Was that likely? There were certainly plenty of people in Ohio and Washington who thought Ashley was not above breaking the law. After all, he had freely admitted on numerous occasions that he had violated the Fugitive Slave Law and helped slaves flee bondage since he was teenager working on the Ohio River. He had also encouraged others to do the same.

But would he also resort to bribery for what he believed was a good cause? His old nemesis, Clark Waggoner, had no doubts on this score. Indeed, Waggoner spent much of his newspaper career trying to prove that Ashley would resort to bribery any time it fit his needs. He insisted that Ashley as chairman of the House Committee on Territories had sold government jobs, forcing applicants like Frank Case, for example, to agree to hire Ashley's brothers, William and Eli, and go along with an illegal land deal in order to get the lucrative post of surveyor general of the Colorado Territory. Waggoner first made this specific charge in 1862. And although Congress investigated the matter and cleared Ashley, Waggoner never let up. He was still at it in 1890, nearly thirty years later.[28]

But Cox, in his second account, never hinted that Ashley was the source of the bribes. Instead, he mentioned "New-York parties." And here he was going along with others, who for years had pointed their fingers at Secretary of State Seward's operatives and, by implication, the entire Lincoln administration.

Was there any validity to this charge? Without question, the Lincoln administration was anxious to get the amendment passed. The president not only said so in his annual message on December 6, but he also lobbied hard for the amendment, meeting privately with at least six House members who had voted nay back in June. Did he make promises? If so, he left no tracks. Nothing was in writing.

One of the men Lincoln called into his office that December for a "long talk" was the Missouri slaveholder, James S. Rollins. The two men had at one time been fellow Whigs and devoted followers of Henry Clay. And from the written record, we know that Lincoln appealed to Rollins as a former Whig and a follower of "that great statesman, Henry Clay," to now support the Thirteenth Amendment. It was something, said Lincoln, that Clay would want his followers to do. And when Rollins indicated that he would now vote for the amendment, Lincoln asked him to use his influence with the other congressmen from Missouri and the other border states. He also assured Rollins that the passage of the amendment would bring the war "rapidly to a close."[29]

Was that all that happened? No one can be certain. One thing is clear, however. By the time of the meeting, Lincoln had been told by Abel Rathbone Corbin, a Republican money man, that he could easily get Rollins's vote by simply leaving a federal judgeship in Missouri vacant and assuring Rollins that he would have a decisive voice in choosing the appointee if he supported the amendment. The same gambit, said Corbin, would also work with Austin King, the other lame duck Missourian on Ashley's list. What did Lincoln do? Did he follow Corbin's advice? Did he tell Rollins on that cold December day that he would have the final say in the choice of a judge? Did he make the same promise to King? There is no proof one way or the other. But he did leave the judgeship vacant.[30]

Deal or no deal, Rollins didn't immediately announce his support for the amendment on leaving his meeting with Lincoln. He waited until January 13, 1865, two days after the Missouri Constitutional Convention abolished slavery in his home state. A few days later, he received a letter from William F. Switzler, an old friend and a prominent Columbia County slave owner. Switzler had just returned home from the Missouri convention. He had been on the losing side. Only three delegates had joined him in voting against emancipating the state's slaves. Having lost that battle, he now saw no point in continuing the fight. Wrote Switzler: "No difference how many or how few governments we may have, slavery is dead. And since it is wiped out in Missouri, you had as well wipe it out elsewhere. . . . Let us now that we are rid of it, make a clean sweep."[31]

Although there is no proof "beyond a shadow of doubt" that Lincoln himself made deals, there is ample reason to believe that he allowed others to do it for him and, also, that he promised to fulfill whatever bargains they made. Nearly every man in Congress had a story to tell.

Years later, for example, two Massachusetts Republicans published their reminiscences. One, John B. Alley, recalled that two of his fellow House members were called into the White House and told to get two more votes. And when they asked how they should do it, Lincoln told them that he was willing to leave it up to them, but they should remember that he had "immense power" and that he expected them to get two votes. Some historians question this account. They claim the language doesn't square with the way Lincoln usually talked.[32]

The other Massachusetts Republican was George S. Boutwell. By the time he wrote his memoir, he had been in politics for sixty years. He had been the state's governor for two years, a House member for six years, secretary of the Treasury for four years, and US senator for four years. And like many old hands in politics, he was careful in what he said. After pointing out that he had not been a major player in getting the amendment passed, that all he had done was vote aye, he then recalled that he had heard a "rumor" at the time that Ashley was engaged "in making arrangements with certain Democrats to absent themselves from the House when the vote was taken." He also indicated that Ashley was making "pledges which no one but the President could keep." Concluded Boutwell: "Such was the exigency for the passage of the resolution that the means were not subjected to any rigid rules of ethics."[33]

Did Lincoln give James Ashley the power to negotiate in his behalf? Without question, he did. The best documented case involves Anson Herrick, a New York Democrat who was affiliated with Tammany Hall.

Anson Herrick, congressman from New York. Matthew Brady photograph,
National Archives and Records Administration (526304).

Herrick had lost his district in the 1864 election because New York
City's former mayor Fernando Wood, the head of the rival Democratic
faction in New York known as Mozart Hall, ran as a Peace Democrat
against him and split the Democratic vote. Thanks to Wood, Herrick
had seen his vote total drop from a whopping 64 percent in the 1862
election to a dismal 29 percent in 1864. Undoubtedly bitter over the
turn of events, Herrick was still reluctant to break with his party and
vote for the amendment. But he was also anxious to find a job for his
brother as a federal revenue assessor. Could Ashley get Lincoln to
make that appointment? Yes, he could. And after Congress adopted
the amendment, Lincoln assured Herrick that "whatever Ashley
promised should be performed" and nominated Herrick's brother for
the post.[34]

Another clear case involves Alexander F. Coffroth, a Peace Democrat from Pennsylvania. Like Herrick, he, too, had lost his district in
the fall election, but he hadn't lost by much. The difference had been
a mere sixty-eight votes out of some twenty-two thousand that were
cast. Like many politicians in this situation, Coffroth claimed that he

had been "robbed," that he would have won except for several "irregularities." But in challenging the outcome, Coffroth had to cope with the fact that the election committee that would decide his fate was in the hands of Republicans. Would they side with him? Yes, if he cut a deal. So, to the great shock of a fellow Pennsylvania Peace Democrat William H. Miller, Coffroth repudiated everything he had said in the past and became a supporter of the amendment. His constituents back home also couldn't believe it. They denounced him as "stool pigeon" who had taken "anxious flight to the [Republicans] well filled feed-troughs."[35]

There are other cases where the evidence is definitely mixed. Of these probably the most controversial involves Andrew J. Rogers of New Jersey. Rogers was a hard-line antiemancipationist. He hated blacks. He hated white abolitionists. And he made sure that everyone knew it. If a fellow congressman even suggested that slavery was the cause of the war, Rogers was on his feet. It was not slavery, he thundered. It was the abolitionists. And if they ever got their way, said Rogers, the country would be ruined. Not only did Rogers follow the standard Democratic line and denounce emancipation as inexpedient, unconstitutional, and disastrous, but he did so repeatedly. And in 1862, he secretly wrote a platform for New Jersey's Fourth District that embodied these thoughts and thus forced the incumbent Democratic representative George T. Cobb to either endorse them or be denied renomination. Cobb refused and Rogers was chosen to run in his place.

So when the Thirteenth Amendment came up for a vote in June 1864, Rogers did what everyone expected. He responded with a loud no. He also lambasted all the amendment's supporters. He made all the usual charges. The amendment was unconstitutional. It was inexpedient. And it would lead to the downfall of white America. He made the same pitch in the fall election campaign and whipped his Republican opponent by nearly two thousand votes. And when debate over the amendment began again in January 1865, he was still at it, denouncing John A. J. Creswell of Maryland, one of the lame ducks on Ashley's list, for supporting emancipation.[36] Was there any chance, then, that Rogers might fail to cast another loud no vote two weeks later? Not a chance in the world, said the pundits. But, to everyone's surprise, Rogers missed the decisive vote.

How did that happen? If one believes the accounts of J. R. Freeze

Andrew J. Rogers, congressman from New Jersey. Brady-Handy Collection, Library of Congress (LC-DIG-cwpbh-02052).

and George Shea, two lobbyists who worked for the Camden and Amboy Railroad, they cooked a deal with Ashley. The railroad had a monopoly on the only line running the length of New Jersey, and a bill before the Senate Commerce Committee being pushed by Senator Charles Sumner of Massachusetts threatened it. The lobbyists promised Ashley that they would round up one or two New Jersey votes for the amendment if he could get Sumner to back off. Having no influence with Sumner, Ashley then took the matter to the White House. What did Lincoln do? According to his private secretary, John G. Nicolay, the president rejected the offer, arguing that it was hopeless even to try to get Sumner to budge on this issue, and that it would probably only make the Massachusetts senator even "more resolute" in pushing the bill forward.

But what became of Sumner's bill? Did it make its way through Congress? No, it didn't. It died in committee. The Senate Commerce Committee didn't report it out. The two lobbyists, of course, took credit for killing the bill. As they told the story, the railroad essentially owned Rogers, and they in effect sold his vote to Ashley and Lincoln to preserve the railroad's monopoly. Was that what happened? Or were they just bragging? No one knows for certain. But Rogers was undoubtedly one of the keys in getting the amendment passed. He, along with seven other Northern Democrats, failed to vote and thus made it possible for Ashley to get the necessary two-thirds majority.[37]

But even if Ashley had somehow bought Rogers's absence, where was the "New-York money" that Cox spoke of? No one linked it directly to Ashley, and only a few eyebrows were raised when he insisted that he spent exactly $27.50 to get the amendment passed. Instead, fingers pointed at Secretary of State Seward and four of his operatives. Did Seward, in turn, act alone? Or did he have Lincoln's blessing? Years later, some of Lincoln's admirers would argue that Seward operated on his own, that Lincoln never would have stooped so low as to use money to get the amendment passed. At the time, however, everyone assumed that Seward must have had Lincoln's approval.[38]

Seward's four operatives were William N. Bilbo, Emanuel B. Hart, Robert W. Latham, and George O. Jones. All were in their fifties. Only one had anything in common with Ashley. That was George Jones, an Ohioan whose father had been active in the Liberty Party, the tiny antislavery party that ran James G. Birney for president in the early 1840s. At age fifty, Jones was also the youngest of the four. He had moved from Ohio to New York in 1850, affiliated with the Know-Nothing Party briefly, and then the Democratic Party in 1859. He would remain a Democrat for the next nineteen years and then become a leader of the Greenback Party, the third party that tried unsuccessfully to stop the nation from shifting from paper money back to a bullion coin–based monetary system.

The other three operatives had no antislavery connections whatsoever. William N. Bilbo was an old-line Tennessee Whig who had been a supporter of the Confederacy at the beginning of the war. On arriving in New York, he had been jailed as a Confederate spy by General John A. Dix. Released on Lincoln's order, he had somehow convinced

Seward that despite his Whig past he had influence with New York Democrats.

If Bilbo was to be believed, he was a mover and shaker of the first order. On January 10, he reported to Seward that he had his work cut out for him, as the Democratic leadership was making "the most strenuous efforts . . . to unite every member against the amendment." But he also indicated that he was up to the task, that he had contact with all elements of the party, including Manton Marble of the *New York World*, Governor Seymour, and Fernando Wood of Mozart Hall.[39]

While Bilbo may have been just bragging about his New York connections, Emanuel B. Hart undoubtedly had them. A Tammany Hall stalwart, Hart had been doing party work in Manhattan and Brooklyn since the 1832 presidential election. But over his long career, he had always been regarded as a proslavery, pro-South Democrat. He had always been identified with the "Hunker" wing of the New York party, the office-holding conservatives who in the years before the Civil War had vehemently opposed the agitation of the slavery question and had sided whenever possible with the slaveholding states. For that service, President James Buchanan had appointed Hart surveyor of the port of New York, a post that had given him control of dozens of patronage jobs.

The fourth operative was Robert W. Latham. The money man in the group, Latham had extensive ties both in Washington and in New York City. He had been a Washington banker in the early 1850s. Then in 1857 he had moved to Brooklyn, become a broker on Wall Street, and acted as a liaison between Manhattan speculators and Democratic leaders in the Buchanan administration. Shortly after the war, he became an ally of Lincoln's successor, Andrew Johnson, and was put in charge of the National Bank of Virginia. Latham had no qualms whatsoever about using money to get support for the amendment. He was even blatant about it. On January 9, he wrote Seward that "money will certainly do it, if patriotism fails." [40]

The main task of the four operatives was to get the support of the six New Yorkers on Ashley's list who hadn't voted for the amendment in June. To accomplish that goal, they divided the labor, with Jones working out of Albany, Hart out of New York City, Latham and Bilbo out of the nation's capital. What Hart accomplished is uncertain, but Jones met with Governor Seymour and with Dean Richmond, the head of the Albany Regency, the party's oldest statewide organization. He tried to talk the two men into putting pressure on the New York delegation to support the amendment. Seymour and Richmond wouldn't go that far. They agreed with Jones that the party's proslavery image was a handicap, but they weren't about to throw their weight behind the amendment. The best they would do was "not advise against voting for it."[41]

Meanwhile, Bilbo and Latham worked directly on the six congressmen in Washington. The six men, according to Bilbo, were being pressured constantly by the Democratic Party leadership to stand firm and vote against the amendment. But one of the six, Homer A. Nelson, proved helpful. A young lawyer from Poughkeepsie, Nelson had once been a rising star in the party. He had become a Dutchess County judge at age twenty-six, a full colonel in the 159th New York Volunteer Infantry at age thirty-one, and a US congressman at age thirty-three. He had won his House seat by twelve hundred votes in 1862. Now, just two years later, he was a lame duck, having lost his bid for reelection by 670 votes.

Nelson was the only one of the six New Yorkers on Ashley's list who had not committed himself fully in June. He had simply missed the vote. So, in moving to an aye vote, he was in a more comfortable position than the others. He wouldn't be repudiating his former stance. He could claim, if he wished, that he was just being clear on where he stood. Nonetheless, he apparently wasn't willing to help Bilbo without getting something in return. He was offered a foreign post when his term expired in March. He turned that offer down and asked Seward instead for a position in the Treasury Department.

Was he also offered money? As in every other case, that is uncertain. There is no paper trail, one way or the other. No one can be certain what Bilbo and his associates did to get six New Yorkers to change their vote. It is not even clear that Seward's team truly made a difference. Everyone said they did, especially the loquacious Bilbo.[42] But that, too, is open to dispute. The Washington correspondents of the *New York Tribune* and the *New York Herald* thought Ashley's man Augustus Frank had far more impact. They credited Frank, the lame duck Republican from western New York and the son of one of the state's first abolitionists, with getting four men in the New York delegation to change their votes.[43]

Ashley initially thought he would have all the changes he needed by January 9. In preparation, on Christmas Day, 1864, he began urging his fellow Republicans to be ready for the upcoming battle. He sent out a printed circular to each man asking for his help, with a handwritten note at the bottom: "*You* must help us with *one vote*. Don't you know of a Sinner in the opposition who is on praying ground."[44]

On January 6, he brought the joint resolution before the House, opening his remarks with a quote from Lincoln: "If slavery is not wrong, nothing is wrong." Then the debate began. On Ashley's side, John A. J. Creswell of Maryland was especially forceful. He said that slavery was a curse that had almost destroyed his home state, that it had degraded labor, scared away Northern capital, and driven small farmers off the land. He also defended black men, said that they proved their manliness on the battlefield. His remarks were immediately attacked by one Peace Democrat after another, James Brooks of New York, George Bliss of Ohio, and especially Andrew Rogers of New Jersey.[45]

Also forceful on Ashley's side was Moses Odell, the Brooklyn Democrat who had been denied renomination because of his stand on emancipation. He chastised his fellow Democrats for failing to recognize that their party had been wrecked by slavery. They might disagree with him, he said, but they should realize that he was a true party man and that for many years slavery had been a "dead weight" on the Democratic Party, and the time had now come "when we as a party ought to unloose ourselves from this dead body." He, too, was immediately attacked.[46]

Then on January 13, Ashley brought forth the first of his many surprises, James S. Rollins, the representative from Boone Country, Missouri, where roughly one-fourth of the population had been in bondage. Rollins shocked his colleagues by announcing a complete change of heart. "I am proud that a man has a right to change," he said. And, "I am gratified that I am not too obstinate to change." He also noted that he had just received "a telegram a morning or two ago" that his state had outlawed slavery and that he was no longer a slave owner. And he thanked God for it. Yes, even if he "had owned a thousand slaves, they would most cheerfully have been given up" for the good of the Union, for peace, and for the Constitution. And he then went on to chastise the Kentuckians for turning a deaf ear to Lincoln's proposal of gradual, compensated emancipation. That, he said, was "the unwisest of all acts," and he had been fool to go along with it.[47]

As various members took the floor, others counted heads. Did Ashley have enough votes to break the two-thirds barrier? Schuyler Colfax, the Speaker of the House, had one count. Cornelius Cole, a member from California, had another. Neither man thought Ashley had the votes he needed. So on January 7 Ashley announced a postponement of the vote. Then on January 13 he asked for another two weeks.[48]

The delays frustrated Laura Julian, who sat in the women's gallery. She had longed to see the day that slavery was killed. So had her husband, George Julian, the radical Republican from Indiana, and her father, Joshua Giddings, Ohio's most prominent antislavery Whig of an earlier generation. She didn't like what she saw. The air in the House chamber, she wrote her sister, was "miserable." And Ashley? He was even worse. "Such a pity he should have the charge of such a matter."[49]

Finally, on January 24, Ashley knew he had the votes he needed. He sent out another circular, telling all Republicans that their presence in the House on January 31 was essential.

On that day, every Republican showed up, eager and ready to vote. Eight Democrats were absent. The galleries were full. Five justices of the Supreme Court were on hand. So, too, were several senators, the new Treasury secretary William Pitt Fessenden, and former postmaster general Montgomery Blair. Laura Julian was also back in her usual seat in the women's gallery. Would Ashley disappoint her yet again?[50]

What Ashley did that day was try the patience of many onlookers. Instead of moving quickly ahead at noon, as was expected, he allowed each of the former "Sinners" to have a chance to "repent" and announce their support for the amendment.

The first in line was Archibald McAllister of Pennsylvania. He didn't actually say anything. Instead, he had the House clerk read a statement in his behalf explaining that the failure of the various peace missions over the past year had convinced him that only independence would satisfy the Confederacy. Therefore, he had decided to cast his vote against "the corner-stone of the Confederacy" and to declare "eternal war" against the enemies of his country.[51]

Next came another Pennsylvanian, Alexander Coffroth. With his hands in his pocket, he mumbled something that most of members couldn't hear. But he essentially tried to present himself as a "man of Peace" who had decided that the end of slavery meant the end of the war. He said nothing, of course, about selling his vote to Ashley for Republican help in his contested election. The logic of the Coffroth's speech made no sense whatsoever to his friend William Miller, another Pennsylvania Democrat, who then ripped into it and mistakenly blamed Coffroth's conversion on still another Pennsylvania Democrat, the renegade Joseph Bailey, who had been the first to vote for the amendment the previous year.[52]

Then came the last man in Ashley's line-up, Anson Herrick of New York. His speech had more meat to it. The recent election, he said, had made it clear to him that the people of the loyal states wanted slavery abolished, and he was in favor of following the wishes of the people. Moreover, as a loyal Democrat, he was worried about the future of his party. For it was now ruining itself, sinking into a "hopeless minority in nearly every State in the Union" and "growing weaker and weaker in popular favor" because it would "not venture to cut loose from the dead carcass of negro slavery." Furthermore, he could see no reason why any Northern Democrat should continue to support the institution of slavery when men like James S. Rollins and Austin King of Missouri were willing to abandon it. Thus he called on his sixty-five fellow Democrats to join him in voting for the amendment.[53]

The vast majority didn't. Instead, they just waited glumly in defeat as Republicans gathered around Ashley's desk and urged him to call the vote. Meanwhile a handful of Democrats tried to derail the upcoming vote. James S. Brown of Wisconsin proposed four amendments to the joint resolution that would have freed the slaves gradually and compensated their owners. No one paid him much attention. Two others simply denounced the resolution, and another tried to table its reconsideration. The tabling motion failed, 111 nays to fifty-seven yeas. Finally, shortly after three o'clock, Ashley nodded to Speaker Colfax to call the vote.

The clerk then went down the roll. He came quickly to Augustus Baldwin, a lame duck Democrat from Michigan. To the surprise of many, Baldwin voted aye. There were murmurs in the gallery. Then the clerk reached Sunset Cox. His no vote also came as a surprise. Wasn't he expected to be an aye? So said many. Then came James English, a lame duck Democrat from Connecticut. His aye vote caused a flurry of applause. The noise got louder when John Ganson, a lame duck New York Democrat, also cast an aye vote. Speaker Colfax then called for order, but it had no effect. The rumbling just got louder, as ten members who had voted against the amendment in June moved into the aye column, and four who had not voted in June now cast aye votes, and one member who had cast a strong no vote in June was nowhere to be seen when his name was called.

Speaker Colfax then asked that his name also be called. That was unusual. The tradition had been for the Speaker not to vote. But Colfax was determined to have his name recorded. He wanted everyone to know that he, too, had backed "that great measure, which hereafter will illuminate the highest page of our history." Then, after his aye vote was recorded, the clerk announced the final tally, 119 to fifty-six, with eight members absent. The amendment had passed, with two votes to spare.[54]

What happened next caught Charles Douglass, the son of the famous black abolitionist, by surprise. Republicans went wild. Some threw their hats to the roof. Others smashed them against their desks. Many cheered. Many wept. Many embraced. Women in the gallery waved handkerchiefs. One woman had trouble keeping her male companion in line. He kept kissing her, even though they were in public among strangers. She protested: "Oh don't, Charlie!" It did no good. "Charlie" was beside himself with joy. The hugs and kisses and the cheering went on for a full five minutes, until Representative Ebon Ingersoll of Illinois called for adjournment. Some Democratic members then tried to prevent adjournment, but the crowd ignored them and poured out into the streets to continue the celebration.

Never before, noted Charles Douglass, had he seen such jubilation among white people. "I wish you could have been here to see it," he wrote his father.[55]

On leaving the House chamber, scores of Republicans rushed to the White House to share the good news with Lincoln and his staff. Lincoln was so pleased that he insisted on signing the measure, even though the Constitution didn't require it. He, too, wanted his name recorded for posterity.

The next day, the president addressed a crowd of enthusiasts celebrating outside the White House. He told them that he had received

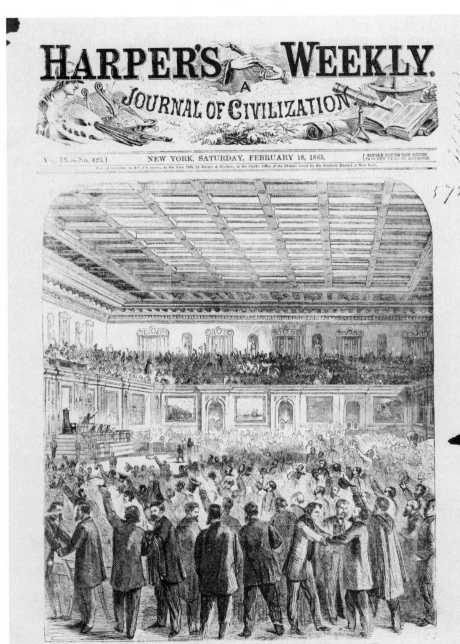

HARPER'S WEEKLY.

A JOURNAL OF CIVILIZATION.

Vol. IX.—No. 425.] NEW YORK, SATURDAY, FEBRUARY 18, 1865. [SINGLE COPIES TEN CENTS.
$4.00 PER YEAR IN ADVANCE.

Entered according to Act of Congress, in the Year 1865, by Harper & Brothers, in the Clerk's Office of the District Court for the Southern District of New York.

SCENE IN THE HOUSE ON THE PASSAGE OF THE PROPOSITION TO AMEND THE CONSTITUTION, JANUARY 31, 1865.

Celebration of the passing of the Thirteenth Amendment. Prints and
Photographs Division, Library of Congress (LC-USZ62-127599).

notice that his home state of Illinois had already ratified the amendment, and he was proud that Illinois was the first state to do so. He also essentially agreed with all those who had insisted that the Emancipation Proclamation had not destroyed the "institution" of slavery, that slavery was still the law of the land in at least thirteen states, and that the proclamation fell "far short of what the amendment will be when fully consummated."

He then called attention to some of the arguments that had been made against the proclamation. That it was not legally valid. That it applied only to slaves who came into Union lines. That it "would have no effect on the children of the slaves born hereafter." The amendment, he pointed out, ended forever all such questions about the future of slavery. No longer would slavery be the law of the land anywhere in the United States. No longer would it be possible for a slave state to reenslave any black child as had happened after the American Revolution. The amendment was "a King's cure for all the evils."[56]

James Ashley was not among those who rushed to the White House bearing the good news. Instead, he hopped into a carriage and drove over to the War Department to share his joy with Secretary of War Edwin Stanton, one of his long time allies. While there, he also fired off a telegram to his constituents back home: "Glory to God in the highest! Our country is free!"[57]

Chapter Seven

THE ENFORCEMENT CLAUSE AND ITS ENEMIES

Though Ashley achieved his dream of getting the Thirteenth Amendment through the House, not all had gone as he had planned. Left undecided was the ticklish question of ratification. Under the Constitution the proposed amendment needed the approval of three-fourths of the states. But eleven of the thirty-six states had seceded from the United States, and most of them were still at war with the United States. Should any of them be included? Congress had failed to make a decision.

On January 6, when Ashley put the amendment before the House, he had shared with the members his thoughts on this matter. In addition to the twenty-five Union states, he proposed that provisions be made to include any state that had returned to the Union and had representatives in Congress "before three fourths of the States now represented adopt the proposed amendment." He obviously had in mind Louisiana, Arkansas, and Tennessee—the three states that the Lincoln administration wanted Congress to accept under the Ten Percent Plan. As for the other Confederate states, the eight that were still in full rebellion, they were clearly not part of the country as it now stood, and therefore they had no right to vote on its Constitution.[1]

If the Congress had followed Ashley's advice, the proposed amendment would have gone to at least twenty-five states and maybe as many as twenty-eight. If it went to just the twenty-five states then in the Union, it would need the support of nineteen to become the law of the land. If it also went to the three states that Lincoln wanted Congress to admit immediately, then it would need the support of two additional states for a total of twenty-one states. But that was it, as far as Ashley was concerned. People at war with the United States should not be able to vote on amending the US Constitution. To insist that they "must" made no sense whatsoever.

In the end, Ashley didn't get his way. The amendment went out for ratification in February. The war was still raging. Grant had yet to crush Lee's army. Lee's surrender at Appomattox Courthouse was still months away. Yet all eleven of the Confederate states, including the eight still in full rebellion, eventually had a chance to ratify the document, and most did so well before they were accepted back into the United States and granted the right to have representatives in Congress.

That happened largely because when the Congress assembled in December 1864, the members had another ticklish issue on their agenda. They had to deal with not only the Thirteenth Amendment but the Louisiana question as well.

Nathaniel Banks had fulfilled the job Lincoln had given him a year earlier to create a free state in Louisiana "in the shortest possible time." Michael Hahn had been elected governor, Louisiana had adopted a new state constitution that abolished slavery, and five representatives and two senators had been elected. They were now in Washington and ready to claim seats in Congress. And the Lincoln administration was pushing hard to have them seated under the president's Ten Percent Plan.

Would they be seated? That was uncertain. Neither the president's Ten Percent Plan nor Hahn's takeover of Louisiana had the backing of the Republican majority in Congress. The strong arm tactics that Banks had used to get Hahn elected had backfired. In installing Hahn as governor, Banks had undercut Thomas Durant, the charismatic leader of the Free State Movement in Louisiana. A tall, thin, forty-six-year-old New Orleans lawyer, Durant had thousands of followers in Louisiana, men who thought he was the true leader of the Free State Movement. Once he was ousted, they gave Banks no peace. They bombarded Congress with complaints that Banks had established a puppet regime in Louisiana, that the Free State that he boasted about creating was a sham, and that he had replaced slave labor with "mock freedom." So effective and persistent had they been with their charges that by the summer of 1864 they had scores of congressional Republicans on their side.[2]

General Nathaniel Banks. Reprinted from *Harpers Weekly*,
December 6, 1862.

To counter this development, Banks and his allies launched a full-scale campaign that summer to undermine the credibility of Durant and his followers and to woo support for the Banks-Hahn regime. And in the fall, Banks went north to defend his program. He made headway, especially in his home state of Massachusetts. By November, he had convinced William Lloyd Garrison, the editor of the Boston *Liberator*, that he was on the right track. But he had no luck with Wendell Phillips, Massachusetts's other leading abolitionist, or with Frederick Douglass. At the annual meeting of the Massachusetts Antislavery Society, both men excoriated Lincoln and Banks. To a cheering audience, Phillips accused them of "sacrificing the very essence of the negro's liberty to the desire for a prompt reconstruction of Louisiana." And Douglass lambasted them for turning the Emancipation Proclamation into "a mockery and delusion."[3]

Banks also had no luck with radical Republicans like Ashley. They, too, remained hostile to the Banks-Hahn regime, even though all five members of the Louisiana congressional delegation had promised to vote for the Thirteenth Amendment.[4] But after the fall election, radical Republicans like Ashley faced another problem. Lincoln was no longer the weak president he had been back in August. At that time, he had appeared to be a sure loser, just another Northern president who would be thrown out of office after one term. It had happened to every Northern president before him, and it seemed certain to happen to him. Standing up against him, therefore, had been relatively easy. Scores of Republicans had done so. Many had shown their disrespect by backing the Wade-Davis Bill. Many had toyed with supporting some other candidate for president. And many like Ashley had done both.

Now all was different. Not only had Lincoln smashed McClellan in the general election. He was the first president since Andrew Jackson to be reelected, and the first Northern president in history to be granted a second term. And when he took the oath of office again in March, the four-year terms of many government officials would expire. He would have loads of patronage to hand out, the power to make or break many careers. Ambitious Republicans thus had to be careful, noted the Indiana radical George Julian. They couldn't afford to get on Lincoln's wrong side.[5]

In light of this reality, the House Committee on the Rebellious States tried to find common ground with the Lincoln administration. On this issue, the committee's Republican majority didn't need to win over some Northern Democrats and border-state Unionists. All they needed to do was get most of eighty-one House Republicans on the same page. If that was accomplished, there would be more than enough votes to ram through any proposal.

With this in mind, Ashley, on behalf of the committee, submitted to the House on December 15 a bill that most of the Republican members regarded as a compromise. The House would recognize the Hahn government and its representatives. In exchange, the main features of the Wade-Davis Bill would be followed in the other Southern states, and in Louisiana all slaves would be declared free and black adult males would be enfranchised.

Banks liked the bill and prodded Lincoln to take a close look at it. Lincoln also saw the bill as a step in the right direction, but he insisted that the black suffrage provision be stricken. At this point, Banks backtracked. He had previously assured his Republican colleagues that he favored black suffrage. He now went along with the president. He,

too, now contended that black enfranchisement would be "a fatal objection to the Bill" in that "the white people under that arrangement
would refuse to vote," and thus the restored governments would end
up solely in the hands of black men.[6]

In response to this objection, Ashley, on behalf of the committee, then offered another compromise. Only black veterans would be
enfranchised. This had the support of many conservative Republicans, and in the eyes of the Washington correspondent of the *New
York Times* it was a sure winner. The bill, predicted the *Times*, would
now easily pass both houses and get the president's signature and the
Louisiana delegation would soon be seated.[7]

Unfortunately, the *Times* forgot that there was also a radical wing in
Ashley's party. Members like Thaddeus Stevens of Pennsylvania and
George Julian of Indiana wanted no part of any bill that recognized
Hahn's government, and members like William D. Kelley of Pennsylvania wanted no restrictions on black male enfranchisement.[8] So
Ashley soon found himself caught in the middle, getting hammered
from both ends, from conservatives who wanted even more compromises, from radicals who wanted none. Hoping to find the magic formula, he offered one modification after another, seven in total, all to
no avail.

While all this was going on, one of the five Louisianans seeking admission to the House made matters worse. Alexander P. Field was a
sixty-four-year-old New Orleans lawyer who had already promised
to vote for the Thirteenth Amendment if given the chance. He was
known to be a man of his word but dangerous when crossed. On the
evening of January 22, he accompanied several Republicans to the
Willard Hotel for food and drink. The most popular meeting place in
Washington, the hotel also had been the scene of many angry disputes.
Ten years earlier, a California congressman, Philemon Herbert, had an
altercation with a waiter, Thomas Keating, and shot him dead. In the
same dining room, Field encountered William Kelley, the Pennsylvania congressman who wouldn't support the restoration of Louisiana
to statehood unless it agreed to black male suffrage. The two men had
words. Then Field went after Kelley with a knife.

News of this incident quickly made its way around Washington.
Opponents of Louisiana admission jumped on it. Ashley's old friend
Salmon P. Chase, who was now chief justice of the United States,
claimed that the assault "was prompted by the very spirit which, if the

blacks are not secured the right of suffrage, will prompt the most cruel legislation against them, and probably produce a renewal of bloody civil strife." He urged Kelley to dig in and fight harder against Banks-Hahn regime. Kelley needed no prompting. He was more determined than ever to block Louisiana's return to statehood.[9]

Finally, on February 18, Ashley brought forth still another version of the bill. It called for the enfranchisement of all black men in all the states without loyal governments but recognized the restoration of Louisiana, Arkansas, and Tennessee—the three states that the Lincoln administration was pushing under the Ten Percent Plan. It, too, got hammered, this time mainly by Henry Dawes, a conservative Republican from western Massachusetts who had been a House member since 1857. Dawes first made sure everyone understood that he personally favored black suffrage. He then ripped into the notion that Congress had the power to require it of any state and came close to censuring Ashley for even making such a suggestion.[10]

The next day, Ashley again was on his feet. He was clearly angry. He claimed that it had been his "earnest desire to conciliate all gentlemen" on his side of the House, and for that purpose he had "consented to what might properly be called a compromise, in providing for the readmission or recognition of the new governments of Louisiana, Arkansas, and Tennessee" in order to secure what he thought was "of paramount importance—universal suffrage to liberated black men of the South." But what had been the results? Had he received "the cooperation of gentlemen who profess to entertain . . . practically the same opinions . . . in favor of securing universal suffrage to the colored men?" Obviously, he had not. As a result, he had concluded that "no bill providing for the reorganization of loyal State governments in the rebel States can pass this Congress."[11]

Ashley then withdrew his last proposal and brought forth still another one. And this time, he made no attempt to conciliate Henry Dawes and the other conservative members of his party. Instead, he eliminated the provisions that had pleased them and irritated his radical friends, including the ones that recognized the restoration of Louisiana, Arkansas, and Tennessee. He also required governments organized under the bill to guarantee the civil rights of all its citizens, regardless of race, and to restrict voting rights to white loyalists and black veterans.

Kelley was then immediately on his feet to amend the bill so that all black males were enfranchised. But others called for the restoration of Louisiana without black suffrage, and still others now agreed with Ashley that the House had reached an impasse. The debate became loud and nasty. Democrats and border-state Unionists then moved quickly. They called for tabling the bill, and with the support of twenty-one of the eighty-one Republicans, the tabling motion passed, ninety-one to sixty-four. The bill's tabling, in turn, meant that the Lincoln administration would be free to follow any Reconstruction policy it saw fit when Congress adjourned in March.[12]

But it didn't mean that the Louisiana delegation would be seated. On January 17, the Committee on Elections headed by Dawes had tried to get around the need for congressional recognition of the Banks-Hahn regime. Over the objections of two Republicans on the committee, it had voted to seat two of the five Louisiana delegates, Max F. Bonzano and the now notorious Alexander Field, on the grounds that the "power to restore a lost state government" rested solely with "'the people,' the original source of all political power in this country," and not with Congress. Then in February, the committee had voted to seat two of the three Arkansas delegates and still another from Louisiana.

But could these resolutions get through the House? No, they couldn't, and thus Dawes didn't bring them up for a vote. So, in the end, Field and his colleagues never became House members.[13]

While the House was busy trying to resolve the Louisiana question, so, too, was the Senate. When the senators convened in December, the Senate Judiciary Committee took charge of the matter. Back in June, the committee had opposed the seating of Arkansas senators. It now advocated the seating of Louisiana senators on the grounds that the Hahn government "fairly represents a majority of loyal voters of the state."[14]

But the committee faced stiff opposition. While most Republican senators were willing to go along, Charles Sumner of Massachusetts, Benjamin Wade of Ohio, Zachariah Chandler and Jacob Howard of Michigan, and B. Gratz Brown of Missouri were determined to kill the proposal. And they were unlikely to bend. Not only were they stubborn and relentless. They regarded Lincoln's Ten Percent Plan as an usurpation of congressional authority. They also regarded the Louisiana constitution as an abomination. It hadn't extended voting rights to black males. It thus had left the freedmen defenseless, totally at the

Charles Sumner, senator from Massachusetts. Prints and Photographs Division, Library of Congress (LC-USZ62-128709).

mercy of white Louisianans, the very people who had enslaved them. Accordingly, Sumner proposed that Congress not admit Louisiana until it rectified this problem, until it had a state constitution under which "all persons shall be equal before the law."[15]

Just as Sumner wanted to block Louisiana's return to statehood, he also wanted to make sure that Louisiana never had a hand in ratifying the Thirteenth Amendment. Here he differed from Ashley, who had been willing to let a rebel state participate in the ratification process if it had gained readmission to the Union and had representatives in Congress "before three fourths of the States now represented adopt the proposed amendment." Sumner insisted that such states be excluded and only the twenty-five Union states be allowed to vote. So, four days after Ashley got the amendment through the House, the Massachusetts senator introduced a resolution in the Senate that excluded Louisiana and all the other rebel states from the ratification process.

The participation of the eleven rebel states was not necessary, argued Sumner. They had lost their status as states when they seceded from the Union, and as a result they had to be accepted back into the Union by Congress before they had any right to participate. It was also absurd to allow "Rebels in arms to interpose a veto upon the National Government in one of its highest functions." And to allow them to participate would also be illogical, said Sumner, for they had no say in the debate that led to the amendment, and their vacant seats were not counted when Congress decided how many votes were needed to meet the two-thirds requirement. Congress therefore must be consistent and allow only those states that were part of the national government when the proposed amendment was passed to ratify it.[16]

While Sumner might have had logic on his side, he didn't have enough votes to get his resolution through the Senate. The Massachusetts senator couldn't even get the support of all his fellow radicals. Jacob Howard of Michigan, among others, wouldn't go along. He suggested that the resolution be dropped as it was not of "so much importance."[17] The normally relentless Sumner thus decided not to pursue the matter and let the resolution die on the table.

Yet, at the same time, Sumner, Howard, and their fellow radicals were able to stop the Judiciary Committee in its tracks. The chairman of the committee, Lyman Trumbull of Illinois, finally brought up the committee's proposal to seat the Louisiana senators in late February. For three days Trumbull tried to get it passed, even calling a late meeting on Saturday night. Hour after hour, the radicals blocked him, with one parliamentary motion after another, and succeeded in killing the bill.

So when Congress adjourned on March 3, the ratification question had yet to be resolved. While Louisiana had not been restored to statehood, the number of states needed for ratification had not been decided either. And until December, when Congress convened again, it would be in the hands of the Lincoln administration, which was now focused mainly on bringing the war to a close.

Five weeks passed. Then on April 9, Lee surrendered the Army of Northern Virginia to Grant. Two days later, an immense crowd gathered on the White House lawn, fired up, waiting to hear Lincoln speak. The president appealed to their better natures. He told them that it was time to be forgiving. At the same time, he rallied their support for the admission of Louisiana. He also suggested that Louisiana should grant voting rights to black veterans and to "the very intelligent" black residents.

And then, finally, Lincoln addressed the issue of ratification. Without mentioning Sumner by name, the president dismissed the Massachusetts senator's contention that only three-fourths of the Union states were needed for ratification. It was "a merely pernicious abstraction," said Lincoln, to question whether the rebel states were still in the Union and thus qualified to ratify the amendment. The fact was that a ratification by only three-fourths of the Union states "would be questionable," whereas a ratification by three-fourths of all the states "would be unquestioned and unquestionable." He also noted that Louisiana had already voted for ratification and, thus, to reject its vote meant the rejection of "one vote in favor of the proposed amendment."[18]

Among those listening to Lincoln's speech was John Wilkes Booth. The well-known Shakespearean actor had long been a vehement opponent of emancipation as well as an ardent supporter of the Confederacy, and for several months he had been planning to either kill or kidnap Lincoln. On hearing the president say that he now favored granting suffrage to some former slaves, Booth declared that it would be the last speech Lincoln would ever make.

Three days later, Booth made good on his promise. He slipped into Lincoln's box in Ford's Theatre and shot him in the back of the head. That shot did more than turn the reluctant emancipator into a martyr. It also handed the presidency over to a man utterly lacking in Lincoln's political judgment, Vice President Andrew Johnson.

Initially, James Ashley along with many of his fellow radicals had high hopes for Johnson. The fifty-seven-year-old Tennessee Unionist seemed to share their desire to punish the traitors who had brought on the war. He was the only Southern senator not to secede from the Union in 1861. He lived in east Tennessee, where slaves were few, and he had spent most of his political career battling the slave barons in his home state. He had also spent years pushing for a homestead act that would benefit poor farmers. And like Lincoln, he had humble origins, even more rock-bottom than Ashley's. Whereas Ashley's parents had

President Andrew Johnson. Brady-Handy Collection,
Library of Congress (LC-DIG-cwpbh-03751).

made sure that their children had learned to read the Bible at an early age, Johnson had grown up in a household where he didn't learn to read at all. His wife had taught him years later.

Surely, thought Ashley, here was a man of the people he could work with. Maybe the new president would even take a close look at Lincoln's Ten Percent Plan and rescind it. Maybe he would even join Ashley in making sure that the Southern states were restored to the Union in such a way that black freedom was truly meaningful. Maybe he would even embrace Ashley's call for "universal suffrage."

Never was Ashley more mistaken. As the country mourned, the new president adopted Lincoln's policy and turned to Secretary of State Seward for advice. Both men feared what the next Congress might do. It was certain to be more radical, more responsive to the pleadings of men like Ashley and Sumner, with the departure of thirty-four House

Democrats and the arrival of fifty-one additional House Republicans. At Seward's urging, Johnson thus decided to move quickly, restore the Southern states to the Union, and obtain the twenty-seven ratifications that the Lincoln administration had deemed necessary before the next Congress convened in December.

Like Lincoln, Johnson regarded the restoration of the Confederate states to the Union as mainly an executive function. He also accepted Lincoln's contention that the states were indestructible, that the states could not legally secede from the Union, and thus they still had all their constitutional rights. The rebellion had not been one of states, said Johnson. It had been one of individuals, and hence only individuals could be punished or pardoned. Accordingly, in late May, just a month after Lincoln's assassination, Johnson advanced his version of Reconstruction. He offered amnesty and restitution of property, except slaves, to the individuals who were responsible for the rebellion, proclaiming that ordinary rebels only had to take an oath of allegiance, while high-ranking Confederate officials and those owning taxable property worth more than $20,000 had to apply to him for individual pardons. Within weeks, thousands of Confederate leaders, including 845 from South Carolina, sought and received pardons.

At the same time, Johnson found traditional leaders in the Old South to do his bidding. He recognized the Lincoln-sponsored governments in Louisiana, Arkansas, and Tennessee, and the loyalist government that had administered part of Virginia under the Union army as the official governments of those four states. And in the seven other Confederate states, he appointed provisional governors, generally men who had opposed secession, and directed them to hold elections in which only loyal white men who had received amnesty could participate. These men, in turn, were to choose from their ranks delegates to statewide conventions that would nullify the state's article of secession, frame a new state constitution, abolish slavery, repudiate the state war debt, and ratify the Thirteenth Amendment. The understanding was that all of this had to be accomplished for a rebel state to gain readmission to Congress and that time was of the essence.

Johnson and Seward thus made an all-out effort to get ratifications from the eleven Confederate states that Congress had yet to recognize. By December 1, three days before the new Congress convened, they had ratifications from five rebel states as well as nineteen Union states. But they had only twenty-four in total, three short of the number they needed. Then in rapid succession, Alabama, North Carolina, and Georgia ratified the amendment, and by December 6, two days after Congress assembled, the magic number of twenty-seven was reached.

Inertia then took over. Congressional Republicans met in caucus and took stock of what had happened since they adjourned in March. Apart from the ratifications, the news was alarming. Black Codes had been established in the rebel states that severely limited the freedom of former slaves. Former rebel leaders, including the vice president of the Confederacy, had been elected to Congress. The caucus thus decided to block the readmission of the Confederate states. But nothing was done to stop the eight Confederate ratifications from being counted, and on December 18 Seward formally announced that the Thirteenth Amendment was now the law of the land.

Did it make any difference that Georgia and the other Confederate states were involved in ratification? In all probability, yes. For at issue during ratification was the second section of the amendment, the one that read: "Congress shall have power to enforce this article by appropriate legislation." In all the earlier amendments to the Constitution, the powers of Congress and the federal government had been curtailed. But in this amendment, for the first time, they had been enlarged.

Having an enforcement section was undoubtedly crucial. The prohibitory language in the amendment came from the Northwest Ordinance of 1787. On paper that ordinance had barred slavery north of the Ohio River. But it had lacked an enforcement mechanism. It didn't give Congress or any government official the power to enforce the prohibition. And even though nearly every US history textbook credits it with ending slavery north of the Ohio, it had failed to do so. On learning about the ordinance, many slaveholders had packed up their belongings and their slaves and left the region. But others had stayed. And those who stayed quickly learned that the ordinance had no teeth. It was just a mandate, just a bunch of nice-sounding words. Congress couldn't enforce it. Nor could the territorial governors. And most of the governors didn't even try. In fact, two of the governors—William Henry Harrison and Ninian Edwards—were themselves slave owners.

The only thing that probably kept proslavery men like Ninian Edwards from completely overturning the spirit of the Northwest

Ordinance were the thousands of white settlers who hated both slavery and blacks. These men and women wanted to keep all blacks, free and slave, out of the territory, and they generally got their way. To satisfy them, Illinois even passed a law in 1813 that promised any black man who entered the territory thirty-nine lashes, repeated every fifteen days, until he left. The next year, the legislature modified the law so that the owners of salt works and mills could hire Southern slaves on a yearly basis. But over the long haul, the sentiments of the white majority prevailed.

Nonetheless, when the US census takers did their count in 1820, they found 917 slaves in the newly created free state of Illinois and 190 in the free state of Indiana. And as late as 1840, they still found 331 slaves in Illinois. Indeed, it wasn't until 1848 that Illinois fully complied with the Northwest Ordinance.[19]

So, if slave owners could get around the law in a place like Illinois, where slavery was always of secondary importance, what might they do in South Carolina or Mississippi, where over half the labor force was black? Obviously, a simple mandate outlawing slavery, like the one appearing in the 1787 Ordinance, just wouldn't do. Enforcement was crucial. And hence Congress had written an enforcement section into the Thirteenth Amendment.

But what did the words mean? What could Congress do? And what could it not do? Was the "power to enforce" broad? Or limited? And how should the phrase "appropriate legislation" be interpreted? Should Congress just make sure that the former slaves were not bought and sold, not kept in chains, not forced to work against their will? Or should it also insist that the former slaves have the same rights as other free persons?

These questions didn't receive much attention when the amendment was going through Congress. But during ratification, they became the central questions. And in this battle, the Southern ratifying conventions made a difference.

In the Union states, the ratification process essentially mirrored the 1864 election. In the states that Lincoln and his party had won easily, the state legislatures endorsed the amendment by huge margins. In states that Republicans barely won, the vote was closer. And in the three states that Lincoln lost—Delaware, Kentucky, and New Jersey—the legislatures rejected the amendment.

Delaware set the tone of much that followed. The general assembly took up the amendment on February 8, a week and a day after it was approved by Congress. Leading the attack against it was Gove Saulsbury, the older brother of Willard Saulsbury, the often tipsy US senator who had vehemently denounced the amendment's women supporters back in April 1864. The Saulsbury brothers played the race card every chance they got and never missed an opportunity to denounce everything the Republican Party stood for. And, as the president of the upper house, the sixty-year-old Gove Saulsbury was in an ideal position to vent their rage.

The older Saulsbury didn't even pretend that slavery had any economic significance in Delaware. The number of slaves in the state had dwindled to about twelve hundred, and he readily acknowledged that fact. Yet he still insisted that the abolition of slavery would be disastrous. At stake, he said, was white supremacy. Blacks had to be kept in their place, and nothing did it better than slavery. As for the enforcement provision in the Thirteenth Amendment, it made matters worse. It opened the door for all sorts of Black Republican chicanery. Men like Ashley and Sumner, he predicted, would next "demand for the negro the right of suffrage, and seek to place him, politically at least, upon an equal with the white man." Every Democrat in the legislature agreed with Saulsbury. One after another repeated his lament. The upper house then voted against the amendment, six to three, the lower house, twelve to seven.

Three weeks later, the governor of Delaware, William Cannon, died. As senate president, Saulsbury automatically took his place, was elected on his own right the next year, and held the office until 1871. Under his leadership, Democrats in the legislature did everything in their power to frustrate the implementation of the amendment and, at one point, even called for laws to sell black convicts back into slavery. They failed in this effort, but they were so successful in lambasting the amendment that few dared to bring it up for a second vote. It wasn't ratified by the state until thirty-five years later, on February 12, 1901.[20]

Sixteen days after Delaware initially rejected the amendment, it came up for consideration in Kentucky. Again, much of the debate centered on the enforcement clause. All the naysayers agreed that it "opened the door" for the federal government and especially the Black Republicans to interfere in the "domestic matters" of the state. It was a dangerous clause, said one legislator after another. In short order, men like Ashley and Sumner would be imposing their will on the state, insisting that blacks should have the same rights as whites—including the right to marry, to bear arms, to testify in court, to sit on juries, to vote, and even to hold office.

Yet, while the Kentucky debate mirrored that of Delaware in this respect, it differed in another. That was initially because of Governor Bramlette. When he met with the legislature, he repeated much of what he said in the past. He denounced Union tactics, and he still claimed that Kentucky had been badly treated by the Lincoln administration and hoodwinked into believing that the war was a war to preserve the Union and not a war to end slavery. But he no longer held out any hope of preserving the institution of slavery in Kentucky. He now believed it was "irrevocably doomed." So he urged passage of the Thirteenth Amendment but with a hitch. He wanted the ratification to count only after Congress paid the state $34 million for its slaves— their assessed value in 1864.

The legislature thus spent much of its time debating the governor's call for compensation. House leaders said they wouldn't be bribed into giving up their principles. They rejected the amendment outright, fifty-seven to twenty-nine, and the governor's proposal, sixty-three to twenty-one. In the state senate, the governor's proposal got a better hearing. John F. Fisk recommended ratification with compensation. This was rejected, twenty-two to eleven. Then the former governor, James F. Robinson, put forth another compensation plan. He wanted $2 million more than Bramlette. He wanted Congress also to pay for the removal of every free black in Kentucky. This, too, was rejected, twenty-four to nine. Finally, the Senate joined the House in rejecting the amendment outright, twenty-one to thirteen.[21]

Nine months later, after learning that Johnson and Seward had the twenty-seven states they needed, Bramlette again called on the legislature to ratify the amendment. It was time, he said, for Kentucky to join the rest of the country in supporting emancipation. He insisted that the fears that Kentuckians had about the second section of the Thirteenth Amendment were overblown. It didn't "open the door" for Congress to run roughshod over white Kentuckians. Members of the Union Party then met in caucus and issued a public address. It de-

234 * CHAPTER SEVEN

clared that Congress had no power "under the Second Section of the Thirteenth Amendment . . . to pass any law granting the right of suffrage in the States to persons of African descent."[22]

With this understanding, a resolution was introduced in both houses to ratify the amendment. But it was a lost cause. The legislators were defiant. They refused to budge, insisting that the earlier vote was final. They were still defiant the next year, and the year after that. And that remained the case in Kentucky for the next 110 years, until March 18, 1976, when a motion to ratify finally passed.

Five days after Kentucky initially rejected the amendment, it came up for consideration in New Jersey. The state had been a Democratic stronghold throughout the war. Democrats had consistently won three of the state's five congressional districts, and in 1862, a good year for the party throughout the nation, they had won four out of five. McClellan had whipped Lincoln in 1864 by roughly six percentage points.

The state legislature not only had a majority of Democrats, but it also had more than its share of Peace Democrats. In 1863, they had composed one-third of the assembly, and nearly half of the Democratic assemblymen. They had enough strength that year to ram through resolutions that denounced the war as futile and called for the appointment of peace commissioners. By 1865, their numbers had dwindled, but they were still a powerful force.

The New Jersey party was also vehemently hostile to emancipation. In 1862, the state Democratic convention had condemned the Emancipation Proclamation, and the party had run against it in every congressional district. That year, the party had also purged from its ranks the only New Jersey Democrat who had shown any signs of supporting black freedom. That was George T. Cobb, who had voted for compensated emancipation in the District of Columbia. He was replaced by Andrew Rogers, who like the Saulsbury brothers in neighboring Delaware had a long history of relentlessly heaping abuse on the state's black population.

So on March 1, when the Thirteenth Amendment came before the New Jersey House, the thirty Democratic members jumped on it. And like Democrats in other states, they made much of the enforcement clause, pointing out again and again that it "opened the door" for the Black Republicans in Washington to try to impose on the nation's white majority "negro equality" and the much dreaded "amalgamation" of the races. And in defense of their position, they insisted that God Himself had decreed that the black man should be subservient to the white man. All of this had been heard before, on many different occasions.

Up against the thirty House Democrats were thirty Republicans. They were anything but the champions of the black man. They gave lip service to all the old arguments about "government being made for white men by white men." They were just less vociferous about it. At the same time, however, they defended the amendment and lambasted the Democrats for protecting the interests of the slaveholding "traitors" who had brought on the war and cost the state thousands of its best men. They also dismissed as trivial Democratic complaints about the enforcement provision. In the end, however, they came out on the losing side. After a long and nasty debate, the assembly rejected the amendment by a tie vote, thirty to thirty. The vote was strictly along party lines, with all the Republicans voting aye and all the Democrats voting no. Two weeks later, the state senate also rejected the amendment, again in a strict party vote, twelve to eight.

The rejection lasted but one year. When the next legislature convened, the Republicans were in the majority. They now outnumbered Democrats in the assembly by a margin to thirty-six to twenty-four, and in the senate by eleven to ten. And on January 17, 1866, when ratification came again before the assembly, it passed forty-two to ten. Six Democrats now voted aye, and eight absented themselves. And on January 23, the senate also ratified, thirteen to eight, with two Democrats joining the Republicans in voting aye.[23]

The initial rejections of Delaware, Kentucky, and New Jersey were significant. Not only did they reflect the sentiments of most Northern Democrats and border-state Unionists. They also reflected the true sentiments of the white majority farther south. Had the Deep South ratifying conventions been free to do whatever they pleased, no one had any doubt what they would have done. They, too, would have sent in rejection notices. But unlike Delaware, Kentucky, and New Jersey, they couldn't afford to thumb their noses at the Republican majority in Congress. They were trying to get back into Congress. They were also hoping to get Union troops, especially black troops, out of their states and to get help in repairing the devastation that the war had brought.

Governor Benjamin Franklin Perry. Reprinted from B. F. Perry,
Reminiscences of Public Men (Philadelphia: J.D. Avil & Co., 1883).

Louisiana was the first of the Deep South states to ratify the amendment. It did so on February 17 under the auspices of the Lincoln-sponsored government. Then came a long lull. Eight months passed. Then on November 13, word arrived in Washington that South Carolina, long believed to be the most radical of the Confederate states, had also ratified the amendment. That brought a sigh of relief to Johnson and Seward. For they had worked hard and gone the extra mile to bring it about.

To oversee the operation, they had turned to Benjamin Franklin Perry. At age fifty-nine, Perry was an impressive figure, tall and ramrod straight, with a prominent chin and gold-framed eye glasses. He had been a slaveholder up until the time Sherman's army conquered South Carolina. He had also been a strong supporter of the institution of slavery, never doubting its morality and vehemently opposing its abolition.

But like Johnson, the Tennessee Unionist, Perry had bucked the dominant voices in his home state in 1860. He had been the loudest voice against secession in South Carolina, the proverbial sore thumb in a state that had voted to secede by a margin of 169 to zero. Yet when the war came, he declared: "You are all now going to the Devil and I will go with you." He then helped raise troops, especially among the mountain people in the Greenville District, where he had a large following. He also served as a colonel in the local home defense unit and as a district judge of the Confederate States Court, and thus maintained a close working relationship with many of the state's leading secessionists.[24]

So on June 30, 1865, Johnson appointed Benjamin Franklin Perry provisional governor of South Carolina. The task that Johnson gave Perry was to get all those who had received amnesty together and bring South Carolina back into the Union. Accordingly, Perry called for an election of delegates on September 4. Nine days later, 101 of the 115 delegates assembled at the Baptist Church in Columbia, the same church where twelve of them had first taken up the Ordinance of Secession in 1860. Back then, Columbia had been a beautiful little city with broad streets, magnificent trees, and flowers everywhere. Now it was "a mass of blackened chimneys and crumbling walls," a grim reminder that Sherman and his men had been there.

None of the delegates, noted one observer, would ever get over the devastation or forgive "the Yankees" for what had happened. But only a few of them were still fire-eaters, anxious to denounce the "fanatics of the North" at every turn. Most were still rebels but "subdued Rebels" and, in some cases, "conquered Rebels." And nearly all had accepted the admonition of their former governor, Francis Pickens, that those South Carolinians who wanted "to vapor or strut or brag or bluster or threat or swagger" were just wasting everyone's time.[25]

Two days after the delegates assembled, Perry got them to nullify the Ordinance of Secession. The vote was 105 to three. Then came the ticklish matter of abolishing slavery, which few of them wanted to do. But as T. N. Dawkins explained to the resistant, they had no choice if they wanted to ever get rid of "military rule." They could, however, shift the blame. Accordingly, he proposed language that would indicate that emancipation had been forced on them by the North. The delegates then spent many hours debating and voting down various ways to make that point. Finally, by a vote of fifty-nine to forty-three, they agreed on the following: "The slaves in South Carolina having been emancipated by the action of the United States authorities, neither slavery nor involuntary servitude, except as a punishment for crime whereof the party shall have been duly convicted, shall ever be re-established in this State." Then, by a 98–8 vote, they agreed to insert this language into the new state constitution.[26]

Perry thus completed two of the tasks that Johnson had given him. He failed, however, to get the convention to repudiate the state war debt and to ratify the Thirteenth Amendment. Then on October 18, he held an election for the state legislature under the new constitution. A week later, the legislature met. In his opening message, he didn't even bother to mention the need to ratify the amendment. He didn't think it was important. Hadn't the convention abolished slavery? What else was needed? He was far more concerned with the presence of black troops in South Carolina and wanted the legislature to know how hard he was working to get Johnson and Seward to remove them.[27]

Three days later, on October 28, President Johnson telegraphed Perry. "I hope your legislature," wrote Johnson, "will have no hesitancy in adopting the amendment. . . . It will set an example which will no doubt be followed by the other states. . . . I trust in God that it will be done." Three days passed, and there was still no sign that Perry had got the message. So Johnson sent another telegram, this one more pointed. "If the action of the Convention was in good faith," wrote Johnson, "why hesitate in making it part of the constitution. . . . I trust in God that the restoration of the Union will not be defeated and all that has so far been well done thrown away."[28]

Finally, on November 4, Perry responded. He telegraphed Johnson that the state war debt was trivial and that South Carolina had abolished slavery in good faith and never intended or wished to restore it. He then indicated that there were two problems with the Thirteenth Amendment. One was that the legislature had never received official notice of its existence. And the other was the second section of the amendment. It could be "construed to give Congress power of local legislation over the negroes, and white men." His state would never consent to that.[29]

Johnson then turned the matter over to Seward. And on November 6, Seward telegraphed Perry. He first made it clear that the president was unhappy with Perry. He then told Perry that there was no constitutional requirement that the state be officially notified, but he would do it anyway. Finally, Seward addressed the controversy over the second section. What did "appropriate legislation" mean? Did the wording of the second section grossly expand the power of Congress? No, said Seward: "The objection which you mention to the last clause of the constitutional amendment is regarded as querulous & unreasonable, because that clause is really restraining in its effects, instead of enlarging the power of Congress."[30]

Perry then passed on this construction of the amendment to the legislature and told them to incorporate it into the ratification. That they did. On November 13, after much wrangling, both houses ratified the amendment with this proviso: "Resolved, That any attempt by Congress towards legislating upon the political status of former slaves, or their civil relations, would be contrary to the Constitution of the United States, as it now is, or as it would be altered by the proposed amendment, in conflict with the policy of the President declared in his Amnesty Proclamation, and with the restoration of that harmony upon which depends the vital interests of the American Union."[31]

So on November 13, after much work, Johnson and Seward finally got the ratification of South Carolina, a state where over half the population had once been in bondage. And as knowledge of Seward's interpretation of the amendment became widespread, other Confederate states soon fell into line. Two weeks later, Alabama sent in its ratification with the "understanding that it does not confer upon Congress the power to Legislate upon the political status of Freedmen in this State." Then two days later, Johnson and Seward received word that North Carolina had ratified and, two days after that, Georgia, giving them the twenty-seven states they needed.[32]

Mississippi, however, held out. Despite Johnson and Seward's best efforts, they couldn't get ratification through Mississippi. On November 1, Johnson sent virtually the same telegram to William L. Sharkey, the provisional governor of Mississippi, that he had sent to Perry. It did no good. Although the state had agreed to abolish slavery, it wouldn't budge when it came to ratification. On December 5, the Mississippi House rejected the amendment by a vote of forty-five to twenty-five. The problem, said one legislator after another, was the enforcement clause. It would "open the door for congressional legislation concerning the State's domestic affairs." It might even "admit federal legislation in respect to persons, denizens and inhabitants of the State." It was too dangerous. The rejection lasted for the next 130 years, until March 16, 1995.[33]

While Mississippi and the other Southern states were busy coming to terms with the Johnson administration, most of the nation's Northern lawmakers were miles away from Washington. In Ashley's case, he spent most of the long congressional break between March and December in the Far West, traveling along dusty roads in stage coaches, taking in the sights, giving speeches in San Francisco and Sacramento, and calling for the enfranchisement of all loyal Southerners, black as well as white. Yet when he returned to Washington in late November 1865, he knew that trouble lay ahead.

The news from back East had upset him. Yes, Johnson and Seward had gotten state endorsements for his pride and joy, the first change to the US constitution since 1804. But it had been done with the understanding that the power of the Congress to enforce the change was limited. And Andrew Johnson, to Ashley's dismay, had turned out to be a fraud. All the new president's remarks about the infamy of treason and the need to punish traitors had been deceiving. When it came time to act, Johnson had proved that he was no friend of black rights or the Republican Party. He had been too soft on the former Confederates and too eager to forgive and forget. Would he have made provisional governors out of radical abolitionists, men like William Lloyd Garrison and Wendell Phillips, if they had brought on the war? No, he definitely would not. Yet he had turned the South over to a bunch of "traitors." And now waiting to be seated in Congress were six Confederate cabinet officers, four Confederate generals, and the vice president of the Confederacy.

Equally upsetting was the news from the South. Race riots were now commonplace, and while the causes were disputed the victims were almost always blacks and their white supporters. Also, most of the states that Johnson had restored to the Union had enacted Black Codes to regulate the conduct of former slaves. In some states, the codes forbid blacks from assembling, possessing firearms or alcohol, or pursuing a skilled trade. In others, black children could be apprenticed to white masters without their parents' consent, black vagrants could be bound out, and petty criminals could be sold at auction. The South Carolina code allowed blacks to work only as farm laborers or domestic servants, while the Mississippi code prohibited blacks from owning or leasing farm land.

To Ashley and many like him, such legislation amounted to the restoration of slavery in all but name. It was abominable. It meant that the war had accomplished nothing. And it was mainly Johnson's fault. The man had encouraged Southern intransigence, and now it had to be stopped in its tracks.

Accordingly, the Republicans in Congress refused to admit the representatives of the new Southern state governments. They also extended the life of the Freedmen's Bureau, a wartime organization to supervise and aid ex-slaves. And, to prove the Thirteenth Amendment had real teeth, they passed a Civil Rights Act that recognized the citizenship of all blacks born in the United States, conferred on them the same civil rights as white citizens, and authorized US attorneys to bring enforcement suits in federal courts. Republicans thus demanded that the federal government, not the individual states, assume responsibility for the civil rights of the freedmen.

Johnson, in turn, became even more obstinate. In the spring of 1866, he vetoed both the Freedmen's Bureau Bill and the Civil Rights Act, arguing that such measures were unconstitutional and that blacks were not ready for full citizenship. Both measures were repassed over his veto, and together those resolutions made it clear that the federal government—at least for short haul—was determined to protect the former slaves. This change was then spelled out in the Fourteenth Amendment. Submitted to Congress in June 1866, this amendment recognized the citizenship of anyone born in the United States and prohibited the states from infringing on the liberties of any citizen, black or white, and from denying to any citizen "the equal protection of the laws."

This time, Johnson urged the Southern states not to ratify. Only his home state, Tennessee, ignored his wishes. The other ten followed his advice. Congress, in turn, then moved on to still more drastic action, dividing the "sinful ten" into five military districts, wiping out their existing state governments, and calling for new constitutional conventions elected by the whole adult male population, black as well as white, but excluding former Confederate leaders. Then when the new constitution had the approval of the state's new electorate and the Congress, and when the state ratified the Fourteenth Amendment, its representatives might be admitted to Congress. Added to the mix was the Fifteenth Amendment, forbidding suffrage discrimination on the basis of "race, color, or previous condition of servitude."

All of these actions were vehemently opposed by Johnson. Seward called on him to compromise. So did others. But he became even more obstinate by the day and thus turned the entire Republican Party against him and won the support of Democrats. In the 1866 congressional elections, he went out on the road, campaigned hard for Democrats, and denounced his Republican opponents as traitors. Along with Thaddeus Stevens and Charles Sumner, he singled out Ashley for special abuse. It did no good. Ashley won his seat handily. So did most radical Republicans. And in response, Ashley, among others, began looking for ways to render Johnson powerless. They settled on impeachment.

In this effort, Ashley was a zealot. He was so eager to have Johnson thrown out of office, and to protect the interests of the former slaves, that he got a new nickname of the Great Impeacher. On January 7, 1867, just three months after his reelection, Ashley introduced an impeachment resolution. He accused the president of usurping the legislative power of Congress, of misusing his power of appointment, pardon, and veto, of illegally disposing of public property, and of corruptly interfering in elections.[34]

Then, in the months that followed, Ashley made all sorts of allegations, some true, some false, some pure fantasy. He accused Johnson of dealing with thieves and pardon brokers, of being drunk at Lincoln's second inaugural, and of being drunk on the campaign trail. He also implied that Johnson was involved in Lincoln's assassination and spent weeks trying to find evidence to prove it. At one point, he even said that two earlier presidents—William Henry Harrison and Zachary Taylor—had been killed by poison to get them out of the way.[35] But his main concern was that as long as Johnson was in the White House, there would be no protection for loyal black men of the South. The president wouldn't enforce the laws of the land, and the former slaves thus would be abandoned to the evil machinations of their former masters.

Ashley's charges electrified the House. But many doubted that he had the evidence to convict the president of "treason, bribery, high crimes or misdemeanors," and some undoubtedly thought he had gone off the deep end. Thus, after months of hard work, the resolution failed, fifty-seven to 108.

The radicals in Congress then settled on another dubious charge: that Johnson had violated the Tenure of Office Act of 1867 in removing Secretary of War Stanton without congressional sanction. On February 24, 1868, the House endorsed this resolution, 126 to forty-seven, and thus brought the president up on charges before the Senate. Finally, after an eleven-week trial in the Senate, thirty-five senators voted on May 16 to convict Johnson. But to the disgust of Ashley and other radicals, seven Republican senators joined twelve Democratic senators in voting for acquittal, and thus the Senate was one vote shy of the two-thirds majority required for conviction.

That fall, the impeachment fiasco cost Ashley dearly. He was again up for reelection. Given his radicalism, he had always had to work hard to keep his House seat. On black suffrage, moreover, he was out of step with most of his constituents, who in 1867 had opposed enfranchising black Ohioans by a 965-vote margin. And now on impeachment, even some of his old supporters thought he had gone too far. The Johnson administration had accused him of manufacturing evidence. Was that true? Had he tried to bribe men into saying that Johnson had a hand in Lincoln's assassination? And what about his statement that two earlier presidents had been killed by poison? Did he really believe that? Viewing him as a political liability, the Ohio Republican Party rejected his cries for help. He lost by 932 votes out of over thirty thousand cast.

Ashley's political career went downhill from there. Republicans in Congress pressured incoming president Ulysses S. Grant into appointing him territorial governor of Montana. The defeated congressman then set off for Montana in July 1869 with the hopes of turning the Big Sky Country into a Republican stronghold and having the pleasure of naming various places in the territory after some of the heroes of the antislavery movement, such as John Greenleaf Whittier, William Lloyd Garrison, Wendell Phillips, and Charles Sumner.[36]

To his dismay, Ashley found that the territorial legislature was loaded with Democrats, particularly Southern Democrats, who wanted nothing to do with him or his goals. He was thus constantly on the defensive and had to keep assuring his detractors that he was no amalgamationist even though he supported black citizenship and black male suffrage. He even told one Helena audience that he was an enemy of

amalgamation and thought that it would be a mistake for them to promote the immigration of anyone "with whom they cannot properly
intermarry." At the same time, however, he irritated many of Montana's leading citizens by opposing the importation of Chinese coolie
labor, likening it to slavery and denouncing it as a "pernicious crime"
that would drive down the wages of other American workers, black
and white, and benefit only "capitalists and monopolists." [37]

Never welcome in Montana, Ashley soon lost what little support
he had in the Grant administration and was sacked in December 1869.
Returning to Ohio, he became a businessman and the owner of a railroad. But as a politician, he was now just a voice from the past.

As Ashley lost political clout, so, too, did the enforcement section of
the Thirteenth Amendment. For a few years after the war, there was
some hope that the amendment might give free blacks the same free-
doms white men and women enjoyed. That, to be sure, had never been
the case before the war. Nearly every state, North and South, had set
limits on what free blacks could do. One state after another had barred
them from testifying against whites in court, sitting on juries, voting,
holding office, bearing arms, and being in the militia.

Did the Thirteenth Amendment change that? In fashioning the Civil
Rights Act of 1866, Lyman Trumbull, the chairman of Senate Judiciary Committee, clearly said yes. The amendment not only outlawed
slavery, said Trumbull, but it also outlawed the "badges of slavery," and
thus Congress had the right to nullify "all provisions of State or local
law" that infringed on a person's right to movement, right to property,
right to make contracts, right to sue, and right to give testimony.[38]

For a short while, this was more than just talk. Laws forbidding
blacks from testifying against whites, for example, had once been
the rule in five free states as well as in the slave states. Soon after the
war, such restrictions were repealed in one state after another. Moving in the same direction were several state courts. In 1868 the Texas
Supreme Court held that the old Texas law prohibiting black testimony against whites was void and that blacks now had the equal right
to testify. In 1869 the Arkansas Supreme Court declared unconstitutional the old Arkansas state law forbidding blacks to testify against
whites. That same year, the California Supreme Court also declared
unconstitutional the California law that prohibited nonwhites from
testifying against whites.[39]

Several states, however, still clung to their old ways. The most notable was Kentucky. In June 1867, just fourteen months after the Civil Rights Act of 1866 was passed, the Kentucky Supreme Court reversed a white man's larceny conviction on the grounds that it was based on the testimony of a black witness. The court held that the Civil Rights Act of 1866 was unconstitutional, that the Congress had overstepped its authority in granting blacks the right to testify against whites, that it had intruded on state sovereignty, and that the Thirteenth Amendment did nothing more than free slaves and gave them no additional civil or political rights. The decision was unanimous.[40]

In making this decision, moreover, the Kentucky court blatantly ignored a ruling handed down the previous year by US Supreme Court Justice Noah Swayne. A devout Quaker who had fled Virginia some forty years earlier to get away from slavery, Swayne was Lincoln's first appointment to the Supreme Court. His circuit included Kentucky, and before him had come a case involving several white men who had burglarized the house of a black woman, Nancy Talbot. The burglars obviously thought they could get away with it because she couldn't testify against them in a Kentucky court. But, to their surprise, a federal prosecutor under the Civil Rights Act brought charges against them in a federal court and got a conviction on the basis of her testimony. They, in turn, appealed on the grounds that her testimony should have been prohibited. In rejecting their argument, Swayne held that the Civil Rights Act was constitutional and that "the spirit" of the Thirteenth Amendment clearly gave Nancy Talbot the right to testify.[41]

Justice Swayne's reasoning, however, didn't have lasting impact. Five years later, all but one of his fellow justices on the US Supreme Court rejected his position in another case. The case involved two white Kentuckians, John Blyew and George Kennard, who in August 1868 had hacked to death four members of a black family with an ax. One victim, seventeen-year-old Richard Foster, didn't die immediately. Although a bloody mess, he crawled two hundred yards to a neighbor's house, identified the two killers under oath, and then died two days later from his wounds. Corroborating his statement was that of his thirteen-year-old sister Laura, who had witnessed the attack from her hiding place in a trundle bed. Investigators also found the murder weapon and a bloody trail of footprints leading to Blyew's mother's house. Determined to get a conviction, federal authorities weren't about to let Blyew and Kennard be tried in a Kentucky court. So, with much fanfare, they had the trial removed under the Civil Rights Act to a federal court where Richard's dying words and Laura's testimony would be admissible. The federal court found both men guilty and sentenced them to death by hanging.

The behavior of the federal officials, in turn, infuriated many Kentucky Democrats. In response, Governor John W. Stevenson got the state legislature in January 1869 to finance an appeal and to hire as legal counsel Jeremiah S. Black, the former attorney general of the United States under President Buchanan. Now a Pennsylvania lawyer, Black's hatred of blacks and their white supporters was legendary. Before the war, he had repeatedly denounced the antislavery movement. He had also blamed abolitionists for the Senate's refusal to confirm his nomination to the US Supreme Court. After the war, he had served as an adviser to Andrew Johnson, drafted Johnson's veto of the Reconstruction Act of 1867, and represented Johnson briefly in his impeachment trial. Since then, Black had devoted his legal talent to defeating the new federal civil rights law in the courts.[42]

On appeal, Black and his cocounsel argued that in "a proceeding by the State against white men" for the crime of murder, only those directly involved in the proceeding—namely, the state and the accused— could request removal to a federal court. And since they didn't, the convictions must be reversed. In April 1872, the US Supreme Court, in its wisdom, agreed. To Swayne's chagrin, the majority held that the Kentucky court was the sole arbiter even though it barred black testimony. The decision had far-reaching repercussions. It both made a mockery of Congress's intentions in the Civil Rights Act and made it much easier for members of the Ku Klux Klan and other white supremacist groups to get away with murder and mayhem.[43]

A year later, in the famous Slaughterhouse cases, the Supreme Court further emasculated the Thirteenth Amendment. The case involved some white butchers who had lost work because the Louisiana legislature allegedly had been bribed into granting a monopoly to a single slaughterhouse company in the New Orleans area. The butchers sued on the grounds that the state had violated both the Thirteenth and Fourteenth Amendments in excluding them from lawful work. The lawyers for the state insisted that bribes had nothing to do with the state's decision. They maintained, instead, that the state had granted the monopoly to a single slaughterhouse company as a police measure,

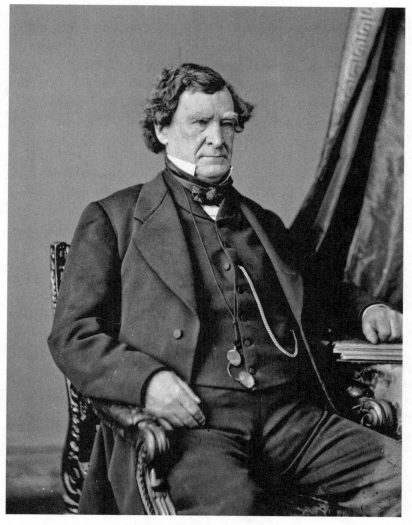

Jeremiah S. Black. Brady-Handy Collection,
Library of Congress (LC-DIG-cwpbh-00583).

mainly to protect the public from renegade butchers who were dump-
ing carcasses and other trash into the Mississippi River.

To make that argument before the Supreme Court, the state of
Louisiana followed the lead of Kentucky and turned to Jeremiah S.
Black, now widely regarded as the most successful legal opponent of
the two amendments. In a five-to-four decision, the court sided with
the state. Disregarding the bribery charges, it held to a narrow in-

terpretation of the Fourteenth Amendment, which had become the centerpiece in the dispute, and ruled that it did not restrict the police powers of a state.

As for the Thirteenth Amendment, the Court dismissed it as irrelevant. Writing for the majority, Justice Samuel F. Miller ignored what was said at the time of the amendment's creation, especially by its Republican sponsors, like James Ashley who had insisted that the amendment's prohibition of "involuntary servitude" should be broadly construed to protect the rights of all workers, white as well as black. Instead, Miller claimed that Congress had never intended the amendment to pertain to white men like the butchers, that its "obvious purpose" was to abolish slavery and guarantee the freedom of the "slave race," and that the word "servitude" in the phrase "involuntary servitude" was obviously intended to apply only to slave-like conditions. Hence, in dashing the hopes of the butchers, he also made it clear that the powers of Congress were narrow, that the amendment had empowered Congress to prohibit chattel slavery and perhaps a few forms of peonage but nothing else.[44]

By this time, Ashley's Republican colleagues were also in deep trouble. The nation's economy tanked in 1873, and in the South the tactics of the Ku Klux Klan and other white terrorists succeeded in keeping many black voters and a dwindling number of white Republicans away from the polls. Thus, in the 1874 congressional election, Republicans lost control of the House. But before they turned the chamber over to Democrats, who vowed to end Reconstruction and put black men and women "back in their proper place," some of Ashley's fellow radicals decided to make a last-ditch effort in behalf of black freedom.

The result was the Civil Rights Act of 1875. The new law declared "that all persons within the jurisdiction of the United States shall be entitled to the full and equal enjoyment of the accommodations" in restaurants, theaters, hotels, and railroads. But before its final passage, Congress eliminated its federal enforcement provisions and turned the enforcement burden over to individual litigants. Nonetheless, the new law wasn't completely toothless. A few blacks had the money as well as the fortitude to pursue their rights in courts, and by 1883 they had generated a host of lawsuits. They won many of them, and that led to a barrage of appeals.

The justices decided to hear five of them—one case each from California, Kansas, Missouri, Tennessee, and New York—and bundled the five together under the caption "Civil Rights Cases." At issue was whether an inn or hotel could refuse to serve a black man, whether Maguire's Theater in San Francisco could exclude a black patron from its dress circle, whether the Grand Opera House in New York could stop a black ticket holder from entering, and whether a conductor on the Memphis & Charleston Railroad could keep a black woman with a first-class ticket out of the ladies car. Although there were five defendants, only one bothered to have a lawyer appear before the court and present an argument. It didn't matter. All five defendants came out on the winning side.

Of the nine justices, only one had any sympathy for the black litigants. That justice, ironically, was John Marshall Harlan. Back in 1865 Harlan had been one of the many slaveholding Kentuckians who had vehemently opposed the ratification of the Thirteenth Amendment on the grounds that it violated the property rights of slave owners. But the outrages committed by the Ku Klux Klan and other racist thugs had subsequently driven him into the camp of his former antislavery adversaries. And while he never regarded black men and women to be socially his equals, he became strongly committed to treating them as his equals under the law.

Thus in 1883, Harlan tried to convince his brethren on the court that the Thirteenth Amendment should guarantee black Americans all of the "civil rights as belong to freemen of other races." He also contended that the United States must not enter into "an era of constitutional law, when the rights of freedom and American citizenship cannot receive from the nation that efficient protection which heretofore was unhesitatingly accorded to slavery." But Harlan's was a lonely voice. He couldn't get the support of a single one of his fellow justices. None of them wanted any part of his notion that the Supreme Court should protect black freedom and black citizenship to the degree that it had once protected slavery.[45]

All sided, instead, with Justice Joseph P. Bradley, who wrote the majority opinion. A former New Jersey railroad lawyer and a Grant appointee, Bradley had been one of the dissenters in the Blyew case. At the time, he had contended that the Thirteenth Amendment and the Civil Rights Act of 1866 had not only abolished slavery but also put "persons of African descent on an equality of rights and privileges with other citizens of the United States."

Justice John Marshall Harlan. Brady-Handy Collection,
Library of Congress (LC-DIG-cwpbh-04615).

Yet, despite those words, Bradley had been determined to kill the Civil Rights Act of 1875 since the day it was written. He had privately denounced it in his journal and insisted that it would deprive "white people of the right to choose their own company" and thus "introduce another kind of slavery." So when he got the opportunity to declare the act unconstitutional, he did it with a relish. And in doing so, he made it clear that the Thirteenth Amendment was relevant only in cases of chattel slavery, not in those involving civil rights violations and, especially, not in those involving "the denial of equal accommodations in inns, public conveyances, and places of public amusement."[46]

For the next two decades, the majority of the court continued to hold to this line. Then in October 1905, the court dealt its harshest blow against the enforcement clause. An Arkansas case came before the court involving a white mob that had driven eight black men away from their lumber mill jobs and thereby prevented them from fulfilling their labor contracts. An Arkansas federal grand jury had indicted the mob leaders under two federal laws, one that criminalized such behavior and another that gave the right to enforce contracts to all persons. With Justice Harlan again dissenting, the court, in a seven-to-two decision, held that the federal statutes were unconstitutional, that Congress had overstepped its Thirteenth Amendment powers in enacting them, and that the power to prevent mob obstructions of liberty remained solely with the states.[47]

Thus the Supreme Court accomplished what President Andrew Johnson, Governor Benjamin Perry, and virtually the entire Democratic Party had once hoped. It severely limited the impact of the Thirteenth Amendment.

Epilogue

EMANCIPATION DAY, 1893

As the struggle for civil rights gave way to resurgent white supremacy in the 1880s and 1890s, the Nashville chapter of the Afro-American League decided that for their children's sake they had to resurrect the writings and orations of James Ashley. Their children and grandchildren had to know that in the battle for black freedom they weren't alone, that even in the worst of times they had some white men and women on their side, and that they were especially in debt to an obscure congressman from Toledo that white historians had all but forgotten.

With this in mind, the president of the Nashville chapter, William Henderson Young, wrote Ashley on March 8, 1892, and told him that the league wanted to publish in book form all his papers, statements, and public addresses "against the crime of slavery." For the complete record of his "unselfish devotion in behalf of human liberty" was not to be found in any public library or school, and the league thought it should be readily available so "that future generations may have in their homes and their schools a perennial fountain of inspiration." Young asked for permission to publish such a memorial and for Ashley's help in collecting the pertinent material. He also told Ashley that the league would be happy to present him with a copy of the book in the near future as a "souvenir."[1]

The request was enthusiastically received by Ashley. He was now sixty-eight years old, feeling his age, suffering from the first signs of diabetes. Two years earlier, he had tried to make a political comeback. He had run for his old House seat, this time promising to fight in behalf of the "working man," but had lost by a narrow margin. All the old

Bishop Benjamin W. Arnett. Ohio House of Representatives
Photograph Collection (P206).

charges, dating back more than thirty years, had been raised against
him. His old nemesis, Clark Waggoner, had published a broadside
portraying him as a crook. He had also been dismissed as a bumbling
fool by one of the Washington's most prominent journalists, Benjamin
Perley Poore, mainly for his role during the impeachment controversy. Neither man had given him any credit for getting the Thirteenth
Amendment through Congress.[2] And now, with little to do, he spent
much of his time traveling, swimming, and fishing.

So to be treated like a hero by "the colored citizens of Tennessee"
brought him great joy. But, unfortunately, he no longer had most of
his personal papers. They had been destroyed in a fire. All he could do
was provide the league with the papers and public addresses that had
appeared in print, or had been saved by his friends, as well as some of
the speeches that he had given since leaving Congress. In total, it came
to over nine hundred pages.

To edit the project, the league then turned to Bishop Benjamin W.
Arnett, a leading figure in the African Methodist Episcopal Church.
As a young pastor, the fifty-four-year-old Arnett had served in Toledo
and knew Ashley well. He had also been in the House gallery when
the Thirteenth Amendment finally passed. Since then, he had been a
member of the Ohio legislature—the elected representative of a dis-

trict that was overwhelmingly white—and had written the legislation for the repeal of Ohio's infamous Black Laws. He was now the president of Wilberforce University, a small black college near Xenia, Ohio. By the time Arnett finished the project, he had over forty years of Ashley's speeches, beginning in the early 1850s and ending in the 1890s. To write the introduction, he turned to Frederick Douglass, the most famous black man in America. And to present the completed souvenir to Ashley, he turned to his eight-year-old son Daniel.

The ceremony took place on Emancipation Day, September 22, 1893, at the Art Palace in Chicago, in the Columbian Hall of the World's Parliament of Religions. It was part of the Chicago World's Fair, the famous white-city extravaganza that drew some twenty-six million visitors and dignitaries from forty-six nations. Technically, the exposition was to celebrate the four hundredth anniversary of Columbus's discovery of the New World. In fact, many were there for the carnival rides, especially the original Ferris wheel built by George Ferris, which was 264 feet high and had thirty-six cars, each of which could accommodate sixty people, and for Buffalo Bill Cody's Wild West Show, which had been denied a spot in the six hundred–acre fairgrounds, but held forth anyway to huge crowds just outside the exposition.

During its six-month existence, the fair's directors scheduled many conferences. The largest of these by far was the World's Parliament of Religions. The first formal gathering of representatives of the Eastern and Western spiritual traditions, it ran from September 11 to September 27. Each day was special to one faith or another. The day set aside especially for black churches was September 22, the same day that Lincoln in 1862 had announced the preliminary Emancipation Proclamation, now known as Emancipation Day.

By the date of the ceremony, a number of black activists led by Ida B. Wells had decided to boycott the Chicago fair, largely because its managers had given in to the demand of white Southerners that black men and women be "kept in their place" and assigned only to the most menial jobs. The boycott had received wide attention. But to the well-educated black elite of the Southern states, the leaders of the African Methodist Episcopal Church, and Ohio's Wilberforce University, the fair presented a golden opportunity to display black achievements and black talent. And that they did. The Hampton Institute in Virginia, Atlanta University, and Wilberforce University set up impressive exhibits that drew thousands of admirers. They also decided to ignore the boycott and make the most of Emancipation Day.[3]

So, at their urging, over five thousand men, women, and children crowded into the Art Palace on Emancipation Day to hear Bishop Arnett speak and to pay tribute to James Ashley. Some in the crowd were white, including Prince Serge Wolkonsky, who had come all the way from Saint Petersburg, Russia, to attend the fair. But most were black. And especially prominent were the members of the African Methodist Episcopal Church. At least eleven bishops and 150 pastors were in attendance. Bishop Arnett gave a long speech on black accomplishments since emancipation. He then had his young son Daniel present the seven hundred–page souvenir to James Ashley. And then, to thunderous applause, Ashley took the podium.

The former congressman was obviously in good spirits. After thanking young Daniel, the league, and everyone in the audience for "the monument" they had given him, he pointedly assured them that he wasn't dead yet, that he still had another fifteen to twenty years of "fighting material" left in him. Otherwise, his speech was much like his old ones, filled with anecdotes, and loaded with references to the slave barons. Yet, at the same time, he also tried to sum up what the Civil War and the Thirteenth Amendment had accomplished.[4]

What, indeed, had the Thirteenth Amendment accomplished?

First of all, it obviously changed fundamental law under the Constitution. The Founding Fathers had written a document in 1787 that protected slaveholding interests. For them, protecting the interests of slaveholders had been more important than a bill of rights. While they purposely excluded a bill of rights from the original document, they included numerous clauses that not only protected the owners of slaves but also enhanced Southern power. How many clauses? That has been a matter of dispute. Some historians say just three, others five, still others eight, nine, ten, and eleven.[5]

One clearly was the three-fifths clause that provided for counting three out of five slaves for representation in Congress. Since the slaves couldn't vote and had no political voice whatsoever, the clause enhanced the power of the Southern white man. It made his vote count more than a Northern white man's vote. It gave the white South extra political clout in both the House of Representatives and the Electoral College. And over the years, it had a huge political impact. It determined the outcome of at least one presidential election, the election of Thomas Jefferson in 1800, and at least a dozen congressional bills.[6]

Another was the slave trade clause. This provision was a major exception to the general power granted to Congress to regulate all commerce. It prohibited Congress from banning the African slave trade at any time before the year 1808, and it could not be amended. But, contrary to popular belief, it did not require Congress to ban the trade in 1808 or thereafter. However, Congress did abolish the trade in 1808, but by then South Carolina and Georgia had imported more slaves than they needed. By then, in fact, South Carolina was about to join Virginia as a major exporter of surplus slaves.

Still another was the fugitive slave clause. This clause prohibited states from emancipating fugitive slaves and required that runaways be returned to their owners "on demand." How this was to be done was then spelled out in congressional legislation, the first act passed in 1793, the second in 1850. From the beginning, scores of Quakers denounced this provision as unholy, as a violation of their religious faith. It didn't matter. Under the law, they still had to abide by it. It was the law of the land.

Still another was the domestic insurrections clause. This provision empowered Congress to call "forth the Militia" to "suppress Insurrections." When this clause was written, its authors undoubtedly had in mind Shays's Rebellion, the western Massachusetts uprising that had frightened George Washington out of retirement. But they also were well aware that it would be used to put down potential slave rebellions. Coupled with this clause was still another, the domestic violence provision. It guaranteed that the United States would protect states from "domestic Violence," which obviously included slave rebellions. It came into play several times before the Civil War, notably with the Louisiana slave revolt in 1811, Nat Turner's insurrection in 1831, and John Brown's raid on Harpers Ferry in 1859.

Finally, and probably most important, the Constitution created a government of limited powers. Under the federal system that was established, Congress did not have the power to interfere in the "domestic institutions of the states." Only a state could interfere with slavery within its borders. It could even outlaw slavery if it wished. But Congress could not. In 1860, when Lincoln ran for president, he made it clear that he had no intention of interfering with slavery in the states where it existed. In fact, he didn't think the federal government, much less the president, had the power to do so. And later, he had his doubts about the Emancipation Proclamation. Was it constitutional? Did it violate the Fifth Amendment? Would it stand up in court? Many legal scholars thought it wouldn't. And then, what about the institution of slavery? Wasn't it still the law of the land in South Carolina, Georgia, and eleven other states? Yes, it was. And that, in his eyes, was why the Constitution in 1865 had to be amended. It was the "king's cure."

The Civil War and the decision to outlaw slavery also had an impact on the nation's power structure. For fifty of the seventy-two years between Washington's election and Lincoln's, slaveholders had held the presidency. The only presidents to be reelected—Washington, Jefferson, Madison, Monroe, and Jackson—had all been slave owners. For forty-five of those years, slaveholders had also occupied the position of Speaker of the House. And during those years, eighteen of the thirty-three justices on the Supreme Court had been slave owners. Those days were now over.

Similarly, the nation's top wealth holders in 1860 had tended to be its major slaveholders. In total, the United States in 1860 had about four million slaves, and on the open market they were worth at least three billion dollars. That was roughly three times the amount of capital invested in manufacturing, three times the amount invested in railroads, seven times the amount invested in banks, and forty-eight times the amount the federal government spent that year. Only the nation's real estate was more valuable. During the Civil War, the market price for slaves undoubtedly went down in much of the country. Nonetheless, as one Southern leader after another pointed out, the Thirteenth Amendment was the biggest confiscation of capital in history.

Among the top wealth holders affected by the Thirteenth Amendment was a woman whom the members of the Nashville chapter of the Afro-American League knew well. That was Adelicia Acklen. She was one of the few Americans in 1860 who owned more than five hundred slaves, and on that notable list probably no more than four or five plantation owners had more slaves than she did.[7] Known locally as "the mistress of Belmont," she was a Nashville native who in 1839 at age twenty-two had married the city's most famous slave trader, fifty-year-old Isaac Franklin. By then, Franklin had made more than a million dollars from slave trading, and when he died in 1846 he left her with seven Louisiana cotton plantations, a two thousand–acre plan-

Adelicia Acklen. C. C. Giers photograph, Belmont
Mansion, Nashville, Tennessee.

tation in Gallatin, Tennessee, more than fifty thousand acres of unde-
veloped land in Texas, stocks and bonds, and at least 750 slaves, 659 in
Louisiana alone.[8]

Three years later, the wealthy widow selected from her many
suitors an Alabama planter, Colonel Joseph A. S. Acklen, to be her
second husband, but only after he agreed in writing that she would be
the sole owner and final authority over all the properties she brought
into the marriage. The colonel turned out to be a good manager, and
he was given credit for tripling the value of her holdings. Together,
they also built Belmont, which became the talk of Nashville. A twenty
thousand–square-foot summer villa, it had thirty-six rooms, including
an art gallery and conservatories, along with several lavish gardens, an
aviary, a lake, and a zoo. At the beginning of the war, she was undoubtedly the wealthiest person in Tennessee and probably the wealthiest
in Louisiana as well.

By war's end Adelicia Acklen was a widow again. She also had lost
all her slaves. But she wasn't as financially strapped as a radical Republican like Ashley might have hoped. He wanted the slave barons
dispossessed of their land as well as their slaves. He wanted to see
them flat broke. That didn't happen in her case. After her second hus-

band died in 1863, she somehow managed to cut a deal with Union authorities and got the last of her slave-grown cotton shipped to Liver-
pool where it was sold to the Rothschilds of London for a reported
$960,000 in gold. She thus held onto her land, which had been devas-
tated by the war, and soon had tenants working it. She also held onto
Belmont, her thirty-six-room summer home. And in 1867, at her Belmont mansion, she was married again, this time to a Nashville doctor,
before some two thousand well-fed guests. He, too, had to sign a pre-
nuptial agreement.

The Acklen story was fairly typical in that, while the great planters lost their slaves and suffered from the devastation of the war, they
usually managed to hold onto their land. Right after the war, however,
many believed that this wasn't the case. They were also led astray by
the federal census takers, who in 1870 and 1880 failed to distinguish
between landlords and tenants. Instead, they recorded rented land
under the renter's name and thus led many to believe that the number of landowners had doubled, while the average farm had been cut
in half. Although people who lived in the cotton belt probably knew
better from the beginning, this fiction lasted for forty years. Then, in
1910, the federal government did a special census of 310 cotton counties and found that the old plantations had not only survived but also
increased in size.[9]

The cotton belt also had more power in Congress than ever before. It was still the home of most the nation's black people, and with
the end of the three-fifths rule these men, women, and children now
counted a full five-fifths. That meant more seats in the House of Representatives and more votes in the Electoral College. For a while during Reconstruction black men in the cotton belt had voted, and for a
while they had seen members of their race elected to public office. In
Mississippi, Hiram Revels, in 1869, had even won the US Senate seat
once held by Jefferson Davis.

But by the time Ashley gave his speech, this period of black participation was coming to an end. Throughout the cotton belt, state
governments claiming to represent "poor whites" came to power. Denouncing the alleged collaboration of "aristocrats" and blacks, they
effectively nullified the Fifteenth Amendment and drove Southern
blacks out of politics, partly by violence, and partly by poll taxes, lit-
eracy tests, grandfather clauses, and other legal shenanigans. Yet, in

the national government, the cotton South still had all the additional seats that the end of slavery had brought.

Finally, the Thirteenth Amendment obviously made a big difference to nearly everyone in Ashley's audience. It was undoubtedly central to his hosts, the members of the Nashville chapter of the Afro-American League, who along with some 275,000 other Tennessee slaves had been excluded from the Emancipation Proclamation. It was their badge of freedom. But it was also important to men and women like Bishop Arnett. The bishop had been born free. He also had been born in Pennsylvania, a free state. Nevertheless, when he was a youngster, he had encountered scores of people, maybe a hundred or more, who assumed that he was a runaway slave.

That wasn't unusual. It had been experienced by every free black American before the Civil War. Now, that was no longer the case. No one would ever ask the bishop's son for his "freedom papers." No one would wonder who his owner was. No one would even think of turning him over to the local sheriff and maybe collecting a handsome reward. The road ahead for young Daniel would be hard. He would never experience freedom in its fullest. Nor would his children. Nor would his children's children. And even more than a century later, when the country for the first time had a black president, his great, great grandchildren would still have to watch their step. But the old assumption that every black person in America was a slave or a runaway was now history.

Appendix A:
Significant Events Leading to
the Thirteenth Amendment

1860

November 6: Lincoln elected president.

December 18: John J. Crittenden proposes six constitutional amendments and four resolutions to appease secessionists.

December 20: Secession of South Carolina. Six other Deep South states soon follow.

1861

March 2: Congress adopts Corwin Amendment prohibiting any subsequent amendment abolishing slavery. Never ratified.

April 12: Confederate attack on Fort Sumter. Lincoln calls for troops. Four more states secede and join Confederacy.

May 24: First fugitive slaves arrive at Fortress Monroe.

August 6: First Confiscation Act authorizes the confiscation of slaves employed in Confederate war effort.

August 30: General Frémont declares free the slaves of disloyal Missouri slave owners. Countermanded by Lincoln.

November 26: Lincoln drafts bill for gradual compensated emancipation in Delaware. Subsequently rejected.

1862

April 16: Congress abolishes slavery in Washington, DC, with compensation to loyal owners and money for voluntary colonization.

May 9: General Hunter declares free all slaves in South Carolina, Georgia, and Florida. Countermanded by Lincoln.

July 12: Lincoln appeals to border-state congressmen to support gradual, federally compensated emancipation with colonization of freed slaves outside United States. Rejected.

July 17: Second Confiscation Act frees all rebel-owned fugitive slaves and authorizes president to employ "persons of African descent" in any capacity to suppress the rebellion. Militia Act provides for employment of "persons of African descent" in "any military or naval service for which they may be found competent."

July 22: Lincoln announces to his cabinet his intention to issue the Emancipation Proclamation but agrees to wait for a military victory.

September 17: Battle of Antietam.

September 22: Announcement of preliminary Emancipation Proclamation.

November 8: Fall elections cost Republicans twenty-three House seats; Democrats gain twenty-eight seats.

1863

January 1: Emancipation Proclamation issued.

May 27: Black soldiers partake in assault on Port Hudson, Louisiana.

June 7: Black soldiers distinguish themselves at Milliken's Bend, Louisiana.

July 3: Battle of Gettysburg.

July 4: Confederate surrender of Vicksburg, Mississippi.

July 18: Fifty-Fourth Massachusetts spearheads failed assault on Battery Wagner, South Carolina.

October 3: War Department orders recruitment of black soldiers in Maryland, Missouri, and Tennessee.

December 8: Lincoln offers pardon and restoration of all property except slaves to Confederates who take an oath of allegiance.

December 14: James Ashley proposes amendment outlawing slavery.

1864

April 8: Senate approves amendment outlawing slavery.

June 7: War Department orders full-scale recruitment of black soldiers in Kentucky.

June 15: House of Representatives rejects amendment outlawing slavery.

October 13: Maryland electorate approves new state constitution outlawing slavery.

November 8: Lincoln reelected. Republicans gain fifty-one House seats; Democrats lose thirty-four.

1865

January 11: Missouri state constitutional convention abolishes slavery.

January 31: House of Representatives approves constitutional amendment outlawing slavery.

April 9: Surrender of Lee's army at Appomattox Courthouse.

April 14: Assassination of Lincoln.

December 18: Thirteenth Amendment ratified.

Appendix B:
A Historiographical Note

The Thirteenth Amendment, in setting free over 3.5 million slaves and their unborn offspring, undoubtedly had far more impact on American society than any other amendment. It also transformed the handiwork of the nation's Founding Fathers, the original US Constitution of 1787, far more than any other amendment. Yet Civil War historians, in trying to explain the outcome of the war, have rarely said much about it. Instead, they have devoted their attention almost entirely to the strategically vital but legally less decisive Emancipation Proclamation. Meanwhile, constitutional historians have preferred to write about the more complex Fourteenth Amendment that became constitutional law three years later.

Yet, while the amount of attention given to the Thirteenth Amendment has generally been sparse, the books and articles devoted to it have often been first rate. For the most part, these scholarly works have focused on the more technical issues related to the amendment, especially the legal debates over its legitimacy. In addition, they have tended to follow the lead of Harold M. Hyman, *A More Perfect Union: The Impact of the Civil War and Reconstruction on the Constitution* (New York: Alfred A. Knopf, 1973), in contending that the more radical members of Lincoln's party were the driving force in overcoming the widespread resistance to changing the Constitution, making it "more perfect," and thus bringing freedom to the slaves. Quietly taking exception with this interpretation, however, are the two most acclaimed studies of recent years—namely, Michael Vorenberg, *Final Freedom: The Civil War, the Abolition of Slavery, and the Thirteenth Amendment* (Cambridge: Cambridge University Press, 2001), which insists that War Democrats were also an impetus behind the amendment, and James Oakes, *Freedom National: The Destruction of Slavery in the United States, 1861–1865* (New York: W. W. Norton & Co., 2013), which argues that the gap between Lincoln and the more radical members of his party has been grossly exaggerated.

On the resistance to changing the text of the original 1787 Constitution, which by the time of the Civil War had often been hailed as "sacred," "inspired," and "untouchable," several other recent scholarly works are also especially helpful: David E. Kyvig, *Explicit and Authentic Acts: Amending the U. S. Constitution, 1776–1995* (Lawrence: University Press of Kansas, 1996), 154–87; Bruce Ackerman, *We the People*, vol. 2: *Transformations* (Cambridge, MA: Harvard University Press, 1998), 99–252; and Michael Les Benedict, "Constitutional Politics, Constitutional Law, and the Thirteenth Amendment," *Maryland Law Review* 71 (2012): 163–88.

As for the long-term impact of the amendment, especially valuable is Alexander Tsesis, *The Thirteen Amendment and American Freedom: A Legal History* (New York: New York University Press, 2004), which contends that the Radical Republicans who propelled the amendment through Congress intended to produce full-fledged freedom for all Americans, not just some halfway legal status between freedom and slavery for black Americans, and that the enforcement clause provided Congress with the power to act against a "slew" of discriminations. But in the end that didn't happen, thanks mainly to the federal courts. Also insisting that the amendment could and should have been far more productive are several essays in Harold Holzer and Sara Vaughn Gabbard, eds., *Lincoln and Freedom: Slavery, Emancipation, and the Thirteenth Amendment* (Carbondale: Southern Illinois University Press, 2007) and especially in Alexander Tsesis, ed., *The Promises of Liberty: The History and Contemporary Relevance of the Thirteenth Amendment* (New York: Columbia University Press, 2010).

Just as the Thirteenth Amendment has received little attention from scholars, so, too, has James Ashley. In his case, of course, the reasons are different. He was never a major figure except on two occasions in his life, first, in the fight over the Thirteenth Amendment and, then, in the impeachment of Andrew Johnson. Moreover, learning about Ashley has always been difficult, as the bulk of his private papers were destroyed in a fire. In the early 1890s, the Nashville chapter of the Afro-American League tried to remedy this problem. With Ashley's help, they assembled most of Ashley's speeches and public statements. That material is now available both in book form and on the Internet in Benjamin W. Arnett, ed., *Orations and Speeches: Duplicate Copy of the Souvenir from the Afro-American League to the Hon. James M. Ashley* (Philadelphia: AME Church, 1894).

There have also been two biographies of Ashley, the first written by his son, Charles S. Ashley, "Governor Ashley's Biography and Messages," *Contributions to the Historical Society of Montana* 6 (1907): 142–289, and the second by Robert F. Horowitz, *The Great Impeacher: A Political Biography of James M. Ashley* (New York: Brooklyn College Press, 1979). The Horowitz biography is especially valuable, as he did the hard work of digging up most of Ashley's political connections. Helpful, too, is W. Sherman Jackson, "Representative James M. Ashley and the Midwestern Origins of Amendment Thirteen," *Lincoln Herald* 80 (Summer 1978). For Ashley's legal perspective, especially worthwhile are two recent articles by Rebecca E. Zietlow, "James Ashley's Thirteenth Amendment," *Columbia Law Review* 112 (2012): 1697–1731, and "Ideological Origins of the Thirteenth Amendment," *Houston Law Review* 49 (2012): 393–458.

Notes

Prologue

1. The contrary notion that the Emancipation Proclamation somehow outlawed slavery, which is the popular view today, came much later. People at the time knew better. Civil War historians have pointed this out repeatedly, largely to no avail. Among the more recent of the many fine scholarly works are Eric Foner, *The Fiery Trial: Abraham Lincoln and American Slavery* (New York: W. W. Norton & Co., 2010); James Oakes, *Freedom National: The Destruction of Slavery in the United States, 1861–1865* (New York: W. W. Norton & Co., 2013); and Michael Vorenberg, *Final Freedom: The Civil War, the Abolition of Slavery, and the Thirteenth Amendment* (Cambridge: Cambridge University Press, 2001). For a far more controversial perspective, see Lerone Bennett Jr., *Forced into Glory: Abraham Lincoln's White Dream* (Chicago: Johnson Publishing, 2000).

2. Charles S. Ashley, "Governor Ashley's Biography and Messages," *Contributions to the Historical Society of Montana* 6 (1907): 152–55; Benjamin W. Arnett, ed., *Orations and Speeches: Duplicate Copy of the Souvenir from the Afro-American League to the Hon. James M. Ashley* (Philadelphia: A. M. E. Church, 1894), 601–29.

3. Arnett, ed., *Orations and Speeches*, 616–17.

4. Ibid., 615.

5. Ibid., 616–17.

6. Minutes, House of Representatives Committee on Territories, 37th Cong., 2d Sess. (1861–62), RG 233, National Archives; David Donald, ed., *Inside Lincoln's Cabinet: The Civil War Diaries of Salmon P. Chase* (New York: Longmans Green, 1954), 50–51; Herman Belz, *Reconstructing the Union: Theory and Policy during the Civil War* (Ithaca, NY: Cornell University Press, 1969), 55.

7. James L. Huston, *Calculating the Value of the Union: Slavery, Property Rights, and the Economic Origins of the Civil War* (Chapel Hill: University of North Carolina Press, 2003), 36, 80.

8. Minutes, House of Representatives Committee on Territories, 37th Congress, 2d Session (1861–62), RG 233, National Archives.

9. Belz, *Reconstructing the Union*, 177, 179; William C. Harris, *With Charity for All:*

Lincoln and the Restoration of the Union (Lexington: University Press of Kentucky, 1997), 236–37.

10. *Congressional Globe*, 38th Cong., 1st Sess. (1863–64), 19, 21, 521–22, 1203; Leonard Schlup, "Republican Loyalist: James F. Wilson and Party Politics, 1855–1895," *Annals of Iowa* 52 (Spring 1993): 123–49; Floyd C. Shoemaker, "John Brooks Henderson, 1826–1913: Author of the Thirteenth Amendment Abolishing Slavery in the United States," in *Missouri's Hall of Fame: Lives of Eminent Missourians* (Columbia: University of Missouri Press, 1918), 213–17; David Donald, *Charles Sumner and the Rights of Man* (New York: Alfred A. Knopf, 1970), 147–49.

11. *Congressional Globe*, 38th Cong., 1st Sess. (1863–64), 1490; Vorenberg, *Final Freedom*, 251.

12. Arnett, ed., *Orations and Speeches*, 706; W. Sherman Jackson, "Representative James M. Ashley and the Midwestern Origins of Amendment Thirteen," *Lincoln Herald*, 80 (Summer 1978): 87.

13. *Congressional Globe*, 38th Cong., 1st Sess. (1863–64), 2995; Vorenberg, *Final Freedom*, 252.

14. Ashley, "Governor Ashley's Biography," 176–79; *Congressional Globe* 38th Cong., 1st Sess. (1863–64), 2962; "Address of Hon. James M. Ashley Before the 'Ohio Society of New York,' Feb. 19, 1890," in Arnett, ed., *Orations and Speeches*, 707–8, 712, 713.

Chapter 1

1. Benjamin W. Arnett, ed., *Orations and Speeches: Duplicate Copy of the Souvenir from the Afro-American League to the Hon. James M. Ashley* (Philadelphia: AME Church, 1894), 618.

2. For an incisive analysis of Ashley's basic argument, see Rebecca E. Zietlow, "James Ashley's Thirteenth Amendment," *Columbia Law Review* 112 (2012): 1697–1731, and "Ideological Origins of the Thirteenth Amendment," *Houston Law Review* 49 (2012): 393–458.

3. For detailed analysis, see Harold M. Hyman, *A More Perfect Union: The Impact of the Civil War and Reconstruction on the Constitution* (New York: Alfred A. Knopf, 1973); Phillip S. Paludan, *A Covenant with Death: The Constitution, Law, and Equality in the Civil War Era* (Urbana: University of Illinois Press, 1975); Herman Belz, "Abraham Lincoln and American Constitutionalism," *Review of Politics* 50 (Spring 1988): 169–97.

4. Leonard L. Richards, *The Slave Power: The Free North and Southern Domination, 1780–1860* (Baton Rouge: Louisiana State University Press, 2000), 23–25, and passim.

5. Arnett, ed., *Orations and Speeches*, 706.

6. For details on Ashley's life, see Robert F. Horowitz, *Great Impeacher: A Political Biography of James M. Ashley* (New York: Brooklyn College Press, 1979); W. Sherman Jackson, "Representative James M. Ashley and the Midwestern Origins of Amendment Thirteen," *Lincoln Herald* 80 (Summer 1978): 83–95; Charles S. Ashley, "Governor Ashley's Biography and Messages," *Contributions to the Historical Society of Montana*, 6 (1907): 142–289.

7. Clark Waggoner, *History of Toledo and Lucas County, Ohio* (New York: Munsell and Co., 1888), 601. Alma Buchanan, *History of Warren AME Church* (Toledo: Warren AME Church, 1977).

8. Arnett, ed., *Orations and Speeches*, 140–41; Ashley to William Schouler, February 17, 1861, Schouler Papers, Massachusetts Historical Society, Boston.

9. *Toledo Blade*, May 21–June 11, 1861.

10. *Chicago Tribune*, February 1, 1861.

11. For details on Crittenden's life, see Albert D. Kirwan, *John J. Crittenden: The Struggle for the Union* (Lexington: University Press of Kentucky, 1962).

12. Damon R. Eubank, *In the Shadow of the Patriarch: The John J. Crittenden Family in War and Peace* (Macon, GA: Macon University Press, 2009); Tom Chaffin, *Fatal Glory: Narciso Lopez and the First Clandestine U.S. War against Cuba* (Charlottesville: University of Virginia Press, 1996).

13. Combined Books, comp., *Civil War Book of Lists: Over 300 Lists, from the Sublime . . . to the Ridiculous* (Conshohocken, PA: Combined Books, 1993), 19, 21, 27.

14. Kentucky Constitution (1792), article 9; Joan Wells Coward, *Kentucky in the New Republic: The Process of Constitution-Making* (Lexington: University Press of Kentucky, 1979), 16–25, 35–45; Frank Mathias, "Kentucky's Third Constitution: A Restriction on Majority Rule," *Register of the Kentucky Historical Society* 75 (January 1977): 18; Richard Sutton, official reporter to the convention, *Report of the Debates and Proceedings of the Convention for the Revision of the Constitution of the State of Kentucky, 1849* (Frankfort, KY: Printed at the Office of A. G. Hodges & Co., 1849), 857–58.

15. For the importance of the interstate slave trade in Kentucky and elsewhere, see Michael Tadman, *Speculators and Slaves: Masters, Traders, and Slaves in the Old South* (Baton Rouge: Louisiana State University Press, 1989); Walter Johnson, *Soul by Soul: Life Inside the Antebellum Slave Market* (Cambridge, MA: Harvard University Press, 1999); Steven Deyle, *Carry Me Back: The Domestic Slave Trade in American Life* (New York: Oxford University Press, 2005); and David L. Lightner, *Slavery and the Commerce Power: How the Struggle against the Interstate Slave Trade Led to the Civil War* (New Haven, CT: Yale University Press, 2006).

16. *Kentucky Statesman* (Lexington), January 6, 1860.

17. John V. Mering, "The Constitutional Union Campaign of 1860: An Example of the Paranoid Style," *Mid-America* 60 (1978): 99.

18. *Congressional Globe*, 36th Cong., 2d Sess. (1860–61), 409; David M. Potter, *Lincoln and His Party in the Secession Crisis* (New Haven, CT: Yale University Press, 1942), 108–10, 182–200.

19. For details on Seward, see Glyndon Van Deusen, *William Henry Seward* (New York: Oxford University Press, 1967); Walter Stahr, *Seward: Lincoln's Indispensable Man* (New York: Simon and Schuster, 2012).

20. *Congressional Globe*, 36th Cong., 2d Sess. (1860–61), 1264, 1283–85, 1305, 1338–40, 1375, 1403; R. Alton Lee, "The Corwin Amendment in the Secession Crisis." *Ohio Historical Quarterly* 70 (January 1961): 1–26.

21. *New York Tribune*, March 2, 4, 1861; James M. Ashley, "Address of Hon. James M. Ashley before the 'Ohio Society of New York,' February 19, 1890," in *Orations and Speeches*, ed. Arnett, 699–700.

22. *Toledo Blade*, May 2–27, 1861; Ashley to Salmon P. Chase, May 5, 1861, Salmon P. Chase Papers, Library of Congress.

23. *Congressional Globe*, 36th Cong., 1st Sess. (1859–60), app., 374; Eric Foner, *Free Soil, Free Labor, Free Men* (New York: Oxford University Press, 1970), 119–21.

24. Giddings to Salmon P. Chase, May 4, 1861, Salmon P. Chase Papers, Historical Society of Pennsylvania, Philadelphia.

25. [Edward Lillie Pierce], "The Contrabands at Fortress Monroe," *Atlantic Monthly* (November 1861); Writers' Program of the Work Projects Administration, comp., *The Negro in Virginia* (New York: Hastings House, 1940), 210; Benj. F. Butler to Lt. Gen. Winfield Scott, May 24, 1861, in *The War of the Rebellion: A Compilation of the Official Records of the Union and Confederate Armies*, by Robert N. Scott et al., 128 vols., ser. 2 (Washington, DC: Government Printing Office, 1880–91), 1:752; Louis S. Gerteis, *From Contraband to Freedman: Federal Policy toward Southern Blacks, 1861–1865* (Westport, CT: Greenwood Press., 1973), 19, 22, 39; Charles Wilder, "Testimony before the American Freedmen's Inquiry Commission, May 9, 1863," in *Freedom: A Documentary History of Emancipation, 1861–1867*, by Ira Berlin et al., ser. 1 (Cambridge: Cambridge University Press, 1982–90), 1:89.

26. For details on Butler, see Hans L. Trefousse, *Ben Butler: The South Called Him Beast!* (New York: Twayne, 1957).

27. *Toledo Blade*, June 3, 7, 1861.

28. *Congressional Globe*, 31st Cong., 1st Sess. (1860–61), 242.

29. Ibid., 222–23, 265; Ashley, "Address to the 'Ohio Society of New York,'" 697.

30. Edward Magdol, *Owen Lovejoy: Abolitionist in Congress* (New Brunswick, NJ: Rutgers University Press, 1967); *Congressional Globe*, 37th Cong., 1st Sess. (1861), 24, 32.

31. Arthur T. Pierson, *Zachariah Chandler: An Outline Sketch of His Life and Public Services* (Detroit: Post and Tribune Co., 1880); *Congressional Globe*, 37th Cong., 1st Sess. (1861), 11.

32. James G. Blaine, *Twenty Years of Congress*, 2 vols. (Norwich, CT: Henry Hill Publishing, 1884), 1:342.

33. *Congressional Globe*, 37th Cong., 1st Sess. (1861), 411–34; Silvana R. Siddali, *From Property to Person: Slavery and the Confiscation Acts, 1861–1862* (Baton Rouge: Louisiana State University Press, 2005), 251–54.

34. Blaine, *Twenty Years of Congress*, 1:343; Howard K. Beale, ed., *The Diary of Edward Bates, 1859–1866* (Washington, DC: Government Printing Office, 1933); Mark Grimsley, *The Hard Hand of War: Union Military Policy toward Southern Civilians, 1861–1865* (New York: Cambridge University Press, 1995), 34–35, 63–66, 88–89; John Beatty, *Memoirs of a Volunteer, 1861–1863* (Cincinnati: Baldwin and Co., 1879), 91–92.

35. Allan Nevins, *Frémont: Pathmarker of the West* (New York: D. Appleton Century Co., 1939), 503–5; Mark W. Geiger, *Financial Fraud and Guerrilla Violence in Missouri's Civil War, 1861–1865* (New Haven, CT: Yale University Press, 2010); William Parish, *Turbulent Partnership: Missouri and the Union, 1861–1865* (Columbia: University of Missouri Press, 1962), 60; Vernon Volpe, "The Frémonts and Emancipation in Missouri," *Historian* 56 (Winter 1994): 339–54.

36. Roy C. Basler, ed., *The Collected Works of Abraham Lincoln*, 9 vols. (New Brunswick, NJ: Rutgers University Press, 1952-55), 4:506.

37. Joshua Speed to Abraham Lincoln, September 7, 9, 1861, Abraham Lincoln Papers, Library of Congress; Lowell H. Harrison, *Lincoln of Kentucky* (Lexington: University Press of Kentucky, 2000), 225.

38. Sceva B. Laughlin, "Missouri Politics during the Civil War," *Missouri Historical Review* 24 (October 1929): 89, 92; William E. Parrish, *Frank Blair, Lincoln's Conservative* (Columbia: University of Missouri Press, 1998); Norma L. Peterson, *Freedom and Franchise: The Political Career of B. Gratz Brown* (Columbia: University of Missouri Press. 1965).

39. Ruhl J. Bartlett, *John C. Frémont and the Republican Party* (New York: Da Capo, 1970), 74-5; Nevins, *Frémont*, 503-7; John Medill to Salmon P. Chase, September 15, 1861, Salmon P. Chase Papers, Library of Congress; *Chicago Tribune*, September 16, 1861; Erastus Wright to Abraham Lincoln, September 20, 1861, and Orville H. Browning to Abraham Lincoln, September 17, 1861—both in Abraham Lincoln Papers, Library of Congress.

40. Benjamin F. Wade to Zachary Chandler, September 23, 1861, Zachary Chandler Papers, Library of Congress.

41. Lincoln to Orville H. Browning, September 22, 1861, in *Collected Works of Lincoln*, ed. Basler, 5:531-32.

42. *Toledo Blade*, September 7, 1861.

43. Ashley to Salmon P. Chase, September 6, 1861, Salmon P. Chase Papers, Library of Congress.

44. *Toledo Blade*, November 26, 1861.

45. Ezra J. Warner, *Generals in Blue: Lives of the Union Commanders* (Baton Rouge: Louisiana State University Press, 1964), 195-97.

46. Ira Berlin et al., eds., *Destruction of Slavery* (Cambridge: Cambridge University Press, 1985), 47, 26.

47. Grimsley, *Hard Hand of War*, 126-27.

48. Michael Burlingame, ed., *With Lincoln in the White House: Letters, Memoranda, and Other Writings of John G. Nicolay, 1860-1865* (Carbondale: Southern Illinois University Press, 2000) 59.

49. *Louisville Journal*, as quoted in *Frankfort Daily Commonwealth*, December 13, 1861, as quoted in Siddali, *From Property to Person*, 118.

50. *Congressional Globe*, 37th Cong., 1st Sess. (1861-62), 414; Margaret Shortreed, "The Antislavery Radicals: From Crusade to Revolution, 1840-1868," *Past and Present*, no. 16 (November 1959), 77.

51. *Congressional Globe*, 37th Cong., 2d Sess. (1861-62), 15.

52. Ibid., 76; Grimsley, *Hard Hand of War*, 125.

53. Mark M. Krug, *Lyman Trumbull: Conservative Radical* (New York: A. S. Barnes and Co., 1965), 200; Ralph J. Roske, *His Own Counsel: The Life and Times of Lyman Trumbull* (Reno: University of Nevada Press, 1979), 83.

Chapter 2

1. 33 Annals of Cong. 1170, 1236 (1818-19).

2. Arthur Zilversmit, *The First Emancipation: The Abolition of Slavery in the North* (Chicago: University of Chicago Press, 1967), 181-84; David N. Gellman, *Emancipating New York: The Politics of Slavery and Freedom, 1777-1827* (Baton Rouge: Louisiana State University Press, 2006), 176-83.

3. For the complete story, see Betty L. Fladeland, "Compensated Emancipation: A Rejected Alternative," *Journal of Southern History* 41 (May 1976): 169-86.

4. Gailllard Hunt, ed., *The Writings of James Madison*, 9 vols. (New York: G. P. Putnam's Son, 1900-10), 8:439-47; Jefferson to Jared Sparks, February 4, 1824, in *The Writings of Thomas Jefferson*, ed. Paul L. Ford, 10 vols. (New York: G. P. Putnam's Son, 1892-99), 10:289-93.

5. Leonard L. Richards, *The Slave Power: The Free North and Southern Domination, 1780-1860* (Baton Rouge: Louisiana State University Press, 2000), 83-84; 37 Annals of Cong. 1168-70 (1820-21).

6. Richard K. Craile, ed., *The Works of John C. Calhoun*, 6 vols. (New York: D. Appleton and Co., 1888), 3:169-75.

7. Ibid., 6:290-313.

8. William Lloyd Garrison, *Thoughts on African Colonization* (Boston: Garrison and Knapp, 1832), 10-14.

9. Herman V. Ames, ed., *State Documents on Federal Relations* (Philadelphia: Department of History of the University of Pennsylvania, 1906), 203-13.

10. For the complete details on the Delaware story, see Patience Essah, *A House Divided: Slavery and Emancipation in Delaware, 1638-1865* (Charlottesville: University Press of Virginia, 1996), 161-77; H. Clay Reed, "Lincoln's Compensated Emancipation Plan and Its Relations to Delaware," *Delaware Notes* 7 (1931): 27-78.

11. Harold B. Hancock, *Delaware during the Civil War: A Political History* (Wilmington: Historical Society of Delaware, 1961), 129; P. J. Staudenraus, ed., *Mr. Lincoln's Washington: Selections from the Writings of Noah Brooks Civil War Correspondent* (South Brunswick, NJ: Thomas Yoseloff, 1967), 88.

12. As quoted in Hancock, *Delaware during the Civil War*, 109.

13. Roy C. Basler, ed., *The Collected Works of Abraham Lincoln*, 9 vols. (New Brunswick, NJ: Rutgers University Press, 1952-55), 5:144-46, 152-53, 160-61; John G. Nicolay and John Hay, eds., *The Complete Works of Abraham Lincoln*, 12 vols. (New York: Century, 1905), 7:112-13, 115, 119.

14. "Memorandum of the Meeting written by Representative John W. Crisfield of Maryland," in *Conversations with Lincoln*, ed. Charles M. Segal (New York: G. P. Putnam's Sons, 1961), 164-68; Sceva B. Laughlin, "Missouri Politics during the Civil War," *Missouri Historical Review* 24 (October 1929): 94.

15. George P. Fisher to Abraham Lincoln, August 14, 1862, and Lincoln to Fisher, August 16, 1862, Abraham Lincoln Papers, Library of Congress; Wilson Lloyd Bevan, ed., *History of Delaware*, 4 vols. (New York: Lewis Historical Publishing, 1929), 2:650.

16. David Donald, ed., *Inside Lincoln's Cabinet: The Civil War Diaries of Salmon P. Chase* (New York: Longmans, Green, 1954), 50–51.

17. "Majority Report of the Committee on Territories of a Bill to Establish Temporary Governments in Disloyal States, March 12, 1862," National Archives, RG 233; Herman Belz, *Reconstructing the Union* (Ithaca, NY: Cornell University Press, 1969), 70–77.

18. "Minority Reports of the Committee on Territories"; *Congressional Globe*, 37th Cong., 2d Sess. (1861–62), 986, 1084, 1117, 1193, 1198; Belz, *Reconstructing the Union*, 80–81.

19. James M. Ashley, "Address of Hon. James M. Ashley before the 'Ohio Society of New York,' February 19, 1890," in *Orations and Speeches: Duplicate Copy of the Souvenir from the Afro-American League to the Hon. James M. Ashley*, ed. Benjamin W. Arnett (Philadelphia: AME Church, 1894), 701–4; James M. Ashley, "The Passage of the Thirteenth Amendment to the Constitution," *Magazine of Western History* 13 (April 1891): 670–71.

20. For details on the bill, see Page Milburne, "The Emancipation of the Slaves in the District of Columbia," *Records of the Columbia Historical Society* 16 (Washington, DC: Columbia Historical Society, 1913), 96–119; Michael J. Kurtz, "Emancipation in the Federal City," *Civil War History* 24 (September 1978): 250–67; Henry Wilson, *History of the Antislavery Measures of the Thirty-Seventh and Thirty-Eighth Congresses, 1861–65* (Boston: Walker, Fuller, and Co., 1865), 40–49.

21. Basler, ed., *Collected Works of Lincoln*, 5:49, 145; T. C. Pease and J. G. Randall. eds., *The Diary of Orville Hickman Browning*, 2 vols. (Springfield: Illinois State Historical Society, 1925), 1:541.

22. David Hunter to Edwin M. Stanton, January 29, 1862, Stanton Papers, Library of Congress.

23. Basler, ed., *Collected Works of Lincoln*, 5:219, 222–23.

24. *Congressional Globe*, 37th Cong., 2d Sess. (1861–62), app., 224–25.

25. For the Wickliffe-Stanton-Hunter exchange, see Charles G. Halpine, *Baked Meats, by Private Miles O'Reilly* (New York: Carleton, 1866), 171–89. Halpine, a former newspaperman, was the officer on Hunter's staff who drafted most of the documents that Hunter signed.

26. *Congressional Globe*, 37th Cong., 2d Sess. (1861–62), 3087, 3102, 3109, 3121–27.

27. Jessie Ames Marshall, comp., *Private and Official Correspondence of Gen. Benjamin F. Butler*, 6 vols. (Norwich, MA: [Plimpton Press], 1917), 2:125–26, 148; Otis F. R. Waite, *Vermont in the Great Rebellion: Containing Historical and Biographical Sketches, Etc.* (Claremont, NH: Tracy, Chase, and Co., 1869), 258–61; Dudley Taylor Cornish, *Sable Arm: Black Troops in the Union Army* (Lawrence: University Press of Kansas, 1956), 56–63; Benjamin Quarles, *The Negro in the Civil War* (Boston: Little, Brown and Co., 1953), 115–16.

28. George B. McClellan, *McClellan's Own Story* (New York: Charles L. Webster and Co., 1887), 487–89.

29. Basler, ed., *Collected Works of Lincoln*, 5:219, 222–23.

30. Ibid., 5:317–19.

31. *New York Tribune*, July 19, 1862.
32. Laughlin, "Missouri Politics during the Civil War," 94; Leonard P. Curry, *Blueprint for Modern America* (Nashville: Vanderbilt University Press, 1968), 53–55; *Congressional Globe*, 37th Cong., 3d Sess. (1862-63), 207–9, 586–97, 611–25, 776–805, 897–903, app. 137–38, 143–51.
33. Gideon Welles to Mary Welles, July 13, 1862, Gideon Welles Papers, Library of Congress; Howard K. Beale, ed., *Diary of Gideon Welles* (New York: F. Unger, 1960), 1:70–71; Gideon Welles, "The History of Emancipation," *Galaxy* 14 (December 1872): 842–43.
34. For full and recent accounts of the Second Confiscation Act, see Silvana R. Siddali, *From Property to Person: Slavery and the Confiscation Acts, 1861-1862* (Baton Rouge: Louisiana State University Press, 2005), 120–250; and Daniel W. Hamilton, *The Limits of Sovereignty: Property Confiscation in the Union and the Confederacy during the Civil War* (Chicago: University of Chicago Press, 2007), 20–81.
35. *Congressional Globe*, 37th Cong., 2d Sess. (1861-62), 1784–85, 1874, 2196.
36. Ibid., app., 224–5.
37. For a breakdown of the vote, see Siddali, *From Property to Person*, 255–57.
38. *Congressional Globe*, 37th Cong., 2d Sess. (1861-62), app., 325–27.
39. Ibid., 3374–83.
40. Where Lincoln wrote the proclamation, like virtually everything else about it, has been questioned. The telegraph office account, which has been accepted by scores of Lincoln scholars, came originally from Major Thomas Eckert of the telegraph office. See David Homer Bates, *Lincoln in the Telegraph Office: Recollections of the United States Military Telegraph Corps during the Civil War* (New York: Century Co., 1907), 138–41. For those who have questioned it, see Matthew Parker, "Lincoln's Summer of Emancipation," in *Lincoln and Freedom*, ed. Harold Holzer and Sarah Vaughn Gabbard (Carbondale: Southern Illinois University Press, 2007), 79–99.
41. Paul Finkelman, "Lincoln and the Preconditions for Emancipation," in *Lincoln's Proclamation: Emancipation Reconsidered*, ed. William Blair and Karen Fisher Younger (Chapel Hill: University of North Carolina Press, 2009), 19.
42. Basler, ed., *Collected Works of Lincoln*, 5:336–37.
43. Cornish, *Sable Arm*, 64–68; Quarles, *Negro in the Civil War*, 116–18.
44. Wendell H. Stephenson, *The Political Career of General James H. Lane* (Topeka: Kansas State Historical Society, 1930); Cornish, *Sable Arm*, 69–78; Quarles, *Negro in the Civil War*, 113–15; Richard S. Brownlee, *Gray Ghosts of the Confederacy: Guerilla War in the West, 1861-1865* (Baton Rouge: Louisiana State University Press, 1958), 37–41; Robert N. Scott et al., *The War of the Rebellion: A Compilation of the Official Records of the Union and Confederate Armies*, 128 vols., ser. 2 (Washington, DC: Government Printing Office, 1880-91), 2:294, 311–12, 417, 431, 445.
45. Scott et al., *War of the Rebellion*, ser. 1, 14:377; Worthington Chauncey Ford, ed., *A Cycle of Adams Letters, 1861-1865*, 2 vols. (Boston: Houghton, Mifflin Co., 1920), 1:174–75; Cornish, *Sable Arm*, 52–55, 80.
46. Thomas Wentworth Higginson, *Army Life in a Black Regiment* (1890; repr., Bos-

ton: Beacon, 1970), 2–4; Brenda Whiteheat, *The Friendship of Emily Dickinson and Thomas Wentworth Higginson* (New York: Alfred A. Knopf, 2008), 125.

47. James Mitchell, *Report on Colonization and Emigration Made to the Secretary of the Interior by the Agent of Emigration* (Washington, DC: Government Print Office, 1862).

48. *Douglass Monthly*, September 1862.

49. Paul J. Scheips, "Lincoln and the Chiriqui Colonization Project," *Journal of Negro History* 37 (October 1952): 418–53.

50. Benjamin R. Curtis, *Executive Power* (Boston: Little, Brown, 1862); Joel Parker, *The War Powers of Congress, and of the President* (Cambridge, MA: H. O Houghton, 1863); Robert C. Winthrop, *Speech of Hon. Robert C. Winthrop, at the Great Ratification Meeting in Union Square, New York, September 17, 1864* (New York, 1864). For a summary of the positions of the Emancipation Proclamation's supporters and critics, see Allen C. Guelzo, *Lincoln's Emancipation Proclamation* (New York: Simon & Schuster, 2004), 190–98.

51. Basler, ed., *Collected Works of Lincoln*, 6: 48–49.

52. Ibid., 5:433–36, 462–63, 470–71, 500.

53. David Herbert Donald, *Lincoln* (New York: Simon & Schuster, 1995), 397–98.

54. Ashley to Dr. George Cheever, December 22, 1862, George B. Cheever Papers, American Antiquarian Society, Worcester, MA.

55. Willis D. Boyd, "The Île a Vache Colonization Venture, 1862–1864," *Americas* 16 (July 1959): 45–62; Virginia Jeans Lass, ed., *Wartime Washington: The Civil War Letters of Elizabeth Blair Lee* (Champaign: University of Illinois Press, 1999), 223; Howard K. Beale, ed., *Diary of Edward Bates* (Washington, DC: Government Printing Office, 1933), 268; Phillip W. Magness and Sebastian N. Page, *Colonization after Emancipation: Lincoln and the Movement for Black Resettlement* (Columbia: University of Missouri Press, 2011).

Chapter 3

1. *Toledo Commercial*, January 6, 1863.

2. *Frankfort Tri-Weekly Commonwealth*, November 19, 1862, January 5, February 27, 1863.

3. Robert N. Scott et al., *The War of the Rebellion: A Compilation of the Official Records of the Union and Confederate Armies*, 128 vols., ser. 3 (Washington, DC: Government Printing Office, 1880–91), 1:106, 133.

4. Benjamin Quarles, *The Negro in the Civil War* (Boston: Little, Brown and Co., 1953), 27–28; James M. McPherson, *The Negro's Civil War* (New York: Pantheon Books, 1965), 19.

5. McPherson, *Negro's Civil War*, 22, 34–5; Peter H. Clark, *The Black Brigade of Cincinnati* (Cincinnati: J. B. Boyd, 1864), 4–5.

6. *Douglass Monthly*, 4 (September 1861), 516.

7. Gerrit Smith, *Sermons and Speeches* (New York: Ross & Tousey, 1861), 186–96.

8. Russell Duncan, ed., *Blue-Eyed Child of Fortune: The Civil War Letters of Robert Gould Shaw* (Athens: University of Georgia Press, 1992), 123.

9. *Douglass Monthly*, 4 (September 1861), 516.

10. Robert N. Scott et al., *War of the Rebellion*, ser. 4, 1:409; James G. Hollandsworth Jr., *The Louisiana Native Guards: The Black Military Experience during the Civil War* (Baton Rouge: Louisiana State University Press, 1995), 2; Lawrence Lee Hewitt, "The Ironic Route to Glory: Louisiana's Native Guards at Port Hudson," in *Black Soldiers in Blue*, ed. John David Smith (Chapel Hill: University of North Carolina Press, 2002), 78.

11. Henry Cleveland, *Alexander Stephens in Public and Private* (Philadelphia: National Publishing Co., 1866), 721-23.

12. Alfred N. Hunt, *Haiti's Influence on Antebellum America: Slumbering Volcano in the Caribbean* (Baton Rouge: Louisiana State University Press, 1988); Don E. Fehrenbacher, *The Slaveholding Republic* (New York: Oxford University Press, 2001), 111-18.

13. Rayford W. Logan, "The Negro in the Quasi War, 1798-1800," *Negro History Bulletin* 14 (March 1951): 128; Lorenzo J. Green, "The Negro in the War of 1812 and the Civil War," *Negro History Bulletin* 14 (March 1951): 133; Gerard T. Altoff, *Amongst My Best Men: African Americans and the War of 1812* (Put-in-Bay, OH: Perry Group, 1996).

14. *Congressional Globe*, 27th Cong., 2d Sess. (1841-42), 805-7, and 3d Sess., 175.

15. Okon Edet Uya, *From Slavery to Public Service, Robert Smalls 1839-1915* (New York: Oxford University Press, 1971).

16. *New York Tribune*, August 5, 1862; Roy C. Basler, ed., *The Collected Works of Abraham Lincoln*, 9 vols. (New Brunswick, NJ: Rutgers University Press, 1952-55), 5:356-57, 423.

17. James Speed to Abraham Lincoln, July 28, 1862, Robert Todd Lincoln Papers, Library of Congress; George Julian, *Political Recollections, 1840-1872* (Chicago: Jansen, McClurg and Co., 1884), 227; Cassius M. Clay, *The Life of Cassius M. Clay* (Cincinnati: J. Fletcher Brennan, 1886), 310; *Louisville Journal*, October 3, December 18, 1862; *New York Tribune*, November 14, 1862.

18. George Robertson to A. Lincoln, November 19, 1862; William Utley to Alexander W. Randall, November 17, 1862; William Utley to Abraham Lincoln, November 17, 19, 1862 — all in Robert Todd Lincoln Papers, Library of Congress.

19. Basler, ed., *Collected Works of Lincoln*, 5:502, 512.

20. Edwin S. Redkey, "Brave Black Volunteers: A Profile of the Fifty-fourth Massachusetts Regiment," in *Hope and Glory*, ed. Martin H. Blatt et al. (Amherst: University of Massachusetts Press, 2001), 21-27.

21. William F. Cheek and Aimee Lee Cheek, *John Mercer Langston and the Fight for Black Freedom, 1829-65* (Urbana: University of Illinois Press, 1996), 395; Norwood P. Hallowell, *The Negro as a Soldier in the War of the Rebellion* (Boston: Little, Brown and Co., 1897), 3-11.

22. Redkey, "Brave Black Volunteers," 23-24; Hallowell, *Negro as a Soldier*, 3-11.

23. Robert N. Scott et al., *War of the Rebellion*, ser. 3, 3:100.

24. Michael D. Meier, "Lorenzo Thomas and the Recruitment of Black Troops in the Mississippi Valley, 1863-1865," in *Black Soldiers in Blue*, ed. Smith, 249-69; Joseph T. Glatthaar, *Forged in Battle: The Civil War Alliance of Black Soldiers and*

White Officers (New York: Free Press, 1990), 37-38, 67-71; Dudley Taylor Cornish, *Sable Arm: Black Troops in the Union Army, 1861-1865* (Lawrence: University of Kansas Press, 1987), 112-31; Scott et al., *War of the Rebellion*, ser. 3, 3:1190, 5:121, 5:124.

25. Hollandsworth, *Louisiana Native Guards*; Stephen J. Ochs, *A Black Patriot and a White Priest: Andre Cailloux and Claude Paschal Maistre in Civil War New Orleans* (Baton Rouge: Louisiana State University Press, 2000); Lawrence Lee Hewitt, "An Ironic Route to Glory: Louisiana's Native Guards at Port Hudson," in *Black Soldiers in Blue*, ed. Smith, 78-106; Joseph T. Glatthaar, "The Civil War through the Eyes of a Sixteen-Year-Old Black Officer: The Letters of Lieutenant John H. Crowder of the 1st Louisiana Native Guards," in *Louisiana History* 35 (Spring 1994): 202-3.

26. Hewitt, "An Ironic Route to Glory," 97; Cornish, *Sable Arm*, 142-43; *New York Times*, June 11, 1863.

27. Richard Lowe, "Battle on the Levee: The Fight at Milliken's Bend, in *Black Soldiers in Blue*, ed. Smith, 107-35; Scott et al., *War of the Rebellion*, ser. 3, 3:453-54.

28. Scott et al., *War of the Rebellion*, ser. 1, vol. 24, pt. 1: 106; Charles A. Dana, *Recollections of the Civil War* (New York, 1898), 86-87; John Q. Anderson, ed., *Brokenburn: The Journal of Kate Stone, 1861-1868* (Baton Rouge: Louisiana State University Press, 1955), 218-19.

29. Duncan, ed., *Blue-Eyed Child of Fortune*, 343. For more on the sacking of Darien, see E. Merton Coulter, "Robert Gould Shaw and the Burning of Darien, Georgia," *Civil War History* 5 (Fall 1959): 363-73; Duncan, *Blue-Eyed Child of Fortune*, 43-45, 331, 342-46, 361, 369.

30. For the casualties, see Redkey, "Brave Black Volunteers," 28-32.

31. Donald Yacovone, "The Fifty-Fourth Massachusetts Regiment, the Pay Crisis, and the Lincoln Despotism," in *Hope and Glory*, ed. Blatt et al., 35-51.

32. For samples of Higginson's numerous protests, see his *Army Life in a Black Regiment* (Boston: Fields, Osgood and Co., 1890), app. D.

33. Frederick Douglass, *Life and Times of Frederick Douglass* (Hartford, CT: Park Publishing Co., 1881), 348.

34. Marvin R. Cain, *Edward Bates of Missouri* (Columbia: University of Missouri Press, 1965), 234.

35. Fred B. Joyner, "Robert Cumming Schenck, First Citizen and Statesman of the Miami Valley," *Ohio State Archaeological and Historical Quarterly* 58 (July 1949): 286-97.

36. For more details on Birney and Maryland recruitment, see Donn Piatt, *Memories of the Men Who Saved the Union* (New York: Frank F. Lovell & Co., 1887), 43-47; John W. Blassingame, "The Recruitment of Negro Troops in Maryland," *Maryland Historical Review* 58 (March 1963): 20-29; Charles L. Wagandt, *The Mighty Revolution: Negro Emancipation in Maryland* (Baltimore: Johns Hopkins Press, 1964), chaps. 9, 13.

37. For black recruitment in Missouri, see Blassingame, "Recruitment of Negro Troops," 326-38; Earl J. Nelson, "Missouri Slavery, 1861-1865," *Missouri Historical Review* 28 (July 1934): 260-74; Michael Fellman,"Emancipation in Missouri," *Missouri Historical Review* 83 (October 1988): 36-56; Ira Berlin et al., eds., *The Black Military*

Experience during the Civil War (Cambridge: Cambridge University Press, 1982), 187–90. For Schofield's viewpoint, see John M. Schofield, *Forty-Six Years in the Army* (New York: Century Co., 1897), chap. 6.

38. For the long and involved story of black recruitment in Kentucky, see John W. Blassingame, "The Recruitment of Colored Troops in Kentucky, Maryland and Missouri, 1863–1865," *Historian* 29 (1967): 533–45; Victor B. Howard, *Black Liberation in Kentucky* (Lexington: University Press of Kentucky, 1983), 45–71; John David Smith, "The Recruitment of Negro Soldiers in Kentucky, 1863–1865," *Register of the Kentucky Historical Society* 72 (October 1974): 364–90; Berlin et al., eds., *Black Military Experience*, 191–97; Richard D. Sears, *Camp Nelson, Kentucky: A Civil War History* (Lexington: University Press of Kentucky, 2002), xxxv–xxxix, 54–96.

39. Scott et al., *War of the Rebellion*, ser. 3, 3:416, 418–20.

40. Hallowell, *Negro as a Soldier in the War of the Rebellion*, 3–11.

41. Scott et al., *War of the Rebellion*, ser. 3, 4:60, 138, 145; James Larry Hood, "For the Union: Kentucky's Unconditional Unionist Congressmen and the Development of the Republican Party in Kentucky, 1863–1865," *Register of the Kentucky Historical Society* 76 (July 1978): 197–215.

42. *Congressional Globe*, 38th Cong., 1st Sess. (1863–64), 333–34, 338, 516, 768, 836, app., 106.

43. Scott et al., *War of the Rebellion*, ser. 3, 4:174–76.

44. Ibid., 4:233–34, 248–49, 422.

45. Ibid., 4:733.

46. Combined Books, comp., *Civil War Book of Lists: Over 300 Lists, from the Sublime . . . to the Ridiculous* (Conshohocken, PA: Combined Books, 1993), 28.

47. *Frankfort Tri-Weekly Commonwealth*, June 23, 1864.

Chapter 4

1. P. J. Staudenraus, ed., *Mr. Lincoln's Washington: Selections from the Writings of Noah Brooks, Civil War Correspondent* (South Brunswick, NJ: T. Yoseloff, 1967), 309, 349–50.

2. Ashley to Salmon P. Chase, February 26, 1856, Chase Papers, Ohio Historical Society, Columbus.

3. For the Blair family, see William E. Smith, *The Francis Preston Blair Family in Politics*, 2 vols. (New York: Macmillan Co., 1933).

4. Blair to Andrew Jackson, May 2, 1844, in *Correspondence of Andrew Jackson*, ed. John S. Bassett, 7 vols. (Washington DC: Carnegie Institute of Washington, 1926–35), 6:281–82.

5. Burton J. Hendrick, *Lincoln's War Cabinet* (Boston: Little, Brown and Co., 1946), 387.

6. For further details on Frank Blair, see William E. Parrish, *Frank Blair: Lincoln's Conservative* (Columbia: University of Missouri Press, 1998).

7. *St. Louis Missouri Democrat*, March 24, 1857, April 8, 1857, and April 15, 1857; *Washington National Era*, April 16, 1857; Kenneth Stampp, *America in 1857* (New York: Oxford University Press, 1990), 141.

8. *Congressional Globe*, 35 Cong., 1st Sess. (1857–58), 183; Frank P. Blair Jr., *Speech of Hon. Frank P. Blair, Jr., of Missouri, on the Acquisition of Territory in Central and South America, to Be Colonized with Free Blacks, and Held as a Dependency by the United States: Delivered in the House of Representatives, on the 14th Day of January 1858 — with an Appendix* (Washington, DC: Buell and Blanchard, Printers, 1858).

9. Frank P. Blair Jr., *The Destiny of the Races of This Continent: An Address Delivered before the Mercantile Library Association of Boston, Massachusetts, on the 26th of January, 1859* (Washington, DC: Buell and Blanchard, 1859), and *Speech of F. P. Blair, Jr., of Missouri at the Cooper Institute, New York City, January 25, 1860* (Washington, DC: Buell and Blanchard, Printers, 1860).

10. Louis S. Gerteis, *Civil War St. Louis*, (Lawrence: University Press of Kansas, 2001), 58–60, 65, 67, 78; James Neal Primm, *Lion of the Valley: St. Louis, Missouri* (Boulder, CO: Pruett Publishing Co., 1981), 244–46.

11. Steven Rowan and James Neal Primm, eds., *Germans for a Free Missouri: Translations from the* St. Louis Radical Press, *1857–1862* (Columbia: University of Missouri Press. 1983), quote on 288, 20–22, 283–96, 311–12. See also Gustave Koerner, *Memoirs of Gustave Koerner, 1809–1896*, 2 vols. (Cedar Rapids, IA: Torch Press, 1909), 2:189–91.

12. Samuel Knox, "Brief," Blair Papers, Library of Congress.

13. *St. Louis Missouri Democrat*, July 9, 23, 30, and August 18, 29, 1853.

14. For a detailed analysis, see Mark W. Geiger, *Financial Fraud and Guerrilla Violence in Missouri's Civil War, 1861–1865* (New Haven, CT: Yale University Press, 2010).

15. *Missouri Republican*, September 27, 1863; *Liberator*, October 16, 1863; Elizabeth Blair Lee to Samuel Phillips Lee, October 24, 1863, in *Wartime Washington: The Civil War Letters of Elizabeth Blair Lee* , ed. Virginia Jeans Lass (Urbana: University of Illinois Press, 2000), 316; Smith, *Blair Family in Politics*, 2:227–45; Parrish, *Frank Blair*, 178–80.

16. Gideon Welles, *Diary of Gideon Welles*, 3 vols. (Boston: Houghton Mifflin Co., 1911), 2:20; Michael Burlingame and John R. Turner Ettlinger, eds., *Inside Lincoln's White House: The Complete Civil War Diary of John Hay* (Carbondale: Southern Illinois University Press, 1997), 123.

17. Montgomery Blair, *Speech of Montgomery Blair, on the Revolutionary Schemes of the Ultra Abolitionists, and in Defence of the Policy of the President* (New York: D. W. Lee, 1863).

18. Ralph Korngold, *Thaddeus Stevens: A Being Darkly Wise and Rudely Great* (New York: Harcourt, Brace and Co., 1955), 219–20.

19. *Missouri Democrat*, October 3, 1863–January 8, 1864; *Proceedings of the American Anti-Slavery Society . . . December 3rd and 4th, 1863* (New York, 1864), 28–29.

20. For details on the Radical Democracy, see Harold M. Hyman, "Election of 1864," in *1848–1868*, vol. 3 of *History of American Presidential Elections*, ed. Arthur M. Schlesinger Jr. (New York: Chelsea House Publishers, 1985), 1155–78.

21. *Missouri Democrat*, January 13, 1865; William E. Parrish, *Turbulent Partnership: Missouri and the Union, 1861–1865* (Columbia: University of Missouri Press, 1962), 186–95; William E. Parrish, *Missouri under Radical Rule, 1865–1870* (Columbia: University of Missouri Press, 1965), 8–13, 18–19, 37–39; Ralph R. Rea, *Sterling Price,*

the Lee of the West (Little Rock: Pioneer Press, 1959); Grace G. Avery, ed., and Floyd C. Shoemaker, comp., *Messages and Proclamations of the Governors . . . of Missouri* (Columbia: State Historical Society of Missouri, 1924), 4:256.

22. See the *Toledo Blade*, June 1, 1864, for Ashley's characterization of Frémont as an ass.

23. For details on Chase, see Frederic J. Blue, *Salmon P. Chase: A Life in Politics* (Kent, OH: Kent State University Press, 1987); John Niven, *Salmon P. Chase: A Biography* (New York: Oxford University Press, 1995).

24. Charles R. Wilson, "The Original Chase Organization Meeting and the Next Presidential Election," *Mississippi Valley Historical Review* 23 (June 1936): 61–79; *National Intelligencer*, February 22, 1864; David Donald, *Lincoln* (New York: Simon & Schuster, 1996), 481–83.

25. *Congressional Globe*, 38th Cong., 1st Sess. (1863–64), app. 46–51.

26. Ibid., 1828–32.

27. Theodore C. Smith, *The Life and Letters of James Abram Garfield*, 2 vols. (Hamden, CT: Archon Books, 1968), 1:255, 376–77; Allan Peskin, *Garfield* (Kent, OH: Kent State University Press, 1978), 238–39; Salmon P. Chase to Jay Cooke, May 5, 1864, in *Correspondence, April 1863–1864*, vol. 4 of *The Salmon P. Chase Papers*, ed. James P. McClure and John Niven, 5 vols. (Kent, OH: Kent State University Press, 1997), 379–80; Albert G. Riddle, *Recollections of War Times* (New York: Putnam, 1895), 269–76.

28. Garfield quote, in Noah Brooks, *Washington in Lincoln's Time* (New York: Century Co., 1958), 28; Sauerwein quotes, in Charles L. Wagandt, *The Mighty Revolution: Negro Emancipation in Maryland, 1862–1864* (Baltimore: Johns Hopkins Press, 1964), 22.

29. Tracy Matthew Melton, *Hanging Henry Gambrill: The Violent Career of Baltimore's Plug Uglies, 1854–1860* (Baltimore: Johns Hopkins University Press, 2005), 65–67, 349–50.

30. Bernard Steiner, *The Life of Henry Winter Davis* (Baltimore: John Murphy Co., 1916), 8–9.

31. Ibid., 144–45; *Congressional Globe*, 36th Cong., 1st Sess. (1859–60), 634, 650; *New York Times*, February 1, 3, 1860; Ollinger Crenshaw, "The Speakership Contest of 1859–1860," *Mississippi Valley Historical Review* 29 (December 1942): 323–38; Congressional Quarterly, Inc., *Congressional Quarterly Guide to U.S. Elections* (Washington, DC: Congressional Quarterly, 1975), 606, 609.

32. Steiner, *Life of Henry Winter Davis*, 13–14.

33. Henry Winter Davis, *Speech . . . at Concert Hall, September 24, 1863* (Philadelphia, 1863), and *Speeches and Addresses Delivered in the Congress of the United States, and on Several Public Occasions* (New York: Harper and Brothers, 1867), 363; *Congressional Globe*, 38th Cong., 1st Sess. (1863–64), app., 46.

34. Montgomery Blair, *Speech of Montgomery Blair, on the Revolutionary Schemes of the Ultra Abolitionists, and in Defence of the Policy of the President* (New York: D. W. Lee, 1863); Henry Winter Davis, *Speeches and Addresses*, 384–92.

35. Wagandt, *The Mighty Revolution*, 97–101; Jean H. Baker, *The Politics of Continuity:*

Maryland Political Parties from 1858 to 1870 (Baltimore: Johns Hopkins University Press, 1973), 77, 87–91.

36. Montgomery Blair to Samuel L. M. Barlow, December 25, 1863, Barlow Papers, Huntington Library, San Marino, CA. Blair continued to press this idea. See Blair to Barlow, December 20, 1864, January 7, 12, 1865, Barlow to Blair, December 22, 1864; Barlow to William H. Wadsworth, December 28, 1864, Barlow to Samuel S. Cox, February 9, 1865 — all in Barlow Papers, Huntington Library, San Marino, CA.

37. Wagandt, *The Mighty Revolution*, 217; statistics 219.

38. Ibid., 1, 2, 225–30; *The Debates of the Constitutional Convention of the State of Maryland* (Annapolis: R P. Bayly, 1864), 1:624, 1:742, 3:1873; Anita Aidt Guy, *Maryland's Persistent Pursuit to End Slavery, 1850–1864* (New York: Garland Publishing, 1997), 440, 520–23.

39. C. Peter Ripley, *Slaves and Freedmen in Civil War Louisiana* (Baton Rouge: Louisiana State University Press, 1976).

40. Ted Tunnell, *Crucible of Reconstruction: War, Radicalism, and Race in Louisiana, 1862–1877* (Baton Rouge: Louisiana State University Press, 1984); Herman Belz, *Reconstructing the Union* (Ithaca, NY: Cornell University Press, 1969), 193–95; Benjamin W. Arnett, ed., *Orations and Speeches: Duplicate Copy of the Souvenir from the Afro-American League to the Hon. James M. Ashley* (Philadelphia: AME Church, 1894), 288–93.

41. "Protest of Senator Wade and H. Winter Davis, M.C.," in *The Radical Republicans and Reconstruction, 1861–1870*, ed. Harold Hyman (Indianapolis: Bobbs-Merrill, 1967), 137–47.

42. William Frank Zornow, *Lincoln and the Party Divided* (Norman: University of Oklahoma Press, 1954), 17–21, 108; *New York Tribune*, August 5, 17, 1864; *Harpers Weekly*, August 20, 1864; Albert G. Riddle, *The Life of Benjamin Wade* (Cleveland: Williams Publishing, 1888), 255; Frederic Bancroft and William Dunning, eds., *The Reminiscences of Carl Schurz*, 3 vols. (New York: McClure Publishing Co., 1909), 3:99; Carl Sandburg, *Abraham Lincoln: The War Years*, 4 vols. (New York: Charles Scribner's' Sons, 1939), 2:561–62; George W. Julian, *Political Recollections, 1840–1872* (Chicago: Jansen, McClurg and Co., 1884), 243; Shelby M. Cullom, *Fifty Years of Public Service* (New York: C. Scribner's' Sons, 1911), 98–99; Winfred A. Harbison, "Zachariah Chandler's Part in the Reelection of Abraham Lincoln," *Mississippi Valley Historical Review* 22 (September 1935): 267–76; Hans L. Trefousse, "Zachariah Chandler and the Withdrawal of Frémont in 1864: New Answers to an Old Riddle," *Lincoln Herald* 70 (Winter 1968): 181–88.

43. Henry Winter Davis to Benjamin Wade, June 21, 1864, Wade Papers, Library of Congress.

44. For details on "Little Dixie," see R. Douglas Hurt, *Agriculture and Slavery in Missouri's Little Dixie* (Columbia: University of Missouri Press, 1992); and Jeffrey C. Stone, *Slavery, Southern Culture, and Education in Little Dixie, Missouri, 1820–1860* (New York: CRC Press, 2006).

45. James S. Rollins to Abraham Lincoln, September 8, 1863, and Rollins to Edward Bates, September 13, 1863, both in Lincoln Papers, Library of Congress.

46. Abel Rathbone Corbin to Abraham Lincoln, December 8, 1864, Robert Todd Lincoln Collection, Library of Congress; Mark W. Summers, *The Era of Good Stealings* (New York: Oxford University Press, 1993), 184–85, and *The Plundering Generation* (New York: Oxford University Press, 1987), 102–3.

Chapter 5

1. American Antislavery Society, *Fifth Annual Report of the Executive Committee of the American Anti-Slavery Society* (New York, 1838), 138–44. On the burned-over district, the classic account is Whitney R. Cross, *The Burned-Over District: The Social and Intellectual History of Enthusiastic Religion in Western New York, 1800–1850* (Ithaca, NY: Cornell University Press, 1950).

2. On Warsaw and its antislavery history, see Andrew W. Young, *History of of the Town of Warsaw, New York* (Buffalo, NY: Press of Sage, Sons, and Co., 1869), 156–63 and passim.

3. P. J. Staudenraus, ed., *Mr. Lincoln's Washington: Selections from the Writings of Noah Brooks, Civil War Correspondent* (South Brunswick, NJ: Thomas Yoseloff, 1967), 299.

4. For biographical information on Fenton, see James C. Mohr, *The Radical Republicans and Reform in New York during Reconstruction* (Ithaca, NY: Cornell University Press, 1973), 8–15.

5. For the Frank family, see Young, *History of the Town of Warsaw*, 265–70 and passim.

6. Leonard L. Richards, *The Slave Power: The Free North and Southern Domination, 1780–1860* (Baton Rouge: Louisiana State University Press, 2000).

7. Leonard P. Curry, "Congressional Democrats, 1861–1863," *Civil War History* 12 (September 1966): 213–29; Jean H. Baker, *Affairs of Party: The Political Culture of Northern Democrats in the Mid-Nineteenth Century* (Ithaca, NY: Cornell University Press, 1983); Joel H. Silbey, *"A Respectable Minority": The Democratic Party in the Civil War Era, 1860–1868* (New York: W. W. Norton, 1977).

8. Frank L. Klement, "Sound and Fury: Civil War Dissent in the Cincinnati Area," *Cincinnati Historical Society Bulletin* 35 (1977): 102; Jennifer L. Weber, *Copperheads: The Rise and Fall of Lincoln's Opponents in the North* (New York: Oxford University Press, 2006), 63–66; Bruce Tap, "Race, Rhetoric, and Emancipation: The Election of 1862 in Illinois," *Civil War History*, 39 (June 1993): 101–25.

9. *New York Times*, October 4–November 4, 1862; De Alva Stanwood Alexander, *A Political History of the State of New York* (New York: H. Holt and Co., 1909), 3:40.

10. Silbey, *"A Respectable Minority,"* 144–46; Frank L. Klement, *The Limits of Dissent: Clement Vallandigham and the Civil War* (Lexington: University Press of Kentucky, 1970), 102–13; Congressional Quarterly, Inc., *Congressional Quarterly Guide to U.S. Elections* (Washington, DC: Congressional Quarterly, 1975), 608, 611.

11. H. S. Bundy to Salmon P. Chase, October 18, 1862, Chase Papers, Library of Congress. For similar comments, see John Sherman to William T. Sherman, November 16, 1862, Sherman Papers, Library of Congress; Isaac Welsh to Benjamin F. Wade, January 31, 1863, Wade Papers, Library of Congress.

12. *Toledo Blade*, October 17, 1862; *Chicago Tribune*, November 6, 1862; *New York*

Times, October 23, 1862. For various explanations of the outcome, see Jamie L. Carson et al., "The Impact of National Tides and District-Level Effects on Electoral Outcomes: The U.S. Congressional Elections of 1862-63," *American Journal of Political Science* 45 (October 2001): 887-98; Arnold Shankman, "Francis W. Hughes and the 1862 Pennsylvania Election," *Pennsylvania Magazine of History and Biography* 95 (1971): 383-93. Bruce Tap, "Race, Rhetoric, and Emancipation: the Election of 1862 in Illinois," *Civil War History* 39 (June 1993): 101-25; Jacque Voegeli, "The Northwest and the Race Issue, 1861-1862," *Mississippi Valley Historical Review* 50 (September 1963): 235-51.

13. William Gillette, *Jersey Blue: Civil War Politics in New Jersey, 1854-1865* (New Brunswick, NJ: Rutgers University Press, 1995), 193-95.

14. For further details, see Irving Katz, *August Belmont: A Political Biography* (New York: Columbia University Press, 1968).

15. Phyllis F. Field, *The Politics of Race in New York: The Struggle for Black Suffrage in the Civil War Era* (Ithaca, NY: Cornell University Press, 1982).

16. August Belmont, ed., *Letters, Speeches, and Addresses* (New York: Privately Printed, 1890), 3-7; Merle Curti, "Young America," *American Historical Review* 32 (October 1926): 51-54; Robert E. May, *The Southern Dream of a Caribbean Empire, 1854-1861* (Baton Rouge: Louisiana State University Press, 1973), 141-42, 164-65.

17. George Winston Smith, "The National War Committee of the Citizens of New York," *New York History* 28 (October 1947): 440-57.

18. Society for the Diffusion of Political Knowledge, *Emancipation and Its Results* (New York: Society for the Diffusion of Political Knowledge, 1863); Katz, *August Belmont*, 120-21 and passim; Alexander Flick, *Samuel Jones Tilden: A Study in Political Sagacity* (New York: Dodd, Mead and Co., 1939), 140-41 and passim.

19. For Marble's life, see George McJimsey, *Genteel Partisan: Manton Marble, 1834-1917* (Ames: Iowa State University Press, 1971).

20. For details on the New York Draft Riot, see especially the *New York Herald*, July 12-15, 1863; *The Bloody Week! Riot, Murder, and Arson . . .* (New York: Coutant and Baker, 1863); Irving Werstein, *July, 1863* (New York: J. Messner, 1957); Adrian Cook, *The Armies of the Streets: The New York Draft Riots of 1863* (Lexington: University Press of Kentucky, 1974); and Iver Bernstein, *The New York Draft Riots: Their Significance for American Society and Politics in the Age of the Civil War* (New York: Oxford University Press, 1990).

21. *New York World*, July 15, 1863; Kenneth Ackerman, *Boss Tweed* (New York: Carroll and Graf, 2005), 15-17; Bernstein, *New York Draft Riots*, 50-1.

22. Cook, *Armies of the Streets*, 177-80; Bernstein, *New York Draft Riots*, 3-72.

23. *New York World*, July 14, 1863.

24. Leonard L. Richards, *"Gentlemen of Property and Standing": Anti-Abolition Mobs in Jacksonian America* (New York: Oxford University Press, 1970), 30-32, 40-46, 94-95, 114-15, 120-23; Linda Kerber, "Abolitionists and Amalgamators: The New York City Race Riots of 1834," *New York History* 48 (January 1967): 28-39.

25. For the basic story of what Croly and Wakeman were up to, see Sidney Kaplan, "The Miscegenation Issue in the Election of 1864," *Journal of Negro History* 34 (July 1949): 284-337; Forrest G. Wood, *Black Scare: The Racist Response to Eman-*

cipation and Reconstruction (Berkeley: University of California Press, 1968), 35, 53–79. Weber, *Copperheads*, 160–61, 168.

26. [David Goodman Croly and George Wakeman], *Miscegenation: The Theory of the Blending of the Races, Applied to the American White Man and Negro* (New York: H. Dexter, Hamilton & Co., 1864).

27. Samuel S. Cox, *Eight Years in Congress, from 1857 to 1865* (New York: D. Appleton and Co., 1865), 354; *Congressional Globe*, 37th Cong., 1st Sess. (1863–64), 35–37; Samuel S. Cox, *Miscegenation or Amalgamation. Fate of the Freedman: Speech of Samuel S. Cox of Ohio Delivered in the House of Representatives, February 17, 1864* (Washington, DC: Printed at the Office of "The Constitutional Union," No. 330 E Street, 1864).

28. *New York World*, March 18, 1864.

29. For Van Evrie's views, see John H. Van Evrie, *Negroes and Negro Slavery: The First, an Inferior Race—the Latter, Its Normal Condition* (Baltimore: J. D. Toy, 1853); *Subgenation: The Theory of the Normal Relation of the Races: An Answer to "Miscegenation"* (New York: J. Bradburn, 1864) and *White Supremacy and Negro Subordination* (New York: Horton & Co., 1868). All of these books went through several editions. The latter two books include numerous articles from Van Evrie's newspapers, the *Caucasian* and the *Weekly Day Book*.

30. Stephen W. Sears, *George B. McClellan: The Young Napoleon* (New York: Ticknor & Fields, 1988), 345–46; William Starr Myers, *General George McClellan* (New York: D. Appleton-Century Co., 1934), 423–24.

31. *New York World*, January 13, 23, 1864; Katz, *August Belmont*, 125.

32. *New York Herald*, February 24–26, 1864; Katz, *August Belmont*, 125–26.

33. *New York World*, June 13–24, 1864.

34. Stephens to Hershel V. Johnson, September 5, 1864, as quoted in Larry E. Nelson, *Bullets, Ballots, and Rhetoric: Confederate Policy for the United States Presidential Contest of 1864* (University: University of Alabama Press, 1980), 115; Clement C. Clay to Judah Benjamin, September 12, 1864, in *The War of the Rebellion: A Compilation of the Official Records of the Union and Confederate Armies*, by Robert N. Scott et al., 128 vols., ser. 4 (Washington, DC: Government Printing Office, 1880–91), 3:637–38.

35. Vallandigham to McClellan, September 4, 1864, McClellan Papers, Library of Congress; Charles R. Wilson, "McClellan's Changing Views on the Peace Plank of 1864," *American Historical Review* 38 (April 1933): 498–505. Wilson's notion that McClellan essentially accepted the peace plank in his earlier drafts has been rejected by McClellan's biographer, Stephen W. Sears, in Sears's "McClellan and the Peace Planks of 1864: A Reappraisal," *Civil War History* 36 (March 1990): 57–64. I don't find Sears's argument convincing.

36. Belmont to McClellan, September 3, 1864, McClellan Papers, Library of Congress; Wilson, "McClellan's Changing Views on the Peace Plank of 1864," 498–505.

37. Jessie Benton Frémont to George Julian, May 1, 1862, in *The Letters of Jessie Benton Frémont*, ed. Pamela Herr and Mary Lee Spence (Urbana: University of Illinois Press, 1993), 319–20.

38. Christopher Dell, *Lincoln and the War Democrats: The Grand Erosion of Conserva-*

tive Tradition (Cranbury, NJ: Associated University Presses, 1975), 137; T. Harry Williams, *Lincoln and the Radicals* (Madison: University of Wisconsin Press, 1941), 70; David Donald, ed., *Inside Lincoln's Cabinet: The Civil War Diaries of Salmon P. Chase* (New York: Longmans, Green and Co., 1954), 57; Bruce Tap, "Amateurs at War: Abraham Lincoln and the Committee on the Conduct of the War," *Journal of the Abraham Lincoln Association* 23 (Summer 2002): 3; Bruce Tap, *Over Lincoln's Shoulder: The Committee on the Conduct of the War* (Lawrence: University Press of Kansas, 1998), 29-30, 162-64, and passim.

39. Nathaniel Bartlett Sylvester, *History of Rensselaer Co., New York* (Philadelphia: Everts and Peck, 1880), 74-108, 272 ff.

40. *Congressional Globe*, 38th Cong., 1st Sess. (1863-64), app. 125; Dell, *Lincoln and the War Democrats*, 305.

41. Charles S. Ashley, "Governor Ashley's Biography and Messages," *Contributions to the Historical Society of Montana* 6 (1907): 176-79; *Congressional Globe*, 38th Cong., 1st Sess. (1863-64), 2962; James M. Ashley, "Address of Hon. James M. Ashley before the 'Ohio Society of New York,' February 19, 1890," in *Orations and Speeches: Duplicate Copy of the Souvenir from the Afro-American League to the Hon. James M. Ashley*, ed. Benjamin W. Arnett (Philadelphia: AME Church, 1894), 707-8, 712, 713.

42. Years later, in telling this story, Ashley said that of the seventeen Democrats on the list, eleven—not twelve—voted with him. In doing so, he probably counted Griswold, who had switched parties before the vote, as a fellow Republican. See James M. Ashley, "The Passage of the Thirteenth Amendment to the Constitution," *Magazine of Western History* 13 (April 1891): 678.

Chapter 6

1. James M. Ashley, "The Passage of the Thirteenth Amendment to the Constitution," *Magazine of Western History* 13 (April 1891): 678.

2. James M. Scovel, "Thaddeus Stevens," *Lippincott's Monthly Magazine* 61 (1898): 550. The authenticity of this remark has sometimes been questioned, partly because it first appeared in print thirty years after the fact, and partly because Stevens, who was at odds with Lincoln, referred to him as "the purest man in America." In my judgment, Stevens was just being sarcastic, taking a poke at Lincoln's reputation for rectitude.

3. Computed from data given in Kenneth Martis, *The Historical Atlas of Political Parties in the United States Congress: 1789-1989* (New York: Macmillan Publishing Co., 1989), 116 and 118.

4. Leonard L. Richards, *The Life and Times of Congressman John Quincy Adams* (New York: Oxford University Press, 1986), 57; Alvin W. Lynn, "Party Formation and Operation in the House of Representatives, 1824-1837" (PhD diss., Rutgers University, 1972), 340-97, 489-95.

5. Martis, *Historical Atlas of Political Parties*, 75 and 76.

6. For the battle over the courts, see Richard E. Ellis, *The Jeffersonian Crisis: Courts and Politics in the Young Republic* (New York: Oxford University Press, 1971).

7. Greeley to Lincoln, July 7, August 8, 1864, Lincoln Papers, Library of Congress.

8. Roy P. Basler et al., *The Collected Works of Abraham Lincoln*, 9 vols. (New Brunswick, NJ: Rutgers University Press, 1953–55), 7:514.

9. William F. Zornow, *Lincoln and the Party Divided* (Norman: University of Oklahoma Press, 1954), 139.

10. Jessie Marshall Ames, ed., *Private and Official Correspondence of General Benjamin Butler* (Norwood, MA: Plimpton Press, 1917), 4:534–36; Louis Taylor Merrill, "General Benjamin F. Butler in the Presidential Campaign of 1864," *Mississippi Valley Historical Review* 33 (March 1947): 555–70.

11. Martis, *Historical Atlas of Political Parties*, 117–19.

12. Jonathan W. White, "Canvassing the Troops: The Federal Government and the Soldiers Right to Vote," *Civil War History* 50 (September 2004); 291–317; Oscar O. Winther, "The Soldier Vote in the Election of 1864," *New York History* 25 (October 1944): 440–58.

13. Winther, "Soldier Vote in the Election of 1864," 455–58; Theodore Gerrish, *Army Life: A Private's Reminiscences of the Civil War* (Portland, ME: Hoyt, Fogg, & Donham, 1882), 209.

14. Charles L. Wagandt, *The Mighty Revolution: Negro Emancipation in Maryland, 1862–1864* (Baltimore: Johns Hopkins University Press, 1964), 258–62; William E. Parrish, *Missouri under Radical Rule, 1865–1870* (Columbia: University of Missouri Press, 1965), 14–49.

15. *New York Tribune*, November 12, 1864. Because some states didn't count the soldier vote separately, it is hard to be certain. But in New York and elsewhere, several Republican candidates won by a margin of less than 1 percent.

16. *Toledo Blade*, May 11 — November 22, 1864; Clark Waggoner, *History of Toledo and Lucas County* (New York: Munsell & Co., 1888), 352, 355; Congressional Quarterly, Inc., *Congressional Quarterly Guide to U.S. Elections* (Washington, DC: Congressional Quarterly, 1975), 614.

17. *Columbus, Ohio, Crisis*, October 16, 19, 1864; *Congressional Globe*, 39th Cong., 1st Sess. (1865–66), 13, 170, 422, 2678; Arnold Shankman, "Soldier Votes and Clement L. Vallandigham in the 1863 Ohio Gubernatorial Election," *Ohio History* 82 (Winter/Spring 1973): 88–104.

18. Michael Vorenberg, *Final Freedom: The Civil War, the Abolition of Slavery, and the Thirteenth Amendment* (Cambridge: Cambridge University Press, 2001), 196–97, 202–3, 243; LaWanda Cox and John H. Cox, *Politics, Principle, and Prejudice, 1865–1866* (New York: Free Press, 1963), 28; Christopher Dell, *Lincoln and the War Democrats: The Grand Erosion of Conservative Tradition* (Cranbury, NJ: Associated University Presses, 1975), 130–31, 217, 300; Jennifer L. Weber, *Copperheads: The Rise and Fall of Lincoln's Opponents in the North* (New York: Oxford University Press, 2006), 210; David Lindsey, *"Sunset" Cox: Irrepressible Democrat* (Detroit: Wayne State University Press, 1959).

19. *Congressional Globe*, 37th Cong., 3d Sess. (1862–63), 95, 637, app. 39.

20. Samuel S. Cox to Manton Marble, December 7, 21, 1864, January 13, 17, 1865, Marble Papers, Library of Congress.

21. Samuel S. Cox to Manton Marble, January 13, 1865, Marble Papers, Library of Congress.

22. William H. Seward, "Speech Delivered October 31, 1868," in *Works of William H. Seward*, ed. George E. Baker, 5 vols. (Boston: Houghton, Mifflin and Co., 1873–84), 5:554.

23. Samuel S. Cox, *Eight years in Congress, from 1857 to 1865* (New York: D. Appleton & Co., 1865), 397–8.

24. What happened at this meeting has long been a matter of dispute. No records were kept, and little was said publicly after the meeting. But if Confederate sources are to be trusted, Lincoln and Seward hinted at ways that Confederate leaders could moderate the impact of the Thirteenth Amendment—or even torpedo it and preserve slavery. For a scathing indictment of what Lincoln and Seward allegedly did, see Lerone Bennett Jr., *Forced into Glory: Abraham Lincoln's White Dream* (Chicago: Johnson Publishing Co., 2000), 611–15.

25. Basler, ed., *Collected Works of Lincoln*, 8:275–76.

26. Alexander Long to Alexander S. Boys, February 13, 1865, Alexander S. Boys Papers, Ohio Historical Society, Columbus; *Cincinnati Gazette*, February 14, 1865; Louis R. Harlan, ed., "The Autobiography of Alexander Long," *Bulletin of the Historical and Philosophical Society of Ohio* 19 (April 1961): 99–127.

27. Samuel S. Cox, *Three Decades of Federal Legislation, 1855–1885* (Providence, RI: J. A. and R. A. Reid, 1885), 329.

28. *Toledo Blade*, August 21–December 6, 1862; Clark Waggoner to Charles Sumner, September 17, 1862, Sumner Papers, Houghton Library, Cambridge, MA; H.R. Rep. No. 37-47, at 3–63 (1862–63); Clark Waggoner, "Seventh Congressional District: J. M. Ashley and His Record," *Toledo Blade*, November 1, 1890.

29. Isaac N. Arnold, *The Life of Abraham Lincoln* (Chicago: Jansen, McClurg and Co., 1885), 358–9.

30. Abel Rathbone Corbin to Abraham Lincoln, December 8, 1864, Robert Todd Lincoln Collection, Library of Congress; Mark W. Summers, *The Era of Good Stealings* (New York: Oxford University Press, 1993), 184–85, and *The Plundering Generation* (New York: Oxford University Press, 1987), 102–3; William S. McFeely, *Grant: A Biography* (New York: W. W. Norton, 1981), 319–29.

31. Parrish, *Missouri under Radical Rule*, 16–19; William F. Switzler to James S. Rollins, January 15, 1865, James S. Rollins Papers, State Historical Society of Missouri, Columbia (microfilm).

32. Allen Thorndyke Rice, ed., *Reminiscences of Abraham Lincoln by Distinguished Men of His Time* (New York: North American Publishing Co., 1886), 585–86; Vorenberg, *Final Freedom*, 198.

33. George S. Boutwell, *Reminiscences of Sixty Years in Public Affairs*, 2 vols. (New York: McLure, Phillips and Co., 1902), 2:36.

34. Anson Herrick to William H. Seward, July 3, August 8, 29, 1865, February 5, 1867; Homer Nelson to Seward, July 29, 1865, November 20, 1866—Seward Papers, University of Rochester, Rochester, NY.

35. United States. Congress. House. Committee of Elections. *Alexander H. Coffroth and William H. Koontz* (Washington, DC 1866); Albert G. Riddle, *Recollection of War Times* (New York: G. P. Putnam's Sons, 1895), 324–25; *New York Tribune*, February 3 1865; *Congressional Globe*, 38th Cong., 2d Sess. (1864–65), 523–24.

36. *Congressional Globe*, 38th Cong., 2d Sess. (1864-65), 120-24, 155-56.

37. For the lobbyists' view, see J. R. Freese to Joseph P. Bradley, January 16, 1865, and George Shea to Bradley, January 16 and 25, 1865—Bradley Papers, New Jersey Historical Society, Newark. For Lincoln's side of the story, see John Nicolay and John Hay, *Abraham Lincoln: A History*, 10 vols. (New York: Century Co., 1890), 10:84-85; Helen Nicolay, *Lincoln's Secretary: A Biography of John Nicolay* (New York: Longmans, Green, 1949), 220-21; Michael Burlingame, editor, *With Lincoln in the White House: Letters, Memoranda, and Other Writings of John G. Nicolay, 1860-1865*, (Carbondale: Southern Illinois University Press, 2006), 171. For the views of New Jersey scholars, see William Gillette, *New Jersey Blue: Civil War Politics in New Jersey, 1854-1865* (New Brunswick, NJ: Rutgers University Press, 1995), 193-95, 258-59, 300-304; Charles Merriam Knapp, *New Jersey Politics during the Period of the Civil War and Reconstruction* (Geneva, NY: W. F. Humphrey, 1924), 97-98; George L. A. Reilley, "The Camden and Amboy Railroad and New Jersey Politics" (PhD diss., Columbia University, 1951), 197-208.

38. *Cincinnati Gazette*, February 14, 1865.

39. W. N. Bilbo to Lincoln, November 22, 1864, January 26 1865, Lincoln Papers, Library of Congress; Bilbo to William Henry Seward, January 10, 14, 23, 26, 1865, Seward Papers, University of Rochester, Rochester, NY; Lincoln to John A. Dix, January 20, 1865, in *Collected Works of Lincoln*, ed. Basler, 8:226; Harold Holzer, *Dear Mr. Lincoln: Letters to the President* (Carbondale, IL: Southern Illinois University Press, 2006), 136-37; William Charles Harris, *Lincoln's Last Months* (Cambridge, MA: Harvard University Press, 2004), 129-30.

40. R. W. Latham to William Henry Seward, January 9, 1865, Seward Papers, University of Rochester, Rochester, NY; Cox and Cox, *Politics, Principle, and Prejudice*, 28.

41. W. N. Bilbo to William Henry Seward, December 20, 1864, Seward Papers, University of Rochester, Rochester, NY.

42. For an excellent historical account that gives the credit to Seward and his team, see Cox and Cox, *Politics, Principle, and Prejudice*, 28.

43. *New York Tribune*, February 1, 1865; *New York Herald*, February 5, 1865.

44. Ashley to John G. Nicolay, December 25, 1864, Robert Todd Lincoln Collection, Library of Congress.

45. *Congressional Globe*, 38th Cong., 2d Sess. (1864-65), 120-56.

46. Ibid., 174-75.

47. William Benjamin Smith, *James Sidney Rollins Memoir* (New York: De Vinne Press, 1891), 196-221, provides text of Rollins's speech. For a shorter version, see *Congressional Globe*, 38th Cong., 2d Sess. (1864-65), 174-75, and Arnold, *History of Lincoln*, 581-82.

48. *New York Tribune*, January 10, 14, 1865; *Chicago Tribune*, January 12, 1865; Cornelius Cole to Olive Cole, January 10, 1865, Cornelius Cole Papers, UCLA; *Congressional Globe*, 38th Cong., 2d Sess. (1864-65), 138, 257.

49. Laura G. Julian to "My Dear Sister," January 13, 1865, George W. Julian Papers, Indiana State Library, Indianapolis.

50. P. J. Staudenraus, ed., *Mr. Lincoln's Washington: Selections from the Writings of Noah Brooks* (South Brunswick, NJ: T. Yoseloff, 1967), 408.

51. *Congressional Globe*, 38th Cong., 2d Sess. (1864–65), 523.

52. Staudenraus, ed., *Mr. Lincoln's Washington*, 409; *Congressional Globe*, 38th Cong., 2d Sess. (1864–65), 524.

53. *Congressional Globe*, 38th Cong., 2d Sess. (1864–65), 525–26.

54. Benjamin W. Arnett, ed., *Orations and Speeches: Duplicate Copy of the Souvenir from the Afro-American League to the Hon. James M. Ashley* (Philadelphia: AME Church, 1894), 709–11; *Congressional Globe*, 38th Cong., 2d Sess. (1864–65), 523–31.

55. Charles R. Douglass to Frederick Douglass, February 9, 1865, Douglass Papers, Library of Congress; *New York Tribune*, February 3, 1865; George W. Julian, *Political Recollections* (Chicago: Jansen, McClurg & Co., 1884), 249–50; Cornelius Cole, *Memoirs of Cornelius Cole* (New York: McLoughlin Brothers, 1908), 220.

56. Basler, ed., *Collected Works of Lincoln*, 8: 254; *New York Tribune*, February 3, 1865.

57. Arnett, ed., *Orations and Speeches*, 710–12; *Toledo Commercial*, February 1, 3, 1865.

Chapter 7

1. *Congressional Globe*, 38th Cong., 2d Sess. (1864–65), 140.

2. Of the many fine books on the Louisiana story, I have relied mainly on Herman Belz, *Reconstructing the Union: Theory and Policy during the Civil War* (Ithaca, NY: Cornell University Press, 1969); Michael Les Benedict, *A Compromise of Principle: Congressional Republicans and Reconstruction, 1863–1869* (New York: W. W. Norton, 1974); Peyton McCrary, *Abraham Lincoln and Reconstruction: The Louisiana Experiment* (Princeton, NJ: Princeton University Press, 1978); and Ted Tunnell, *Crucible of Reconstruction: War, Radicalism, and Race in Louisiana, 1862–1877* (Baton Rouge: Louisiana State University Press, 1984).

3. *Liberator*, November 11, December 30, 1864, January 13, 1865; Wendell Philips," The Immediate Issue," in *The Equality of All Men before the Law Claimed and Defended*, comp. George Luther Stearns (Boston: Press of George C. Rand & Avery, 1865), 29–35; Frederick Douglass, "What the Black Man Wants," in *Equality of All Men*, comp. Stearns, 36–39.

4. A. P. Field et al. to Nathaniel Banks, December 12, 1864, Banks Papers, Library of Congress.

5. Harry J. Carman and Reinhard H. Luthin, *Lincoln and the Patronage* (New York: Columbia University Press, 1943); "George W. Julian's Journal," *Indiana Magazine of History*, 11 (December 1915): 228.

6. *Congressional Globe*, 38th Cong., 2d Sess. (1864–5), 53; 38th Cong., House Report 602; Tyler Dennet, ed., *Lincoln and the Civil War Diaries and Letters of John Hay* (New York: Dodd, Mead and Co., 1939), 244–6.

7. *New York Times*, December 19, 1864.

8. *Congressional Globe*, 38th Cong., 2d Sess. (1864–1865), 281, 968, 970, 971, app. 65–8.

9. A. P. Field et al. to Nathaniel Banks, December 12, 1864, Banks Papers, Library of Congress; L. A. Gobright, *Recollections of Men and Things at Washington, During*

the Third of a Century (Philadelphia: Remsen & Haffelfinger, 1869), 160-64; *Congressional Globe*, 38th Cong., 2d Sess. (1864-5), 971; *New York Tribune*, January 23, 1865; Salmon P. Chase to William D. Kelley, January 22, 1865, in Robert B. Warden, *An Account of the Private Life and. Public Services of Salmon Portland Chase* (Cincinnati: Wilstach, Baldwin and Co., 1874), 633.

10. *Congressional Globe*, 38th Cong., 2d Sess. (1864-65), 934-37.

11. Ibid., 968.

12. Ibid., 970-71, 997-1003.

13. Ibid., 870; H.R. Rep. No. 38-13 (1864-65).

14. S. Rep., No. 38-127 (1864-65).

15. Belz, *Reconstructing the Union*, 270-1; *Congressional Globe*, 38th Cong., 2d Sess. (1864-65), 1099.

16. *Congressional Globe*, 38th Cong., 2d Sess. (1864-65), 140, 588; Charles Sumner, *Complete Works* (Boston: Lee & Shepard, 1900), 12:101-3.

17. *Congressional Globe*, 38th Cong., 2d Sess. (1864-65), 1011.

18. Roy P. Basler, ed., *Collected Works of Abraham Lincoln*, 9 vols. (New Brunswick, NJ: Rutgers University Press, 1953-55), 8:399-405.

19. N. Dwight Harris, *The History of Negro Servitude in Illinois* (Chicago: A. C. McClurg & Co., 1904); Emma Lou Thornbrough, *The Negro in Indiana* (Indianapolis: Indiana University Press, 1957); Paul Finkelman, *Slavery and the Founders: Race and Liberty in the Age of Jefferson*, 2nd ed. (Armonk, NY: M. E. Sharpe, 2001), 37-80; Eugene Berwanger, *The Frontier against Slavery: Western Anti-Negro Prejudice and the Slavery Extension Controversy* (Urbana: University of Illinois Press, 1967), 8-29.

20. *Journal of the House of Representatives of the State of Delaware, 1865* (Dover, 1866), 8-17; Patience Essah, *A House Divided: Slavery and Emancipation in Delaware, 1638-1865* (Charlottesville: University Press of Virginia, 1996), 181-85; Harold B. Hancock, "Reconstruction in Delaware," in *Radicalism, Racism, and Party Realignment: The Border States during Reconstruction*, ed. Richard O. Curry (Baltimore: Johns Hopkins Press, 1969), 195-96; Edward B. McPherson, *The Political History of the United States of America during the Great Rebellion* (Washington, DC: Philip and Solomons, 1865), app., 567.

21. E. Merton Coulter, *The Civil War and Readjustment in Kentucky* (Chapel Hill: University of North Carolina Press, 1926), 258-61; *Kentucky Senate Journal* (1865), 21, 274-77; McPherson, *Political History*, app., 598; Thomas E. Bramlette to Abraham Lincoln, March 2, 1865, Lincoln Papers, Library of Congress.

22. *Kentucky House Journal* (1866), 30-32; *Lexington Union Standard*, January 19, 1866; Victor B. Howard, *Black Liberation in Kentucky* (Lexington: University Press of Kentucky, 1983), 88-89.

23. William Gillette, *New Jersey Blue: Civil War Politics in New Jersey, 1854-1865* (New Brunswick, NJ: Rutgers University Press, 1995), 360nn13 and 42, 303-4, 325-26; Charles Merriam Knapp, *New Jersey Politics during the Period of the Civil War and Reconstruction* (Geneva, NY: W. F. Humphrey, 1924), 73-74, 163-65; McPherson, *Political History*, app., 597.

24. For Perry's life, see Lillian A. Kibler, *Benjamin F. Perry: South Carolina Unionist* (Durham, NC: Duke University Press, 1946).

25. Sidney Andrews, *The South since the War* (1865; repr., New York: Arno, 1969), 28-45.

26. Ibid., 45-67.

27. Governor's Message, No. 1, *South Carolina House Journal*, Extra Session, 1865 (Columbia, SC, 1866).

28. Andrew Johnson to Benjamin F. Perry, October 28, 31, 1865, in *The Papers of Andrew Johnson*, ed. Paul H. Bergeron et al., 16 vols. (Knoxville: University of Tennessee Press, 1967-2000), 9:299, 314.

29. Governor's Message, No. 4, *South Carolina House Journal*, Extra Session, 1865, (Columbia, SC, 1866), 69; Benjamin F. Perry, *Reminiscences of Public Men with Speeches and Addresses*, 2nd ser. (Greenville, SC: S. C. Shannon, 1889), 282.

30. William H. Seward to B. F. Perry, November 6, 1865, in *The Works of William H. Seward*, ed. George E. Baker, 5 vols. (Boston: Houghton, Mifflin and Co., 1884), 5:596.

31. *South Carolina House Journal*, Extra Session, 1865 (Columbia, 1866), 88-96; *South Carolina Senate Journal* (Columbia, 1866), 73-77; *New York Tribune*, November 21, 1865.

32. Benjamin Butler to Thaddeus Stevens, November 20, 1865, Thaddeus Stevens Papers, Library of Congress; *Documentary History of the Constitution of the United States, 1787-1870*, 5 vols. (Washington, DC: Department of State, 1894), 2:610.

33. Andrew Johnson to William L. Sharkey, November 1, 1865, in *Papers of Andrew Johnson*, ed. Bergeron et al., 9:325; *Mississippi House Journal* (1865), 327; Carl Schurz to Andrew Johnson, August 29, 1865, in *Advice after Appomattox: Letters to Andrew Johnson*, ed. Brooks D. Simpson et al. (Knoxville: University of Tennessee Press, 1987), 107; George H. Thomas to Edwin M. Stanton, December 12, 1865, in *Advice after Appomattox*, ed. Simpson et al., 239; William C. Harris, *Presidential Reconstruction in Mississippi* (Baton Rouge: Louisiana State University Press, 1967), 141-43.

34. *Congressional Globe*, 39th Cong., 2d Sess. (1866-67), 319-20. Ashley's role in the Johnson impeachment has been denounced by one scholar after another. For a sampling, see Claude G. Bowers, *The Tragic Era: The Revolution after Lincoln* (Boston: Houghton, Mifflin and Co., 1929); George Fort Milton, *The Age of Hate: Andrew Johnson and the Radicals* (New York: Coward-McCann, Inc., 1930); C. Vann Woodward, "That Other Impeachment," *New York Times Magazine*, August 11, 1974. For a spirited defense of Ashley, see Robert F. Horowitz, *The Great Impeacher: A Political Biography of James M. Ashley* (Brooklyn: Brooklyn College Press, 1979), 123-43.

35. *Congressional Globe*, 40th Cong., 1st Sess. (1867-68), 18-19; Benjamin W. Arnett, ed., *Orations and Speeches: Duplicate Copy of the Souvenir from the Afro-American League to the Hon. James M. Ashley* (Philadelphia: AME Church, 1894), 438-40; H.R. Rep. No. 40-7, at 1198-99 (1867-68) (Impeachment Investigation).

36. James Ashley to Charles Sumner, July 18, 1869, Sumner Papers, Houghton Library, Harvard University, Cambridge, MA, microfilm.

37. Stanley R. Davidson and Dale Tash, "Confederate Backwash in Montana Territory," *Montana: The Magazine of Western History* 17 (October 1967): 50-58; Clark C. Spence, "James M. Ashley: Spoilsman in Montana," *Montana: The Magazine of Western History* 18 (Spring 1968): 24-35; Charles S. Ashley, "Governor Ashley's Biography and Messages," *Contributions to the Historical Society of Montana* 6 (1907): app. F and passim.

38. *Congressional Globe*, 39th Cong., 1st Sess. (1865-66), 746.

39. *Ex parte Warren*, 31 Tex. 143 (1868); *Kelly v. State*, 25 Ark. 392 (1869); *People v. Washington*, 36 Cal. 658 (1869).

40. *Bowlin v. Commonwealth*, 65 Ky. 5 (Ky. 1867).

41. *United States v. Rhodes*, 27 F Cas 785 (1866).

42. Jeremiah Sullivan Black, *The Doctrines of the Democratic and Abolitionist Parties Contrasted* (Philadelphia: Printed at "Age" Office, 1864); C. F. Black, *Essays and Speeches of Jeremiah S. Black, with a Biographical Sketch* (New York: D. Appleton and Co., 1885).

43. *Blyew v. United States*, 80 U.S. 581 (1872); Victor Howard, "Black Testimony Controversy in Kentucky, 1866-1872," *Journal of Negro History* 58 (April 1953): 158-59, 164-65; Alexander Tsesis, *The Thirteenth Amendment and American Freedom: A Legal History* (New York: New York University Press, 2004), 64-66.

44. *The Slaughterhouse Cases*, 83 U.S. 36 (1873), 67-69. Justice Miller's intentions are a matter of dispute. A host of scholars have argued that he didn't negligently or purposely undermine the work of men like Ashley. For more on Justice Miller, a complicated figure, see Michael A. Ross, "Justice Miller's Reconstruction: The Slaughter-House Cases, Health Codes, and Civil Rights in New Orleans, 1861-1873," *Journal of Southern History* 64 (November 1998): 649-76.

45. Loren P. Beth, *John Marshall Harlan: The Last Whig Justice* (Lexington: University Press of Kentucky, 1992); Frank B. Latham, *The Great Dissenter: Supreme Court Justice John Marshall Harlan, 1833-1911* (New York: Cowles Book Co., 1970); *Civil Rights Cases*, 109 U.S. 3 (1883).

46. *Civil Rights Cases*, 109 U.S. 3 (1883); Michael C. Collins, "Justice Bradley's Civil Rights Odyssey Revisited," *Tulane Law Review* 70 (June 1996): 1979-2002.

47. *Hodges v. United States*, 203 U.S. 1 (1906).

Epilogue

1. Benjamin W. Arnett, ed., *Orations and Speeches: Duplicate Copy of the Souvenir from the Afro-American League to the Hon. James M. Ashley* (Philadelphia: AME Church, 1894), 9-10.

2. Clark Waggoner, "Seventh Congressional District: J. M. Ashley and His Record," *Toledo Blade*, November 1, 1890; Ben Perley Poore, *Perley's Reminiscences*, 2 vols. (Philadelphia: Hubbard Brothers, 1886), 2:201-2.

3. Ida B. Wells, *The Reason Why the Colored American Is Not in the World's Columbian Exposition: The Afro-American's Contribution to Columbian Literature*, ed. by Robert W. Rydell (1893; repr., Urbana: University of Illinois Press, 1999); David F. Burg, *Chicago's White City of 1893* (Lexington: University Press of Kentucky, 1976);

Christopher Robert Reed, *"All the World Is Here!" The Black Presence at White City* (Bloomington: Indiana University Press, 2000).

4. "Mr. Ashley's Response to Bishop Arnett and President Young," in Arnett, ed., *Orations and Speeches.*

5. See, e.g., Don Fehrenbacher, *The Federal Constitution and Slavery* (Claremont, CA: Claremont Institute, 1984); William M. Wiecek, *The Sources of Antislavery Constitutionalism in America, 1760–1848* (Ithaca, NY: Cornell University Press, 1977); Paul Finkelman, *Slavery and the Founders: Race and Liberty in the Age of Jefferson*, 2nd ed. (Armonk, NY: M. E. Sharpe, 2001); David Waldstreicher, *Slavery's Constitution: From Revolution to Ratification* (New York: Hill and Wang, 2009); George William Van Cleve, *A Slaveholders' Union: Slavery, Politics, and the Constitution in the Early American Republic* (Chicago: University of Chicago Press, 2010).

6. Leonard L. Richards, *The Slave Power: The Free North and Southern Domination, 1780–1860* (Baton Rouge: Louisiana State University Press, 2000); Garry Wills, *"Negro President:" Jefferson and the Slave Power* (Boston: Houghton Mifflin, 2003).

7. It is hard to tell exactly where she ranked, because the 1860 census listed slaveholdings by counties, and most of the big operators had plantations in many counties and in several states.

8. Wendell H. Stephenson, *Isaac Franklin: Slave Trader and Planter of the Old South* (Baton Rouge: Louisiana State University Press, 1938); Mark Brown, "Adelicia Acklen," in *Tennessee Encyclopedia of History and Culture* (Nashville: Tennessee Historical Society, 1998).

9. James L. Roark, *Masters without Slaves: Southern Planters in the Civil War and Reconstruction* (New York: W. W. Norton & Co., 1977), 171–73; Barnes F. Lathrop, "History of the Census Returns," *Southwestern Historical Quarterly* 51 (April 1948): 293–312; Jonathan M. Wiener, "Planter Persistence and Social Change: Alabama, 1850–1870," *Journal of Interdisciplinary History* 7 (Autumn, 1976): 235–60; Randolph B. Campbell, *A Southern Community in Crisis: Harrison County, Texas, 1850–1880* (Austin: Texas State Historical Association, 1983); Carl H. Moneyhon, "The Impact of the Civil War in Arkansas: The Mississippi River Plantation Counties," *Arkansas Historical Quarterly* 51 (Summer 1992): 105–18.

Index